A STORY OF SURVIVAL AND SUCCESS, OF REBELLION AND ABUSE, OF COURAGE AND TRIUMPH
CALL ME ANNA

Here Patty Duke tells her personal story, her journey from child star to award-winning adult actress, from confused and abused teenager to a highly respected and refreshingly honest show business personality—and she tells it in a voice so familiar to millions of us, yet so starkly and startlingly frank that you will never see Patty Duke the same way again—or forget the little girl whose real name was Anna Marie. Inside Patty reveals:

* Her terrifying appearances on TV's rigged quiz show, *The $64,000 Challenge*, that led to her testimony before the congressional subcommittee investigating the show.

* Her courageous break from her ruthless managers when they tried to stop her from seeing the first man she fell in love with.

* Her passionate love affair with 17-year-old Desi Arnaz, Jr. that was thwarted by an angry Lucille Ball.

* Her many liaisons that included a most unusual affair with Frank Sinatra, out-of-wedlock pregnancy, a wedding to a stranger, and her long-term stormy marriage to the much older John Astin.

* The diagnosis of manic depression that began her successful rehabilitation.

* The challenge of bringing up two sons who have followed their mother in acting careers.

. . . and much more.
CALL ME ANNA

"Related with such appealing honesty, courage, self-deprecating humor and strong desire to make the reader understand how it all could have happened, that she succeeds in winning you over."
—*The Washington Post*

CALL ME ANNA

The Autobiography of
Patty Duke

PATTY DUKE AND KENNETH TURAN

BANTAM BOOKS
TORONTO · NEW YORK · LONDON · SYDNEY · AUCKLAND

CALL ME ANNA

A Bantam Book
Bantam hardcover edition / August 1987
6 printings through October 1987
Bantam paperback edition / June 1988

Library of Congress Cataloging-in-Publication Data

Duke, Patty.
  Call me Anna.

  1. Duke, Patty.   2. Actors—United States—
Biography.   I. Turan, Kenneth.   II. Title.
PN2287.A78A3   1987   792'.028'0924   [B]   87-47591
                ISBN 0-553-27205-5

Published simultaneously in the United States and Canada

Bantam Books are published by Bantam Books, a division
of Bantam Doubleday Dell Publishing Group, Inc. Its trademark, consisting of the words "Bantam Books" and the portrayal of a rooster, is Registered in U.S. Patent and Trademark
Office and in other countries. Marca Registrada. Bantam Books,
666 Fifth Avenue, New York, New York 10103.

PRINTED IN THE UNITED STATES OF AMERICA

KR   0 9 8 7 6 5 4 3 2 1

This book is dedicated
to
My Husband, my Mother, my Father, my Sister,
my Brother, and my Children and theirs.

And bizarre though it may be,
John and Ethel Ross.

ACKNOWLEDGMENTS

Angel of God, my guardian dear
To Whom his love commits me here;
Ever this day be at my side
To light and guard
To rule and guide.

This little prayer from my childhood occurred to me as I recalled all those who should be thanked for bringing me this far.

Some of them have names that are familiar, some have names that are not and some will remain nameless even to me. Among those guardian angels are those without whom this particular promise could never have been kept. For their love, their light and their guidance, I am grateful to:

Mitchell Dawson for his good counsel as my friend, especially, but also as my good counsel.

Bobbe Joy Dawson, Mary Lou Pinckert, Sam Faulkner and the munchkin, Sandy Smith, the girlfriends I longed for and treasure so much.

Ralph and Rosalie Turner, my friends who insure that the fruits of my labor are now stored safely.

Laureen Lang and Neil Kreppel who've assisted me so lovingly in every way over the years.

Arnold and Lois Peyser, my friends who assured me if I did a *TV Guide* interview with Kenny Turan, I wouldn't be disappointed.

Steve Rubin, who read that article and had the insight, foresight, and faith to reteam Turan and Duke for Bantam.

Kenneth (you'll always be Kenny to me) Turan. You met a gun-shy actress for a magazine interview and won her trust, her friendship, and her deep respect forever.

My children, all of you, for all that you are and all that you give me.

Dr. Harold Arlen for helping me find me at last.

And, of course you, Michael Ray Pearce, for finding me Forever and Our one day.

INTRODUCTION

About two years ago I went to a meeting in the office of Sid Sheinberg, president of MCA and one of the most powerful men in the entertainment industry. I was part of an ad hoc delegation of Screen Actors Guild members, a gracious, dignified lady. Sid looked at me hard and said, "Well, it's been a long time, hasn't it?" And I said, "Yes, it has." Neither one of us went into any details. I just turned to the folks I was with and said, "Sid and I have had a few meetings in here." What I didn't tell them was that the last time I was in Sid's office, I shouted a string of obscenities and threw his Mickey Mouse clock at him for good measure. When people said about me "She's trouble," they weren't kidding.

That all happened in 1970, when I was pregnant but no one knew it. I was guest-starring on an episode of *Matt Lincoln, M.D.*, starring Vince Edwards. We were on location on the palisades near San Pedro, and I was hanging off a cliff, supposedly committing suicide.

There had been a lot of technical problems that morning, the crew was tired and hungry and they wanted to eat, but it was decided that the actors would take lunch first so the crew could continue to set up the suicide shot. It was none of my business—none—but I couldn't keep my nose out of it. I decided I wasn't going to lunch until the crew went to lunch. Very unionistic. An argument ensued and I stormed off to get into a car and leave. I said I was going to Beverly Hills to eat, they said I had only a half hour and couldn't go that far, I said I was taking an hour, maybe even an hour and a half, so they told the Teamster assigned to my car not to drive me anywhere.

I was getting out of control at this point, and, holding my tiny dog, Tara, and wearing a floor-length black and white leather coat over a miniskirt, I must have looked like a court jester. I said, "Fine, the hell with you," and went out to the street to hail a cab. Of course, one didn't exist. What came by instead was, of all things, an army garbage truck. I stuck my thumb out and the driver picked me up. The assistant director started screaming, "Don't you take her anywhere," I was yelling, "Go guys, go, go, go," and suddenly my departure turned into a great rollicking, hysterical chase, with a studio limo coming after the garbage truck with me and the dog in it. We pulled into the army base, closed the gates, and wouldn't let the limo in.

Then came negotiations through the fence:

"Are you coming back?"

"No. It's my lunch hour. I can do anything I want."

"You gotta come back."

"I'll come back when you feed the crew."

"The crew already went to lunch."

"Then I'll eat here with the guys."

"No, no, you've gotta come back."

"Then can the guys come and eat with us?"

Well, it turned out that these guys were Section Eight, genuinely crazy types (who else would pick me up?) who'd been let out on garbage detail as a kind of occupational therapy and had to get permission to go to lunch. Not only did I invite them, but anybody else they cared to invite as well. I went back to the location site, and as I was standing in line, getting my food, over this little ridge came what looked to me like maybe a hundred or a hundred and twenty guys in uniform, looking for lunch. I knew then I was in big trouble. And sure enough I got the call. "Sid Sheinberg wants to see you."

I was driven over to his office on the Universal lot, fuming over a summons calculated to chill the boldest heart. Sheinberg wasn't there, so while I waited around I touched everything on his desk, just like a four-year-old, too self-absorbed to be afraid. I liked his Mickey Mouse clock, one of those little Baby Bens, so I picked it up and put it into my pocket. Sheinberg finally came in and he started reading me the riot act. I said if he didn't like it, he knew what he could do. He said, "You're gonna have to not talk to me that way," and I said, "Who are you, the dean?" Then he said something else that got me very angry and I said, "Go to hell. I don't have to put up with you. Keep your two grand a week." And I threw his Mickey Mouse clock at him (he caught it) and left.

When I got back to the set, I was told I was on suspension. I got into one of those little golf carts, got my stuff out of my dressing room and put it in my car, then I drove the cart as far as I could way out on the back lot, left it there, and threw away the key. Can you imagine? And then I didn't work for a very long time.

Up until very recently that story was extremely painful to me. Every once in a while I'd run into a crew member from that time who'd start to tell it and I'd be mortified, I'd die. I'd even have a physical response to the memory, a tightening of my stomach. But now I'm starting to find it funny, almost as funny as the people who tell it.

The difference is that I know now what I didn't know then, that I was a manic-depressive, crazy as a bedbug. Since I was diagnosed in 1982 and began taking Lithium, my whole life has dramatically changed. The medication has so stabilized me that incidents like that just aren't in the realm of possibility anymore. Also, I've achieved the kind of respectability that I've always wanted. Part of the attraction of being president of the Screen Actors Guild, frankly, was that it conveyed the ultimate stamp of approval. "We accept you," said the membership, the community I live and work in, "as a person who's got enough wits about her to do the job." So now it's okay for me to say, "Yes, wasn't I crazy in my youth."

What's still the toughest thing for me to accept is all

those articles that were written speculating about my abuse of drugs, which I've never used; that that kind of stuff would linger in newspaper morgues and magazine clip files has made me ache. I'd love to destroy every copy of every article that misquotes me, that maligns my mother, that may cause my son, Sean, even if it's only for five minutes, to have to deal with nonsense instead of getting on with his life. But that's not possible. I'll never be that rich—maybe there isn't anybody who's that rich.

What I've done instead is follow a very sound philosophical approach that my sons' father, John Astin, suggested. He would say, "If you keep living the truth of your life, that, not the mistakes or exaggerations, is what will endure. If you live your life in truth, the truth will out." Sure there are times when I have trouble believing that, but for lack of a better way to proceed, that's been working for me.

And, because of a promise I made, I've decided to do something else, something more. Sixteen years ago I promised my mother that I would write something to set the record straight, that I'd put something in those archives that's more accurate, that gives another point of view. I don't mind being thought of as someone who was crazy, because I had no control over that situation. What I don't like is for people to think that I chose to do destructive things. I was someone who didn't have a choice about my actions, yet I fought like a son of a bitch to get to a place where I could have one.

ONE

Though I've been a professional actress since I was seven or eight, acting was never a dream of mine. What I really wanted to be was a nun: nuns were the only people I came in contact with who weren't drinking and screaming! I played nun a lot with my friend Margie Stravelli— she'd play anything. We'd fold scarves a certain way, make a bib with paper from school, put on a bathrobe, and flick our rosary beads as we walked up and down. And then we'd just be mean: that's how you played nun. Assign a lot of homework, whack the table with a ruler, fight about who was in charge. "You were the Mother Superior last week. Let me be Mother Superior." We played nun for hours.

Yet when I think back to my earliest memory, it was of performing. It was Sundays after church and I'd always be wearing a very good dress, looking very neat and spiffy. My father, John Patrick, would be charged with taking me to a park on Second Avenue between Thirty-fifth and Thirty-sixth streets on New York's East Side, but we never quite made it. We'd end up instead at "Grandpa's bar," where his father, a man with pure white hair, very blue and bloodshot eyes and that kind of handsome Irish face with all the veins sticking out from drinking too much, was a bartender. Grandpa was what they called a periodical drinker, and when he drank, my mother says, he was violent.

As early as I can remember I'd be stood on the bar and, even if it was July, I would recite "The Night Before Christmas." Sometimes everyone would give me pennies, but mostly it was pretzels—I could be bought for pretzels and Coca-Cola. Dad, of course, would be throwing back a few boiler-makers. He'd always swear me to secrecy, but he'd get in trouble anyway when we got home, because whether I told or not—and I would, every time—it was obvious where we'd been. But I loved being hoisted up on that bar, I just loved it. And that was probably where my passion for acting began.

Until I was about twelve years old, when the place got so infested with bedbugs that it drove us cuckoo, my family lived at 316 East 31 Street. The five of us (my father; my mother, Frances; my sister, Carol, who was eight years older than me; and my brother, Raymond, who was five years older) all lived in four rooms: a kitchen, a living room, and two bedrooms, all without doors. It was at the top of a four-story walkup: we lived in the back apartment and the Callahans and their dog, Scroungy, lived in the front. Scroungy was a black spaniel, so vicious it lived its entire life with a muzzle on: the Callahans would take it off only to feed the dog when nobody was around. Scroungy was *mean*.

Though we had four rooms, none of them was as big as my den today—you could do submarine work after living in them. The rent was only thirty-six dollars a month, but there was a panic about not being able to make the payment every time it was due. My sister and I slept in the same bed for a while, but she didn't like it because I moved around too much and I didn't like it because she talked a lot and out loud in her sleep. We had a sink, stove, refrigerator, and the washing machine my mother got her hand stuck in. Even after the machine was turned off, she kept screaming. I was just a little kid, I didn't know what to do. I finally figured out I should pull the plug, but I had to get Mrs. Callahan to extricate my mother's hand. Thank God for Mrs. Callahan. My mother might still be there.

We also had pressed tin ceilings, the kind that are becoming really popular again, only these weren't nice and white; they had big rust stains where water had leaked through the tar-paper roof because my mother always walked on it in her high heels—she used it for a spy tower. She'd go up there and embarrass us to death. Maybe Ray was playing stickball in the street, where he wasn't supposed to be, or I had my finger up my nose—whatever it was, she'd start screaming at the top of her lungs. Once she screamed down for Ray to come upstairs, and one of his buddies, a guy named Walter, couldn't take it anymore and yelled, "Jump, Mrs. Duke, jump!" Of course, the moment my poor brother walked in the door, she gave him a slug because of what the other kid had yelled. Well, she figured, he'd been standing there, hadn't he?

The neighborhood we lived in, Kips Bay, was almost all Irish and Italian. We were street-smart city kids, but the kinds of things the older ones did, like the boys shooting off firecrackers or maybe stealing hubcaps, the girls chewing gum and putting on black eyeliner because it made them look hard and tough, seem very innocent now. We never really wanted for anything, and I never remember being hungry. So tabloid stories that say "a piece of bread seemed like birthday cake to her" still make me furious. Sure we were poor, but we weren't desperate, we weren't like homeless people who may have nothing at all to eat. If I was hungry, it was because my mother made pea soup, which I wouldn't eat on a dare.

My mother had a strong sense of responsibility to her family. She used the phrase "these children we brought into the world" again and again. She prided herself on the fact that she raised perfectly clean children. People of her generation in that neighborhood had very little to be proud of, but they were proud of the way they kept a home. It was the old "you could eat off the floor" routine, though what my mother forgets is the reason you could eat off the floor is that my sister was washing it! The household might be threadbare, but it was sparkling clean, and her children were dressed better than lots of rich people's kids; my clothes were much better, much cleaner, much neater than my boys' are today. When you've got the money, you relax and say, "Fine, wear the holes in your jeans, look like a bum." But when you don't have it, you want to look as if you do.

My parents had both grown up in that same Kips Bay neighborhood before me; in fact my father's sister dated my mother's brother for a while. John Patrick Duke's family was Irish as far back as anyone could remember, but my mother's mother was German. She had eleven children and died when my mother, who was the youngest, was only six. It's a terrible story. Apparently my grandmother had emphysema or bronchitis, some ailment that disturbed her breathing. My aunt Lizzie was taking care of Grandma, who was choking, when the doorbell rang and kept ringing. Lizzie went to the window to see who it was—it was little Frances—and in the interim, before she could get back, Grandma died.

When you think what an old-fashioned Irish Catholic wake on Second Avenue must have been like, with the body in the living room, all the drinking, and how many times Lizzie, not meaning to blame Frances, must have told the story about the ringing doorbell, you realize the kind of guilt my mother must have carried around all these years. I think that, and the fact that I was the youngest and smallest and looked like her, made her feel very, very close to me.

I was born on December 14, 1946, in Bellevue Hospital, the first one of my mother's children who wasn't born at home, and named Anna Marie. The Anna is easy to figure; both my parents had sisters named Anna. Who this Marie person is, nobody knows. We figure it might have been a drinking partner of Dad's, or maybe he just thought another name was needed. My mother always says, "It went good with Duke."

At first it was the classic case of the baby everyone was nice to, getting all the presents I wanted while Carol and Ray weren't so lucky. Though I could be a tomboy on the street, I was really a traditional little girl and played with little-girl things. I wanted books and new Crayolas and when I would color outside the line my sister would make me feel dumb. My poor sister. She says I broke everything she ever had. Well, she could play with me. I was a nice toy.

When I was little, it seemed that every holiday, every event that's supposed to be joyous and wonderful—Christmas, Easter, graduations, weddings, birthdays—turned into a nightmare for my family. We were like a family out of O'Neill, with the melancholy and the fire of the Irish. There was, for instance, the tradition of the Christmas trees always going out the window. Almost every Christmas, my father would get angry about something and there would be an argument, and before anybody knew it the tree was gone, out the window and down into the street. Years later, after my father himself was well gone and we were living in a basement apartment in the Astoria section of Queens, my mother and my brother had an argument about the tree: my mother had bought a fake one and my brother came home and freaked. There was screaming and yelling back and forth and the next thing we knew, the tree was going out the window. Except we were in the basement! Ray was so frustrated and embarrassed that he dragged the tree up the stairs and into the courtyard. So we kept the tradition alive.

Funerals were the big family gatherings where relatives who hadn't spoken to each other in fifteen years wound up in the same room. They'd have a few too many, sparks would fly, two or three folks would beg that this wasn't the time or place, and then the free-for-all would begin. We'd hear "Step outside of Skelly and Larney's," the local funeral home, and after they'd had it out, everything would be fine.

Everyone in my family has a temper. My sister has a terrible temper, my brother, too, and, though I'm beginning to have mine under control, I have the same kind of explosive disposition my mother has. Until quite recently I used to throw things (you can still see the holes in my bedroom walls). My brother and my sister had miserable fights. My sister has scars all over her body to prove it. Usually Carol was passing along some order that Mom had given, and he'd tell her to go to hell. She'd scream at him, he couldn't stand that because it sounded just like Mom, and sooner or later he'd get physical. I remember Ray pushing Carol so hard he accidentally sent her out of our fourth-story window. Luckily it was the one with the fire escape.

If my mother found out what Ray had done, he would get killed. Though I got threatened more than I got hit, my mother was very, very physical. The steam would build up in her, she'd go completely out of control, and all of a sudden we'd get a whack, a real unpremeditated backhand whack.

She had a phrase that always terrified me: "Wait till I get you home." Even after I began working, when I made her angry she'd get that stony look on her face, and the minute we walked in the door, there was the payoff. But it inevitably went worse with Ray; all that rage she couldn't release with Dad was directed at him.

The problem with my father was that he was an alcoholic. From what I know and what I hear, he started out a happy drunk who loved his family and enjoyed a lot of dancing and good old times when he was younger. He never got past the eighth grade, and when he left the Navy after World War II, he had a variety of jobs, everything from working for the telephone company to being a parking lot attendant, a cab driver, and a handyman. "If you give me the tools, I'll do it," he used to say to my mother, "but I can't do it on paper." The problem was he used to drink up his salary. My mother remembers all kinds of excuses he'd come up with, like not getting paid or losing his check or getting robbed on the subway. He began getting into trouble, having accidents with the cars in the parking lot, coming in at all hours. Finally, when I was about six years old, my mother told him, "John, this is it. You've gotta leave. I can't take it."

My father moved to a furnished room and over the next ten years—he died when he was fifty—I almost never saw him again. A journalist once said my father sounded like an elegant but sad man. In my memory he is very dignified, which seems contradictory when you remember he was an alcoholic. Then again, I'm not sure if that image is the man who really existed or just a terrific ideal I've created.

What I really remember is so little, just brief flashbacks. Sunday morning lying on top of the bed where my parents were, watching the kids on the *Horn & Hardart Children's Hour* and reading the funnies. Sitting on his lap in the summer while he watched the ballgame and drank beer. Begging for Worcestershire sauce, which I ordinarily wouldn't touch, but if Daddy was eating it, then I wanted it. I remember a strong, strong attraction, almost a physical need to be close to him when he was there, and the longing when he was gone. And my envy of little Pamela who lived next door because she had a great dad who would take us places. I always felt like the poor relation.

And then there was the smell of Camels. And Old Spice. One of my most exact memories is sitting on the kitchen floor early one morning and going through my father's duffel bag. I find this wooden thing and this good-smelling stuff and I'm playing with it while my parents are arguing at the front door. My mother says, "What the hell are you doing here?" And he says, "I live here." She says, "You've been back for three days now, you don't see fit to come home, you don't live here anymore." I'm sitting on the floor with this wooden soap dish that has a top on it, and he picks up his duffel bag and he leaves and I've got the dish. I don't remember him saying good-bye to me or anything, just leaving in a huff. That little wooden dish, you can imagine what a treasure it was to me. And very shortly after, in a rage, my mother threw it away. I used to blame her, but how can you? It wasn't malicious, just the act of a desperate woman.

The other smell I remember is booze. It smelled embarrassing. I intuitively knew it meant trouble. It conjured up that terrible dilemma of wanting him around but not wanting him around, because if he was there, he was going to drink, and if he drank, there was going to be trouble.

A job that my sister or brother usually handled that fell to me once after Daddy had moved out was meeting him at a bar somewhere and getting ten dollars to bring home. It was summertime, all the kids were in the street, and two of my friends came up and said, "Where ya goin'? We'll walk ya." I always wanted somebody to walk me—in broad daylight I was scared of being by myself—but this time I made up lie after lie about why they couldn't. I went blocks out of my way so they wouldn't know where I was going, and I kept looking behind me to make sure they weren't there.

The bar was on Third Avenue and Thirty-first Street and I'd gotten strict instructions from my very angry mother that I wasn't allowed to go in. I had to tap on the window and let him know I was there. It took a while for him to turn around, but others did, too, they began waving, and finally his attention was diverted. We hadn't seen each other for a long time, so when he came out he wanted to hug me, but I wouldn't let him. He smelled of booze. I took the ten dollars and went back the way I'd come. I've felt guilty and ashamed about that from that day to this because I think that's the last time I saw him on his feet, the last time I could've had a hug. If only he knew how important he was to me. But I don't think he did, I don't think he was able to get outside of all that chaos he was in, to notice how much he meant.

My father's drinking has had an effect on us all. My brother, Ray, who had to be brought over from his army post in Germany to identify my father's body when he died about ten years later, hasn't drunk at all since then. Not a drop. With me, part of the legacy is an awareness that I'm an addictive personality so I better keep on my toes. I drink too much coffee, smoke too many cigarettes, and if I'd ever gotten involved in drugs, I would have ended up seriously addicted or dead. But because of my dad I have a built-in censor that says, "No, I don't think *you* should be doing this." What I'd seen firsthand wouldn't allow it.

Yet the fact that I come from a very long line of alcoholics means that I have had some problems with liquor. I have gone through periods of drinking very heavily, never while I'm working, but either in the privacy of my own home or at parties. And when I drink, my personality is sometimes altered to such an extent as to be destructive or disruptive. I could be funny, witty, the belle of the ball, but then, the minute I'd get in the car to go home, I'd become venomous. Every vicious thing I could think of to say, every injustice that I could recall—I was Dr. Jekyll turning into Mr. Hyde. When I finally recognized the effect drinking has on me, which was more than a dozen years ago now, I just stopped cold. Never missed it. Though I now seem able to have *a* glass of wine, if I never have another drink, I won't even notice. That ability to say, "Whoa, let me stop now and see if I *can* stop," that's one of the things my dad left me, because I'd witnessed what happened to someone who couldn't.

I have just a few pictures of Dad: sitting at a desk; dancing at a party; the wedding portrait, with the two of them standing together like little leprechauns. He was always a sharp dresser. I remember gray suits with very sharp creases in the pants, spiffy-looking fedoras: there was no such thing as going to Daddy with sticky hands, you would wash first.

When I look at those pictures, when I talk about him, I still feel the sadness; tears are always very close. And it makes me mad, too; I wonder how long this process has to take. When people ask me when I realized my parents' separation was final, I tell them I'm still not buying it. I've never stopped wrestling with the loss and inevitable romanticization of my father, and I'm sure it's interfered with my marriages: as long as that idealistic figure exists, who could live up to that?

Yet, on the other hand, I think that some of my drive, which in part comes from wanting to succeed for myself, also has a lot to do with evening the score for my father. It's like what Annie Sullivan says at one point in *The Miracle Worker*, talking about the loss of her brother: "I think God must owe me a resurrection." I don't know what made my father the way he was, if it was character flaws or lack of societal knowledge about alcoholism or something else. Whatever it was, my need is to say, through my life and my work, "This was a magnificent soul who didn't get a chance."

TWO

My father, as it turned out, was not the only parent with problems. My mother, though you'd never know it to look at her today, had episodes of severe depression. There were times when my mother could be warm and wonderful and generous, both of spirit and with things like ice cream cones and dolls, but much of the time she was not. She now takes medication that regulates her moods, but before that she did a lot of what we call "acting out." She's had to be hospitalized three times, the first when I couldn't have been more than five or six years old.

We had a fireplace in our apartment, boarded up as many are in New York, and a big cedar chest in front of it. We kids thought this was a great piece of furniture, but at times it was the dreaded cedar chest because whenever anything went wrong—if my parents had had a fight for instance—the three of us were awakened, taken out of our beds, and lined up by that chest. He would be gone, she would be sitting in the chair, and we'd have to sit up all night with her.

Why'd she do it? I'm not sure even she knows. Either she didn't want to be alone or she needed to take revenge, and if she couldn't take it on him, she could take it out on those closest to him. But it was also terribly self-destructive:

how much worse can you make yourself feel than by having your three innocent kids sitting there crying, unable to go to bed, worrying, "Is he gonna come back? Are they gonna throw things?"

Usually these episodes happened after she threw him out, but there was one time when he said enough was enough and he left. That was it for her. She lined us up by the cedar chest, said, "We're all going together," and turned on the gas. Now, she also left the windows open, but I didn't know that, I thought this was it. And we sat there for hours.

I don't remember if someone finally called us or if she made the call because she wasn't getting the attention she wanted, but they came from Bellevue, took her away, and hospitalized her for a week of observation. That had to have been a nightmare, because when she came back, though her temper still existed, the outbursts were fewer and farther between. I think she was petrified of going back to the hospital. She suffered deeply after each of these episodes.

Other times when she was feeling melancholy, my mother used the city bus as a form of recreation. At one or two in the morning, when she was having insomnia, she'd wake me up and we'd take the Lexington Avenue bus back and forth all night from one end of the route to the other until she felt safe enough or relieved enough to go home. After a few trips the excitement of being up late was replaced by a feeling of sadness, and I'd just want to get back.

But the funny thing was, that didn't matter; it really didn't as long as I was with her. Because I was desperately emotionally attached to my mother. If she was around, my hand was always in her hand. It wasn't always the nicest hand-holding, there was a lot of tension in her, but my hand was there, even when she did some things that were very hard for me to forgive. She took my dog, Skippy, to the Bide-A-Wee because nobody would walk him and nobody would feed him, and that was a major drama—I cried and cried and cried. In fact, every New Year's Eve until I was fifteen, when all the grown-ups had something to cry about when they played "Auld Lang Syne" and I didn't, I used to cry about Skippy. I couldn't even remember what he looked like anymore, but when the ball went down in Times Square, I cried.

One thing that was ultra-important to both my parents was religion; Dad even showed up for church on Sundays, though I'm not sure if he ever went to confession. What fascinated me at church was the ritual, what we now in the eighties call the bells and smells. It was drama and show biz rolled into one, with the mystique of Latin thrown in for good measure.

Our church was Sacred Heart, and the grade school there, The Sacred Heart of Jesus and Mary, was the first one I went to. My poor sister went to Immaculata, a high school in the same building, and every time I wet my pants, which I did a lot whenever I got nervous, she would have to be taken out of class to bring me home. Each school had a navy and white uniform. The little girls wore jumpers over a blouse and the older kids wore a skirt and a blouse, and the blouse had to be clean and starched every morning; I can't believe there's any starch left in the world. Every morning would find my sister crying because she was ironing her blouse and she was late. I don't ever remember my sister as being young, being a kid. She was always the responsible one. We used to tease her that she'd be carrying her ironing board down the aisle at her wedding.

When I look at pictures of me at that time, I can see I had a spark and pizzazz, but I never thought of myself that way then. I had skinny, skinny legs and knobby knees, and my mother cut my hair so I looked like Buster Brown, the kid in the shoe. Only I was missing the dog. I felt very mousy, I felt very nervous, I felt very little. Even though my father had always called me Ree-Ree, a diminutive of Marie, it's only when you go to school that you really know you're small. Everybody's calling you Pee Wee or Shrimp, and patting you on the head—they're still doing that—and you get to be first in line. That part was good, especially at church events, because you got to see the most.

As a child I had the kind of acceptance that Catholic priests pray for in their little parishioners. We were supposed to have blind faith and I did, I really believed all the things they told me. I was *the* first in my class to learn the Confiteor in Latin. The priest would come in to teach it to the boys while the girls were supposed to be practicing their Palmer Method penmanship. It wasn't going very well in our class. We had kids like Joey Gallo, who'd smart-mouth the nuns (an attitude I found very attractive) and who wore his uniform just a little more rakishly than the next guy. One Wednesday the priest said to the boys, "Okay, when I come back next Wednesday, I'm going to give a prize to the first person who knows the Confiteor." Notice he did not say "boy," he said "person."

So the priest came back next week and sure enough none of those clowns knew it, and I kept waving my hand and saying, "Fahda, Fahda, would you please, Fahda." Finally, he decided to use me to humiliate the boys. What did I know then? I hadn't learned politics yet, I just wanted that prize. I said the Confiteor letter-perfect and he had to give it to me: a huge, hideous Mary that glowed in the dark. I'll never forget it; it scared the life out of me for years.

But my imagination, which did wonderful things to make me believe, also worked against me. I was really convinced that anything you did that didn't exactly follow what the Commandments said or what the nuns said or what your mother said was going to cause you, truly, to burn in hell. My imagination flourished in this state of absolute terror. In our church there was a case displaying a sculpture of purgatory, complete with fire and tortured souls, people reaching out with scorched arms and anguished faces. I remember going there after school, around four o'clock, with an extra dime. I'd light a candle—there were lots nearby—and kneel there until, in that kind of light, my eyes started to play tricks on me. I'd swear the people were moving. To this day I can see that purgatory scene.

THREE

John and Ethel Ross lived on one floor of an old mansion on Seventy-fourth Street off Riverside Drive. It was a stylish part of Manhattan and a fabulous apartment, all pinks and grays with a round rug: I'd never seen one of those before. It should have seemed like a fairyland to a seven-year-old girl, but when I think back to my first meeting with the Rosses, what I remember most vividly was the sinking feeling I had in the pit of my stomach when my mother and I walked through the big iron grillwork door and into a tiny elevator to go up to their place. If there ever was a premonition I should have paid attention to, that was it.

It was only because of my brother, Ray, that I was meeting with the Rosses in the first place. Ray was the first of us to have an interest in dramatics. He started acting at about age seven at the Madison Square Boys Club, a big building with a gym and a swimming pool on Twenty-ninth Street between First and Second avenues. Some well-known folks, everyone from Ben Gazzara to Huntz Hall of the Bowery Boys, came out of that place. Ray caught the attention of a kind of talent scout named Irving Harris, who hung around the club. He introduced Ray to John and Ethel Ross, managers who worked with child actors. The Rosses, especially Ethel, liked him and, over the next several years, he worked in dozens and dozens of shows and commercials, including *Studio One*, *Armstrong Circle Theater*, and *The U.S. Steel Hour*.

Many people believe I began acting because I wanted all the goodies Ray was getting as a result of his career. Here's what I told Lillian Ross and Helen Ross (no relation to John and Ethel) in 1961 for their book, *The Player*: "Ray went all the way to Bermuda on a plane (for a TV series called *Crunch and Dez*) and when he came back, he told us how wonderful the plane trip was, and how he had fished in Bermuda and gone swimming, and how beautiful the water was, and he told us about how he had driven a boat. It sounded like such fun to me." Maybe that's true, but I don't remember thinking or feeling that. I don't remember any sibling rivalry. When Ray was acting, he just wasn't there with the rest of us— that's all I was aware of.

My father had left by this time, and my mother, even though she worked for a while as a cashier in Wanamaker's department store, needed and eventually depended on the money Ray earned. Though I had none of Ray's passion for acting, he mentioned me to the Rosses and my mother took me to meet them.

They were close to forty, the same age as my parents, but the similarity ended there. Ethel was an ex-dancer, possibly even a former Ziegfeld girl, and she did have great legs. Her background was midwestern; she grew up in a suburb of Detroit with a father who worked in the Ford plant and a mother who made the best apple pie in the world. She must have been about five foot six, but to my little-girl's perspective she seemed *very* tall and thin, slender except for a pot belly that, oddly enough, looked about like mine does now. The shape of her face was like Loretta Young's, with a tiny nose; she stood very straight; and she had great-looking hands with very shapely fingers. Coming from an era in which women shaved or drastically plucked their eyebrows, she had a very hard look. At first I was very impressed with her clothes, because they were much more sophisticated than the clothes I saw at home. Later I realized they weren't really so elegant.

John—I never called him that; first it was Mr. Ross, then Uncle John, then in my teens a pre-*Dallas* J.R.—was shorter than she, very round, with birdlike legs and a round head that was bald in the middle with a fringe around the sides. He wore really thick glasses and his hair had turned white literally overnight from the trauma of surgery he'd had for a congenital eye condition. When I first met them, his hair was like a lion's mane, very long, startlingly white. Then, on Ethel's advice, he cut it into what the kids would call a buzz; that was a mistake. He had a slight speech impediment, sort of a sibilance, and a strange little smile. He never smiled full out, he just pursed his lips; I don't know how he did it, it was really weird. He wore flashy clothes, like what you'd buy in Las Vegas. And he sweated a lot.

As little as I know about Ethel's background, I know less about John's, except that he came from a very poor family from the New York area and his full name was John Valentine Rossi. He changed it because most of the people who were successful in his end of show business were Jewish, not Italian, and he used to say the shortened name allowed people to think he was Jewish. He'd worked in public relations, and Ray remembers his saying that he wanted to be an actor, but even though he knew what to do and why he should do it, the minute he got in front of a camera or in front of people, he couldn't deliver.

Though I wasn't willing to face this for a number of years, John did understand acting. He had a scattershot approach and there was never any follow-through, but he really did have a fine psychological understanding of character and thought processes. If he had gone about it systematically, he would have been, I think, a Lee Strasberg. When I was coached by him, even as a young kid, he would give me subtext. He also gave me line readings until he got secure enough to know that I could do that myself. He was a huge fan of Stanislavsky, read *The Method* I don't know how many times. He knew what it was all about, but Ethel knew only results, whether a performance was good or bad. How you got there was not her job. While he devoured books on every topic, she didn't read at all; her heavy reading was *TV Guide*.

So hers was all street smarts, a jockeying-for-position kind of intelligence, and his was the more educated approach.

Early on, their relationship with each other seemed like something out of a storybook. She was always saying "I love you, baby," and he was always saying "I love you, baby," and that was several times an hour. If either of them entered or exited a room, it was always "Love ya!" I don't remember their having any friends, and they never entertained, not even business dinners. In the beginning he seemed to be the leader, but the balance of power shifted drastically within a few years and he deferred to her about everything. It was "Ethel says this" and "Ethel says that." And they both turned out to be considerable drinkers.

The Rosses may have been genuinely attached to each other, but I think it's more likely that they were simply stuck with their marriage. This was a time when divorce was a major item and they both were so good at pretending, maybe they themselves believed in the pretense. If there was a real love between them, I couldn't see it. My adult perception, now that I know, or think I know, what love can be, is that it was only surface stuff. I do know that as years went on and I reached the age when it occurred to me to listen, I never overheard them making love.

At that first meeting, however, the Rosses couldn't have been more pleasant. They were very opinionated, but seemingly very secure about what they knew and what should be done with me. The feeling they exuded was that they were superior, that they *knew*, and out of the goodness of their hearts they were going to help *you* to be superior too.

The Rosses also had a way of talking about me while I was standing right there as if I didn't exist—"She can't use that New Yorkese" (I sounded like a miniature Jimmy Cagney), "she can't do this, she can't do that." There was talk about my hair, that it was too short and badly cut, and that I was definitely offbeat, not the pretty little blond girl who seemed to be favored for commercials. But the decision was made before my mother and I left the apartment that they were going to give me a chance, we were all going to try this and see if it worked.

I've often wondered what it was the Rosses saw in me at

that first meeting. Maybe they just thought the offbeat look was going to be more in demand. One thing was for sure: there certainly wasn't any enormous desire in me to become an actress. In fact, I hated it at first. If there was any desire, it was the desire to please, which was very important to them. Besides that, I imagine what they saw was intelligence, a bright shiny little kid who would understand the score and who could easily be controlled. And though they never said any of this to me, they must have seen a strong, basic instinct for acting. I do think that is a gift, something you come here with—I've seen it in my own children, who had no schooling whatsoever in acting. When I think back to my childhood playtime, I was very good at those little pretend games. I really *felt* like a nun when we were playing nun. I had a good imagination, but I didn't have the freedom to use it in front of other people. That's what John Ross was able to bring out, the confidence to let my imagination run free.

FOUR

It happened one day while Ethel was trying hard to curl my hair, which was very coarse and straight and difficult to work with. I had overheard telephone conversations with other people, strangers to me, about having to change the kid's name, about how Anna Marie was too long and not "perky" enough. My opinion had not been solicited and I knew it would not be accepted. Besides, I couldn't believe they'd really do that. But without any preamble Ethel said, in between curls, "Okay, we've finally decided, we're gonna change your name. Anna Marie is dead. You're Patty now." Just like that. Little did they know that over twenty years would be spent on a psychiatrist's couch because of that phrase alone.

No bolt of lightning struck then, at least not that I was aware of. Actually, my first reaction was waiting to see what they were going to do with my last name, and when they didn't go on I guessed that Duke was staying. I think the Rosses chose Patty because Patty McCormack, who'd been so successful on Broadway in *The Bad Seed*, was leaving New York for Hollywood. It'd worked for her, so why not for me? I didn't make a fuss that I can remember, but I took an instant dislike to the name, probably because it wasn't mine. I was sitting on a bus with the other extras on one of my first jobs and listening as they kept calling this "Patty" person. Naturally, I didn't respond. Finally, I remembered, "Oh my God, that's me." Someone I barely knew had taken away my name. What I didn't know was that that was the tip of the iceberg, the beginning of the little by little murder of Anna Marie Duke and the rebuilding of the Frankenstein's monster that became Patty Duke.

One of the first things the Rosses tried to do was break me of my New York speech patterns. They did it by giving me an English accent, the theory being to take the pendulum all the way to the other side and then bring it back. Almost every day after school at Sacred Heart my mother would take me to their apartment and I'd work with John. For hours and hours and hours I'd sit in front of a big old reel-to-reel tape recorder and practice reading from *The Innocents*, the play version of the Henry James novella. I'd listen to John's prerecorded version, and then I'd do it. Afterward he'd come in and review my progress. We'd work without the recorder, reading the script together, and he'd correct me—every word. God, I hated those sessions—they were very frustrating and went on for months. John was a perfectionist in that area; later on, when I learned accents for specific roles, there was no such thing as doing a sort of general Southern accent. If the play was set in Tennessee, we did a Tennessee accent. Though it must've gotten tedious for John as well, at least he was dealing with a child who would never think of saying, "I don't want to do this anymore." The kid was obviously trying, so how mad could he get?

What also started immediately was working on my appearance, which meant picking me apart, a constant tearing-down. While I can remember genuine kindness from John—I think he was very taken with me—Ethel was a different story. There was a lot of anger in her, a very hard, opinionated edge, and she got really vicious when she'd been drinking. John was completely intimidated by her at those moments. He'd get a sad look on his face, as if to say, "Don't pay any attention, it's just the booze talking." Ethel always said she liked Ray the best, which of course made me work all the harder so that I would be the favorite. Dream on.

The Rosses' idea was to create another Grace Kelly.

Little white gloves, little white socks . . . the perfect little princess was the role for me, the image I had to live up to. Only Ethel forgot to notice that we'd run out of princes and little countries to rule. She was always saying, "Is that the way Grace Kelly would behave?"

"No. . . ."

"Then why are you doing it?"

"I'm sorry. . . ."

The Rosses began by telling me how plain I was. I didn't look like the cute little girls who usually worked in show business. There was a whole list of things I'd never do right, from the way I walked and the way I talked to the way I brushed my teeth or combed my hair. Ethel was especially hard on my hair. It just *had* to grow, she would say, as if telling it would make it perform. After trying curls and informing me that I could never wear a ponytail because my nose was too big, Ethel decided braids were what I needed. But there was a long way to go. It took two years of her brushing and brushing and literally pulling for my hair to get long enough for French braids. I loved my long hair once I had it, but the Rosses wouldn't let me wear it down because it was too "glamorous," I would get too affected. When I got too old for braids, they simply cut off my hair. I no longer had that luxurious feeling of masses of hair, and I was inconsolable.

The Rosses were also unhappy with the way my mother dressed me, which I can understand, but the clothes Ethel bought were always intended to make me look younger than I was. She was always putting me in little baby dresses instead of an eight-year-old's clothes. Their reason was, "You're so little, people don't believe you're eight so we'll make you look six." Now that I have kids, I realize how important it is for a child to feel secure with her age, how destructive it can be to dress children younger than they are.

Three jobs, none of them speaking roles, came up almost at once for me, and I'm not sure which one came first. Ray thinks my first was working with him on *The Deep Well*, a documentary on a home for wayward children in Pleasantville, New York. Or it could have been as an extra in *I'll Cry Tomorrow*. In that film Susan Hayward got out of a car and walked into a building and I was part of the background, buying one of those fat, salted pretzels. I wasn't a movie fan, so I didn't know who she was, but still I looked at her not so much with envy but rather just a kind of longing. This must be a special person, because she wasn't out there all day waiting with the rest of us, then, *boom*—there she was and things started to happen.

The early job I remember best, though, was a commercial with Paul Winchell and Jerry Mahoney. It was a Christmastime commercial, with what seemed like ten thousand little kids on a train circling a lot of toys while Winchell talked with his dummy. The job came up very suddenly—I remember a lot of panicky hustle and bustle the night before. My mother took me and my white communion dress over to the Rosses and Ethel dyed it, which was devastating to both my mother and me. A communion dress becomes a relic, you don't go and dye it pink. Ethel also starched my crinolines with sugar water; I had no skin left on my legs by the time the day was over. And something that you'd imagine was apocryphal but that really did happen was having to put cardboard in the bottoms of my shoes to hide the holes. Ethel cut three or four pieces out of shirt cardboards, put them inside my Mary Janes, and then painted the bottoms of the shoes with shoe polish. My instructions for the day were, "Don't talk, and keep your feet on the floor."

As soon as it became necessary for me to deal with the outside world, the Rosses started teaching me what to say, turning me into a perfect Stepford child. Every single word, from the moment I left them before a job till the moment I came back, was programmed. Any so-called personal conversation, programmed. All of which still has its effect on me. I still have to fight the impulse that tells me, "You're not supposed to do anything to rock the boat. Just swallow whatever anyone says or does and get on with it." The Rosses were very clever, and they wanted this to be the most unusual creature ever. Most of all they loved the Cinderella idea, the Pygmalion and Galatea image. The problem with Galatea is she can't have any thoughts of her own; it only messes things up.

When I had to give an interview, I would be prepared in

a way that was diabolical but very effective. John Ross would stay up late the night before, writing down every conceivable question, plus my answer. There could be a couple of hundred of them, covering every possible approach an interviewer might take, every possible topic, every potential twist. He'd quiz me to see what my answers would be—I, of course, never gave the right one—and then the appropriate responses would be worked out in words I could actually say. Their tactic was never, "Here are the lies we're going to tell today," but rather, "Ethel and I have been talking and we think the best answer for how you got started is to say that your desire was so great, you were so thrilled that somebody finally picked you off the streets." Then I memorized those, and I memorized variations, in case the same question was asked in a different way. Even pauses were orchestrated: how long to think before answering a question, how long to think during my answer. If it was an amusing answer, I was told to deliver it thus-and-such a way. Nothing was left to chance.

When the interviewer came around, I performed like the perfectly trained young teenager who might have come from a finishing school for midgets. I would show him in, take his coat and hang it up, serve coffee and cookies or whatever. My manner was one step short of a curtsy, and I think if Ethel could have squeezed that in, she would have. While the interview was going on, John stayed in the background and never interrupted; that was so that no one could say he was interfering or that I was being manipulated. Having prepped me, he didn't have to intrude. If I had a memory lapse and said the wrong thing, he wouldn't contradict me, he'd just say, "Well, perhaps another way to look at it is . . ." and that would push the right button and I'd get the information out the way he had planned. Once I got the basic interview down, it would be updated, critiqued regularly, and there would be periodic refresher courses. People were not used to reading interviews with children that age. They were very taken with the idea of a kid who seemed to be at ease with the language—the Rosses' footwork totally dazzled everyone.

The Rosses were also adept at making up stories about me, like my getting a soap commercial because I was the only kid who showed up with a dirty face. They even had me lie

at my first audition. To reinforce the impression my new
clothes made, they told me to say I was six when I was eight,
a lie that wasn't caught until I testified before Congress in
1959. If I could unearth an eight-by-ten photo of me from
that period, with credits on the back, fifty percent or more
would be lies. Like *Somebody Up There Likes Me.* I wasn't in
that movie, my brother was. A credit for *The Arthur Murray
Party*, saying I appeared on it six times, stayed on my picture
past *The Miracle Worker.* I was never on that show; I wouldn't
know Arthur Murray if I fell on him. And, of course, I had
little anecdotes to go with each credit, in case somebody
asked me a question.

The Rosses tried to convince me I wasn't being made to
lie. They'd say, "Everybody does this," or "It's just so they'll
have something to talk about with you." But I was always
afraid I was going to get caught. With that strong Catholic
upbringing, here I was telling bald-faced lies. I realize now
that I never would have gotten caught because I was so good
at it—I was acting. But at the time I was terrified. Every time
I would hand my picture across the table to the person
casting the part, I worried that I would forget which story
went with which show. There were so many lies. They lied
about my weight, they lied about my height, and, of course,
they lied about my name.

And though I didn't feel it at first, that name change
did indeed turn out to be a lightning bolt that reached deep
into my mind and touched a major concern of mine, which
was a fear of death so powerful it precipitated daily anxiety
attacks from the early 1950s to 1983. I was obsessed, truly
obsessed with my mortality. And guilty, as well, about not
worrying about my parents' deaths or my sister's or brother's
or my children's or anyone else's. Just my own.

Because when the Rosses said, "Anna Marie's dead,
you're Patty now," it was as if she really did die. When people
take away your name, they are taking away your identity.
That may seem like a lot of fuss over a bunch of letters strung
together, but your name is an important symbol. What had
happened to that Anna Marie person, I wanted to know.
Could she be dead? Where'd she go? It was all part of the
feeling that nothing about me was good enough for these

people, not the way I talked, not the way I looked, and not the most important thing, my name. I felt as if they'd killed part of me, and in truth they had.

My fear wasn't ever-present. Life would be going along fine and then something, like passing those endless cemeteries out in Queens, would trigger it. Or maybe I'd be reading, and there would be a natural progression from that to contemplating life and the larger questions. All of a sudden the absolute realization of my own mortality would hit and I just felt impelled to scream. Sometimes it was what I'd call a bloody-murder scream, sometimes words like "No! No! No! No!" The screams served the purpose of relieving the fear a little bit, and then I'd force myself, before I got sucked back in again, to immediately think about something else.

Occasionally, once I began working, the fear would hit when I'd be in a cab, say, going over the 59th Street Bridge into Manhattan. I was a *kid*, but I'd get so crazed, I'd tell the driver to stop and I'd get out and run. I remember running over that bridge, running and running and running and running until I was so physically tired that I couldn't think anymore, I couldn't be scared.

Inevitably, though, it happened at night, on the way to sleep. I'd scream every night of my life. I'd be lying there in bed, thinking about what I had to do the next day, and this feeling would come over me. From that moment I wasn't actually thinking anymore, thoughts didn't come, I was overtaken by abject terror. After the scream I'd pretend that I'd been asleep and had had a bad dream. To cover the sound I developed a really annoying habit of making a horrible clearing-my-throat noise that bordered on hyperventilation.

The men in my life have been very comforting and helpful about this, even when I'd bolt out of bed and run right across the night table. John Astin many times had to hold me down on the floor and tell me that whatever it was, it was all right. My children know about it, of course, and feel free to explore answers that suit them. The only people who weren't sympathetic were the Rosses. Finally, one night Ethel had had enough of that strange, strangled sound and she said, "What's the matter with you? Stop that." And I said, "I have something in my throat." She told me, "No, you don't. You do that all the time." And I finally said, "I'm afraid of dying." And she said, "That's just too bad. You don't have to worry about that for a lot of years." Great, I thought, should I wait until the day I'm dying to start? All I could think, was "I'm in agony, somebody *help* me."

When I went through a cursory basic training at Fort Benning, Georgia, in 1985, to prepare me for a TV movie I did called *A Time to Triumph*, I was reminded of my own early training. The idea was the same: taking away individuality, breaking the will in order to have control, erasing the slate so it could be filled in by the authorities. Everyone wears the same clothes, the hair is shaved so everybody looks the same, the goal being the loss of ego and becoming one with your unit. And that was very much like what the Rosses did to me. I was stripped of my parents, I was stripped of my name, I was eventually stripped of my religion, and they had a blank slate to do with as they wished.

When I was with the Rosses, I quickly went into a kind of limbo, similar to the mind-set of people who are in jail or even mental hospitals. You simply cannot think about the bad things because there is nothing you can do about them, you have to live in the reality that you're in. You don't make a conscious decision not to think, you just stop thinking. What you do is lock it all out, put a solid vault door between your feelings and what you're expected to say and do. That led, especially as I got older, to a constant internal tug-of-war, a resentment against myself as part of me began to feel I could in fact do something about it. I could have said, "I don't want to do this anymore" or "I'm going to tell people what you're doing," but my fear was always greater than my intelligence.

I can imagine people reading all this and saying, "For heaven's sake, why didn't she *say* something, *say* she wanted to make a phone call, *say* she wanted to be with her mother? She was on a set every day with forty people—why didn't she *tell* somebody?" It's just not that simple. For one thing, there were practical reasons. I was a kid. They were adults. It was my word against theirs. But it's also more complicated than that. It's almost impossible to understand, unless you've walked in those shoes for a while, that once you've been successfully indoctrinated, it simply no longer enters your mind to act in another way. You know what your sentence is, and you live it out.

The overwhelming irony of the Rosses' plans and schemes is that they genuinely thought they were doing the right thing with all their disparaging comments, helping me become a solid citizen by keeping things in perspective for me. They weren't out-and-out monsters, thinking, "Okay, let's get the little bitch and humiliate her," even though that was often the result. In their heads there was a lot of self-righteousness. When they built this cocoon around me, they probably thought they were saving me from a lot of the difficulties of growing up, but that was really the opposite of what was necessary. I was never allowed to grow and learn at my own pace, the pace of a child. They often talked of the injustice of their not having children because *they* knew what children needed. But everything they gave me in the way of love was very superficial. I used to think, They never loved me. It was all a lie. It was all a scam. But I think now that they really did love me, they just didn't know how.

FIVE

Opinions, as far as the Rosses were concerned, were a luxury I wasn't allowed. I remember once voicing one, who remembers about what, and being sat down in the kitchen and told there was no such thing as an opinion for me. Period. I was to do what I was told. Period. I'm a parent myself, and I can imagine saying to my own children, "You're a kid, you're being very opinionated and you're not seeing the whole picture." But this was, "No opinions about what you wear, how you look, what you say, how often you change your underwear. That's it. None." We're talking about the most basic things here, even down to the kind of toothpaste I used. "You don't like the taste? We'll tell you what taste you like." And especially no opinions about acting.

When the roles I was going to try out for were discussed, I never had any input. It would simply be announced that "you have an audition for this" or "you're going to do that three weeks from Thursday." Even considerations like "Gee, I have tests coming up in school" weren't allowed. I would take my shiny patent leather Mary Janes and a pair of clean socks with me in my school bag, and I would call in and find out what auditions I had that afternoon. If the part was really good, I'd meet John Ross at the audition and we'd work on the script in the stairwell or someplace. But if the audition was just for a commercial, I'd go by myself or with my mother. Then there would be the last-minute reminders. "Are your socks clean?" Ethel was fixated on socks. "Remember, bright-eyed and bushy-tailed! Sparkle! Sparkle-sparkle-sparkle!" It sounds like a bad "movie of the week," but I took it seriously, I became like some mechanical doll run amuck with my eyes rocketing in my head. Sparkle-sparkle-sparkle.

Many of the first jobs I got when I began to work in the mid-1950s were on commercials. And because this was the heyday of live TV, a lot of the spots were live as well. They made me really nervous, but I'm sure they were even scarier for the people who hired children to do them: "Okay, hold your breath, let's see what the kid's gonna do this time!" The worst was for Esquire shoe polish. The announcer talked about how using the polish was so simple, a child could do it, and I'd stand there and polish the shoes on live television, terrified that I would go right up my arm with the stuff. I did get it all over my dress once, and that got me in a lot of trouble.

The spot most people remember me from was for a cleaner called Lestoil. It was memorable for me, too, because it was done in Springfield, Massachusetts, but nobody thought to tell me that. We got in a cab, we headed out to Queens, we went to LaGuardia airport, and we were preparing to take off—yes, actually take off—before John Ross finally said to me, "We're going to Massachusetts by airplane. Isn't that a great surprise?" Surprise? I'd never been on a plane in my life and I was petrified, absolutely petrified. It was one of those four-engine prop jobs where they served you a box lunch and a lot of people barfed it up. But I kept saying, "What a great surprise! This is terrific!"

The setup was a prissy little 1950s girl having a tea party with her dolls. I would serve them ice cream and one of the dolls would drop her portion on the floor. I'd say in a very sophisticated voice, "Dolls are so messy, you know," and I'd clean up with Lestoil. Let me tell you, the smell of Lestoil and ice cream is something that cannot be beat. It was really an annoying commercial but it ran forever in New York.

People would scream at their TVs, "Let's make the kid drink that stuff."

Commercials in which I actually had to eat and drink presented challenges of their own. One that was really disgusting was for Beanie-Weanies, a product that was exactly what it sounds like, a canned frankfurter and beans combination. Though I didn't know it at the time, my husband-to-be, Harry Falk, was a prop man on that shoot. The real problem here was that this was a Friday and I was still Catholic. Another client of the Rosses, a boy named Joey Trent, was working with me, and he wouldn't do any more than pretend. But I ate them, feeling really guilty but also thinking, "Oh, boy, Joey's going to get in real trouble. At least I'm eating." I was more afraid of the Rosses than I was of God.

The commercial that was the worst, however, was for Minute Maid orange juice. After about four glasses of Minute Maid under those hot lights, I started to throw up. I spent the whole day throwing up, drinking more orange juice, and throwing up. Actually, from as early as I can remember, I'd throw up at the drop of a hat. It was the way I dealt with everything that upset me. It certainly was a safe way to take a break—nobody can pick on you for throwing up. You're sick. And the people I dealt with weren't sophisticated enough to know the vomiting was psychologically motivated. To this day, when I'm doing a play I become physically ill from head to toe on opening night. You don't want to be near me. I'm not unpleasant, except that I spend all my time in the bathroom. When in doubt, vomit.

People have told me they heard that I stopped working for about six months early on because I lost interest in acting, that I said, "I hate this, I don't want to do it anymore." Not true. I was too scared to say that. I would have loved to, which is probably why at one point I believed I did. But the fact of the matter was that for a while there were simply no jobs, and I think the Rosses ran out of ideas about how to package this little number.

Then, all of a sudden, as if someone found the lights in a dark room, I would just go on auditions and knock 'em off, one right after another. My first speaking role came in 1956, when I was nine. I played an Italian waif on the *Armstrong Circle Theater*'s production of "The S.S. *Andrea Doria*." There was more excitement than usual on this production because the sinking had just occurred plus there was a great big ship on the set. I played a little girl who gets separated from her mother but then at the last moment, naturally, is rescued and lowered over the side. I remember feeling at first that this was a really big part, but after three days of saying things like "Mama!" and "Help!," in an Italian accent no less, I was thinking, "Is this all there is?"

I also got a continuing role in a soap called *The Brighter Day*. It was done live, without a TelePrompTer, and one day I forgot my lines. I had a 104-degree fever and this time I was sick for real. I'd throw up just before I made an entrance and once again after I made an exit. You know, they say when a person is drowning, his whole life flashes in front of him. That's what happened to me. It was a short life, because I was only a kid, but God, the moment was awful. I was supposed to introduce Hal Holbrook's character, the Reverend Dennis, but I was so sick I couldn't remember even that much. I said, "I've been with . . . I've been with . . . I've been with . . ." and I looked over at Hal. He wanted to save me, but the terror was contagious. He had the same scared look on his face I did and now he couldn't remember his name either. He kept saying, "I'm . . . I'm . . . I'm . . ." and then from nowhere he blurted out, "She's been with—*me*!"

I've always been grateful that I began acting during what's come to be known as the "golden age" of live TV. You got to work with terrific people, like playing opposite Myrna Loy and dancing with Ed Wynn in "Meet Me in St. Louis," plus there was an excitement about it unlike anything I've ever experienced professionally. The electricity in the studio the date the show was going on the air built and built and built all day long, till it was "Fifteen seconds, stand by," at which point, of course, I had to go to the bathroom but couldn't. Being on those elite shows like the *Armstrong Circle Theater, The U.S. Steel Hour, David Susskind Presents,* and the *Hallmark Hall of Fame* was a real high, scary as hell and fun, all at the same time.

Most of the time, I appeared in TV versions of the

classics and those were wonderful for me. In "The Prince and the Pauper" in 1957 I was a little girl in a loft, watching the sun bounce off the windowpanes and having a conversation with the prince. I had my hair down for once and I was wearing a long peasant dress, so I thought it was all *very* romantic, a feeling I've always loved.

The next year came something even better, "Wuthering Heights," starring Richard Burton and Rosemary Harris. Even today, the romance of that story is really transporting. If I watch the Laurence Olivier/Merle Oberon version on late night TV, I can't go out of the house the next day because my eyes are so red. And Richard Burton was, well, *Burton*, bigger than life and exciting to look at. I played Cathy as a child and even though I was crazy about Rosemary Harris, who was the older Cathy, I also resented it when it was time for her to take over. *I* wanted to do those love scenes with Richard Burton.

Besides Burton, what I really enjoyed about "Wuthering Heights" was the rain. Heathcliff kept running away, I'd follow him, and it would rain and rain on the moors during our preteen love scenes. But if you want to talk serious rain, there was "The Swiss Family Robinson" later in 1957. We created a real hurricane, with trees blowing over, the treehouse swaying as if it were going to collapse, monkeys and all kinds of exotic birds flying around. The wind machines were turned on, then the rain, and we all climbed up rope ladders. I cried out, "Help me! Help me! Help me!"

All of a sudden everything stopped and David Susskind, the producer, ran out, grabbed me, and said, very concerned, "What's the matter, honey, what's the matter?"

"What?"

"What's the matter, honey?"

"I'm acting!"

What could he say but "Oh." I felt like such a fool. He turned and walked away, but the whole place fell apart. "I'm acting! Get out of the way!" Oh, brother.

Walter Pidgeon was the star of that show and I had a special rapport with him. He was my pop. He was tall and handsome and gentle, all those good fantasy things you want in a dad. Because we had a scene together in which we talked about tortoises and how long they live, he gave me a turtle-shaped hassock, which I still have, plus a gold turtle from Tiffany that was my first good piece of jewelry. The Rosses, naturally, took it away from me. It was mine, but it was to be worn only when I was told I could wear it.

Actually Walter Pidgeon was only one of a series of surrogate fathers I created on almost every set I was on. I was very affectionate, and I was addicted to sitting on people's laps. That became a running joke in my grown-up years. People still see me at parties and say, "She sat on my lap!" and someone else will chime in, "She sat on *my* lap too! She'd sit on *anybody's* lap." And it was true.

I found another surrogate in one of the first major film roles I did, *Happy Anniversary* in 1959, and that was David Niven. He was even more elegant than the other dads. He and Mitzi Gaynor, who was the costar, and Mitzi's husband, Jack Bean, were all loving, bright, sunshiny people. And Mitzi looked so glamorous. I remember her wearing a sort of negligee thing for a breakfast scene and my being so impressed with her breasts because they would rise and fall when she talked. I was mesmerized by that. Actually, the story line of the film had to do with sex, and the awful consequences of my blurting out on a television quiz show that my parents, David and Mitzi, had had premarital relations. I think I was smart enough to figure out what premarital relations were, but the Rosses led people to believe that I was a total innocent, all sweetness and light. So someone was delegated to take me aside and gingerly tell me that sex was something adults did and which I shouldn't have mentioned, and that was all I needed to know in order to play the scene.

Before *Happy Anniversary*, however, came *The Goddess*. The film was written by Paddy Chayefsky about a Marilyn Monroe–type movie star, played by Kim Stanley. I played her as an eight-year-old girl. It was shot at Ellicott City, Maryland, and my mother, who was delegated by the Rosses to take me there, freaked out on the airplane. It was her first time on a plane and she got frantic, saying, "I want to get off! I want to get off! I want to get off!" And I'd say, "Mama, you *can't* get off. We're ten thousand feet in the air." Then she really started throwing a fit and the stewardess had to come over and calm her down. I was so embarrassed.

My scene in the movie was a brief one, but it was lovely. I was Emily Ann, the little girl no one paid any attention to. She gets her report card at the end of the school term and she goes to tell her mother, who works in a five-and-dime store, that she got promoted to the next grade. Her mother is annoyed and tells her to go home. Then you see her at a girlfriend's house, calling, "Sylvia! Sylvia!" But Sylvia never comes and Emily Ann has nobody to tell. She goes home and you see that she's a latchkey kid before we had the phrase. She's going to eat a snack in this depressing, hideous-looking kitchen, when suddenly a tough alley cat wanders in through an open window. A funny look comes over the girl's face. She very carefully gets up from the table, finds a bowl, pours some milk into it, and puts it on the floor. While the cat is drinking, she swoops it up, envelops it in a hug, and says, "I got promoted today."

It's a strong scene, just a little vignette but very well written, with a beginning, middle, and end. You could have had the whole movie stop there and you would have gotten the message. Getting that part, which involved a pantomime audition for Paddy Chayefsky, after which he called up and raved about me, was one of the few times I was aware that the Rosses were really excited, really proud of me. When I think about what was the first film I ever did, it's always *The Goddess*.

It wasn't until 1973, however, almost fifteen years after it was made, that I got to see *The Goddess*. I was in Milwaukee, doing a play, and one night I was lying on a motel room bed with the TV on, talking to one of my kids, when I heard a child's voice that sounded vaguely familiar to me. I turned over so I could see the TV, and there I was. The Rosses, forever guarding against my getting too big a head, had never let me watch myself on the screen or even read any reviews.

The Rosses couldn't prevent people from coming up and complimenting me in person, but if according to their standards it had been done too much, there would invariably be a humbling session afterward. Or if my thank-yous were not appropriate, if I hadn't said, "Thank you very much. I worked with my manager very hard," the same thing would happen. It usually took place at dinner. Everything would be light-hearted and fine, and then, all of a sudden, I'd hear, "By the way, today you . . ." and the barrage would start. Immediately I would feel, "When am I going to do something right? Even when I do it right, it's not good enough." So I was always on my guard, always trying to figure out what it was they were looking for so that maybe once in a while I could be one step ahead of them.

The cornerstone of these sessions was the idea that without them I'd be nothing. They'd told my brother Ray, "Without us, you'd end up a truck driver or in jail," and with me it was, over and over again, "If it wasn't for us, you'd be a hooker or you'd work in the five-and-dime." Only once, when I was a teenager, did I have the nerve to say, "Well, I hope I would have chosen hooker." Being twelve or thirteen and fairly independent when he started, Ray was much less vulnerable to them than I was. After all, what does a seven-year-old know? The Rosses' threat was, "We will drop you and you'll go back to oblivion," and I came to believe that completely.

SIX

When I was young, I had a dream, a child's nightmare: that I would be taken someplace away from my mother and never know if I was going to be with her again. That's very spooky, considering what eventually happened.

Living with the Rosses didn't start right away, it evolved. First I began staying with them the night before a job, and if I got homesick, they'd make fun of me for being a baby who wanted to be with her mother. Then they started having me stay on weekends, weekends became three days, three days became five, five became seven. Always I was presented with the notion that spending more time with them would further my career. Once I became a Broadway star at age thirteen, that was it. The standard line was, "She'll have to stay here now because the work is going to be so intense." I never lived at home with my mother again.

From the first apartment I met them in, on Seventy-fourth Street, the Rosses soon moved a few blocks to a sixth-floor apartment at 340 West 72 Street, at the corner of Riverside Drive. It was a nice place, but there never was a room for me. I spent innumerable nights there, all through my most successful years, but it was always on a couch in the hallway. I never had more than two drawers to call my own, with my sheets in one and my clothes in the other. Finally, in 1963, when I was sixteen, the Rosses moved to an apartment on Park Avenue and Thirty-ninth Street, where I had my own room. But I was never allowed to close the door. I could close the bathroom door, but if I was in there longer than ten minutes, I had to open it. There was no genuine effort to make me feel at home.

As far as my real mother was concerned, these years marked the beginning of a really dark period that is still very difficult and complicated for me to deal with. When it came to the boring work involved with my career, like baby-sitting me on a set, then she was brought into action. Mostly she sat there as if she were part of the wall. Never opened her mouth, never made a move, just sat there and read the *Daily News* and the *Mirror*. What she was was petrified, because the Rosses had literally told her, "You find a chair, you put it in the corner, and you stay there and don't say a word about anything." That was the directive, and even when people would come up and compliment me, she'd say thank you and then close right up because she was afraid she'd get into trouble.

That fear was in a sense contagious, because I was scared of my mother. She was very unpredictable emotionally, one step away from suicide most of the time, so I never knew what was going to happen. She might turn into an iceberg, with a really mean expression on her face and a rigid body, and withhold any and all affection. At other times everything would be fine and then all of a sudden she'd be screaming and yelling.

One New Year's Eve my sister, who never went anywhere, was going out with the man who would become her fiancé, when my mother threw a tantrum. My sister decided not to go and I kept insisting she should. But when Carol started out the door, my mother began to attack herself—it was astounding to watch. She smashed her face against the doorjamb, pulled out her hair, beat her face until she'd broken her nose and was a bloody mess. Of course my sister came back in, and I kept saying, "Get outta here! Get *outta* here! If you go, she'll stop." And she went. And my mother stopped. And I took care of her. It was not the first time, and it wasn't the last, that she acted that way.

The other thing my mother did to terrible excess was crying. Relentless crying. For days and days and days on end. I'd be at the Rosses', the doorbell would ring at ten A.M., and she'd be standing there in tears. She would come in and sit down, and it would be obvious that she'd been at it for quite a while. She would continue crying and the Rosses would get angrier and angrier. They would try every approach they could think of to defuse the situation. They'd leave her alone, go and do business, come back—she was still the same. Dinner would come and go, the evening would set in, it could be one or two o'clock in the morning, she was still crying. Once you unplugged the dam, this lady did not stop.

My mother would never say why she was doing this, and I know now that she really didn't know why, didn't understand that it was not due to any single cause, it was because of everything. Her fear of the Rosses was ten times greater than mine; she is, in fact, still afraid of them. This was a terrified woman, someone with less than an eighth-grade education, who had no sense of self-worth. The Rosses managed to loom as authority figures; they appeared to her to be educated people of means. And my working represented income that was like a gift from God, which she didn't want to jeopardize. My mother has always felt responsible for everything; anything in the world that goes wrong, she must have caused it. So the Rosses' admonitions and warnings were taken very seriously by her. She figured she could wreck everything for me. Still, she resented the whole situation. There was a lot of fury in my mother in those days.

What my mother's behavior accomplished was exactly what the Rosses hoped it would: it drove an emotional wedge between me and her that made it easier for them to keep me away from home. Although my mother had signed a contract with the Rosses, which neither of us had ever read, they wanted more than that, they wanted to completely control me. But they could never dismiss the threat, minor though it was, that one day my mother might say, "I've come to my senses now. That's my daughter and we're leaving." So they never tried to hide the contempt they had for her. They characterized her as mentally ill, unbalanced. "We just have to put up with Mrs. Duke" was one of their pet phrases.

So even though it troubled me, even though part of me knew better, I bought that point of view. My mother made it easy to buy, especially in the early days before the Rosses got horrible. The Rosses laughed, life was happier at their place, eating dinner out every night was fabulous, at least at first, and on the other side was a woman out of Kafka. They didn't have to do much to diminish her. My mother was giving the Rosses their ammunition; she loaded every gun for them.

Also, my mother was a willing victim a lot of the time. She didn't want to be poor, she wanted to be taken care of. Her weakness was that it was at almost any price, and that price included me. The Rosses saw to it that there was always some cash for Mrs. Duke, and Mrs. Duke would take her cash and go away. Even now she sometimes says things like, "I was her mother. I deserved some of that." A lot of stage mothers have that attitude; it's not unique to mine. But it's more like a sibling attitude than what I think a mother's should be.

It took me a long time to realize the resentment I had against my mother. I was angry at her on the most important level there is, at the very bottom of my soul, and I think I had a right to be angry. A parent makes an unspoken agreement with a kid: "You're here. I got you here. Now I'm going to take care of you." The expectation isn't, "Oh, by the way, there are these two people who live on Seventy-fourth Street who are going to make you an actress, but you have to go live with them and they're going to take care of you—even though you've already given your allegiance to me, your mom."

And my mother still expected my loyalty. When the Rosses weren't around, she would say, "I'm your mother, and I never see you. I'm your mother, and I told you to do this. I'm your mother . . ." It wasn't in me to say then what I feel now, which is, "What are you talking about? I didn't put me here. You did. I didn't invite the Rosses into my life. You did." When my mother was emotionally ill and needed to be hospitalized, she'd always say, "Don't let them lock me up." And the anger I felt came from the fact that she had locked me up. Turning me over to the Rosses was like taking me to Bellevue and throwing away the key.

The Rosses coached other kids besides me and my brother, and occasionally they'd have four or five of us there of a night. That was fun, like the Hollywood Canteen, with all the actor kids hanging out together. But a kind of attrition took place for two reasons. One was that once my success started to happen, the Rosses' energies grew so focused on me that the other kids just fell away. The other was that these kids, like Joey Trent, the gorgeous boy from the Beanie-Weanie commercial, came from very strong families: there was no way that kid was going to live with anybody but his mother and father, no matter how much the Rosses claimed it was hampering his career. The same thing happened with Susan Melvin, a quite talented little girl whose mother was one of the few people who would say, "What are you doing, John and Ethel? This is weird. My kid is not gonna stay here. She has a home. Tell me where you want her and I'll bring her there, but I'm not leaving her here."

The only kid who stayed over at all regularly was a little boy named Billy McNally whom the Rosses discovered shining shoes in front of the Metropole on Broadway near Times Square. His family was also very poor, so the Rosses struck up the same kind of agreement with them that they had with my mother, and Billy came to live with us. He was about two years younger than me, and I adored him because I wasn't alone anymore, I had a colleague, somebody my own age who also thought the Rosses were a little nuts. When they'd go to bed at night we'd get together and whisper. "What'd they say about this?" "What'd they say about that?" "Can you believe what she did?" Billy stayed with us until he reached that "awkward age" young actors do. His presence was very comforting, one of the rare confirmations I got that I wasn't crazy. Before his arrival I sometimes felt like a movie heroine pleading with the psychiatrist, "Doctor, someone *is* chasing me."

Because the Rosses watched me so closely, one of the most difficult things I've had to learn later in life is how to be alone. During my first marriage I would take a bath with the door open, and just being by myself in any room was almost impossible for me until quite recently. When you've been watched and monitored for all your formative years, it's very hard to get used to not being watched and monitored, very hard to be without the background noise of chatter. If you're alone, then you must have thoughts of your own. And those were not permitted when I was growing up.

Though I was the principal earner in the Ross household, I was hardly the center of attention: that honor went to Bambi. Bambi was a light fawn-colored chihuahua that was made, I swear, out of toothpicks and papier-mâché. Bambi would stare at you from her big wet weepy brown eyes and ooze from every orifice. I don't remember a time when this dog wasn't frail and ailing, but she went everyplace with the Rosses, even, eventually, to the Oscars. If the dog couldn't go, we didn't go. Whenever we'd go shopping for anything and happen to notice a purse that Bambi might fit into, Ethel bought it. And when we went traveling, Bambi had her own wardrobe: a dress, a mink stole, a hat.

Bambi rarely walked anyplace, she was carried in her daytime bed: a wicker basket covered by, depending on the temperature, two or three little infant receiving blankets. Bambi had practically no teeth and her tongue hung permanently outside her mouth. I mean, she never even brought it in to get it wet. So when the time came to feed her, which was quite some ritual in itself, the first thing you had to do was get a glass of water and dip Bambi's tongue in it so she could eat at all!

Now, it was a great honor to be among the chosen few who could feed Bambi, who, of course, ate only a special diet. With God as my judge, feeding her was an hour-and-a-half event. First you opened the can at both ends and squished all the food onto wax paper, because Bambi could eat only a can a week and the rest had to be carefully saved. Then you sliced off just the right amount and put it into a special little frying pan that was only for Bambi's food; nothing else could be cooked in this pan. You'd add a tiny bit of water and mush up the food, but not too much, because Bambi didn't like it if it had been mushed up too much. Then you would heat it, but very carefully, because she couldn't feel anything on her tongue, which was like plaster of Paris, and you might burn her.

When the heating was finished, you poured this gray gruel onto a paper plate. Then you took Bambi out of her bed and put her not on the kitchen floor—too slippery!—but into the foyer, which doubled as my bedroom. You held the plate out and you said in a high voice, presumably at a pitch that dogs could hear, "Does Bambi want her dinner?" At which point, this poor decrepit thing jumped up, danced around in a circle, and begged.

Now, you kept saying this until someone threatened to murder you because of the screeching. Then you put down the plate and everybody had to stand there and watch her eat. When about a third of the stuff was gone, which was about all Bambi could handle, there was a serious discussion about whether or not she'd eaten less than usual and questions like, "Is she getting enough nutrition?" were asked.

Now came the pièce de résistance, asking Bambi, in that same high-pitched screechy voice, if she wanted to "make a river." You cannot believe the instructions I used to get about this. One of my mother's jobs was very neatly cutting up the newspapers used to line Bambi's cat litter box, which was also kept in the foyer where I slept. We all had to stand there and watch Bambi make a river, and after she'd finally acquiesced, everybody had to tell her how good she was to have done it. And then, because no river was allowed to stay more than ten seconds, you would lift up and dispose of four pieces of the paper—no more, no less—so that Bambi's box was always clean.

Finally, years later, Bambi became ill, even in the Rosses' eyes, and they took her to a special vet in New Jersey: no one else could be used. They came back without her, heartbroken that Bambi had to stay overnight. That was one of the few times I reverted to my Catholicism, praying fervently that the dog would die. And she did. That really encouraged me and I started praying about the Rosses! If it worked on animals, maybe it would work on people too. Even though I was always giving interviews about how much Bambi meant to me, I really hated that dog. God, she was hideous. And the Rosses were much nicer to Bambi than they were to me:

no demands were made on that animal, she didn't have to perform any function. I'll probably have to pay some karmic price for this, but I can't help it. I loathed that dog.

Life with the Rosses provided few opportunities for escape, and sometimes they came in unlikely situations. In 1959 I made a curious little science fiction film called *The 4-D Man*, which starred Robert Lansing as a scientist who learns the secret of transposing matter and is able to walk through walls and things like that. Unfortunately, he needed human energy to revitalize his powers, and I played one of his victims: a little girl pushing a doll carriage. He takes one look at me and the next thing, my little legs are sticking out from some bushes, next to a broken carriage.

The producer of the film, Jack Harris, owned a studio out in rural Pennsylvania where he'd made *The Blob* and other movies. I was a city kid and this was my first extended time in the country. I hung around with one of the producer's sons, riding bicycles, finding secret places, inhaling the smells of the Pennsylvania countryside. It was a wonderful experience for me because of the location and the tiny sense of freedom, but I always felt as if I were doing something terrible, that I would be caught and get into trouble for having fun.

The only other times I ever got away were occasional weekends when the Rosses would ship me home if they decided they wanted to be alone. My mother had moved to Queens by this time, but my visits weren't like *Lassie Come Home* or the return of the prodigal daughter. It wasn't that those visits were unhappy, they just weren't much of anything, probably because it was obvious that they were only a stopover, that my mother had no autonomy and nothing was going to change. When I wanted to go out, she'd say, "What would the Rosses say?" Invariably the Rosses would have said, "Don't leave the house." Sometimes my mother would get brave and tell me, "The Rosses said you couldn't go out, but go ahead anyway." I'd go out and play with the neighborhood kids, maybe go to somebody's basement and dance, but I was always looking over my shoulder, because I knew if they called and I wasn't home, there'd be hell to pay.

And invariably there would be one call over the weekend and if I wasn't around—how often can you use the she's-in-the-bathroom routine?—my mother would be ordered to get me home immediately. I always let her know exactly where I'd be in case that call came, because Ethel would rant and rave at her. "How dare you let her go out! We told you she couldn't go out!" We were like two little kids being punished because my keeper for the weekend hadn't followed orders.

Ordering my mother around was standard procedure for the Rosses. They would call and say, not, "Could you come in on Thursday?" but "Can you be here in forty-five minutes?" And that was not really a question. It meant, "You will be here." And my mother, of course, never had the courage or whatever it would have taken to say, "No, I can't. I have some things I'm doing." She would stop whatever she was about, throw herself together, and go into the city. Sometimes they gave her all my fan mail to take care of. She'd take the letters home and sit up till three A.M., addressing envelopes and putting pictures in them, and then drag a suitcase full of them back to Manhattan on the subway the next morning.

After I moved in with the Rosses I mostly saw my mother when she showed up about once a week to do their laundry. She would do the hand laundry and Ethel insisted on most things, especially personal items like pajamas, underwear, and socks, being hand-washed. Not only was my mother never paid, this being kind of a "favor among colleagues," she was given very specific instructions about how to do things and a critique when she was finished. It was always done in a very patronizing tone, with Ethel saying things like, "Oh, Mrs. Duke, would you mind very much? Oh, thank you so much, Mrs. Duke. Now, Mrs. Duke, you must use the Woolite here and you mustn't use more than a capful." No wonder my mother went deaf. Who wants to listen to that?

To this day my mother still gets furious over a phrase in the old stock publicity about me that says how filthy my white shoes and socks were before John and Ethel Ross began to manage me; ask her about the phrase "we took her and her dirty white shoes," and you still get the whole chapter and verse. When I was a kid, I wondered, "Why is she making such a big deal about the shoes and socks? What does it matter?" But now I realize it mattered a whole lot. It was an attack on her motherhood, and it underlined her guilt about having relinquished that position with me. That tossed-off phrase did it; that was the stake through her heart.

The image comes to me often now of this woman who came from a shabby apartment in Elmhurst, or, later on, a basement place in Astoria to a seemingly flashy Manhattan apartment to launder the personal underwear of people with whom her child was living. It's cold on West End Avenue, with the wind coming off the Hudson River, and I think of those awful lonely moments she must have had, cold in her heart as well as on the outside, walking those long blocks to the subway in her thin coat. And returning home to a place where there was no one. Who's going to do *her* laundry? Who's going to care if she's had any dinner? What awful demons she must have been living with. It made me ache. It still makes me ache.

SEVEN

When I first started acting, my main motivation was fear, a feeling that if I didn't do what I was supposed to do, something horrible was going to happen. But once I became a hot little number on live TV, once the work changed from "Daddy, I want ice cream," to more meaningful parts and I began to feel myself understanding the concepts and getting better, the acting mechanism in me really clicked. I've never liked to think of myself as very ambitious, but it's been there, underneath, and this was when the drive really kicked in. I was no longer doing the work just because the Rosses wanted me to; now I wanted it as well. I liked the feeling of walking into a studio and not only knowing that I belonged but also having other people know it.

That sense of belonging—the attention and affirmation—was really the key element for me. Most performers are very loving, very willing to show affection, and I made attachments quickly. I would love everybody, and there would always be a couple of favorites who loved me back. They were like the family I'd never really had, so it was wrenching when each show came to an end. I was grief-stricken to the point of feeling inconsolable; every one of the good-byes was a real loss to me.

As determined a little person as I was, I didn't get every part I wanted. One of my biggest disappointments came in 1959 when *Pollyanna* was being cast. Because of the way the Rosses worked, I'd prepared for weeks for that part. That meant not only reading the book but discussing it, imagining dialogue, learning to dress the way Pollyanna dressed and behave the way Pollyanna behaved. If I messed up, their response was, "Pollyanna wouldn't do that, would she?" And after all that, I never even got to the audition. One was set up, with the help of David Niven, but I got very sick, possibly with hepatitis, and during the postponement Hayley Mills, whose look was more classically Pollyanna, was found. I was heartbroken, *heartbroken* at not playing that role. That had nothing to do with a fear of the Rosses' reaction. *Pollyanna* would have meant going to California and working with *Walt Disney*! It took me a while to get over that one.

One of the Rosses' better traits was that they were surprisingly reasonable about rejection. Before I'd go in to try out for something, they'd deliver an effective kind of coach's pep talk, saying, "Okay, it's your part, just go claim it." I've used a similar thing with my own kids when they want to get a hit in Little League: "It's yours, just go do it." And if I didn't succeed, they never openly said, "You blew it." I would feel very frustrated and discouraged, something I now know adult actors go through also, because you never find out why you didn't get the part. Were you too tall, too short, too fat, too skinny, or did your reading stink? Or were you great and they didn't know it? John Ross was very philosophical about all this. He'd say, "Hey, there's another one coming. Don't worry about it."

We went to Long Branch, New Jersey, to audition for a summer stock production of *The Bad Seed*. We'd worked on the part a lot, drilling for days and nights, so I did extremely well, and the reaction was so good afterward that I thought I had the part. We all went out into the lobby and John Ross and the producer went into a corner to talk. I thought they were making a deal, because in the theater in those days, talking in a corner was how all deals were made. I was sitting on a bench, anticipating the summer and my first stage role, when all of a sudden the producer walked up to say good-bye.

I said good-bye back in my best Sparkle Plenty manner, but I noticed that John was acting really disturbed.

We walked down the gravel driveway to the waiting taxi to go to the train station, and John, to his credit, told me how wonderful I had been and how thrilled and proud of me he was, but that I didn't get the part because I had no previous stage experience. He said there was no point in arguing with these people, their minds were set; they were afraid I wouldn't be able to cut it when there was an audience in the house. Actually, that was probably one of the moments when he thought he should have put *more* lies on my credits.

Not getting that role was another tremendous disappointment because I knew I'd been good, I knew that this was a real injustice. We got on the train and Ross said, "Don't you worry, honey. You'll open on Broadway, and you'll never have to set foot on a summer stock stage."

Nineteen fifty-nine was also the year in which, though I didn't know it at the time, I would make the front page of *The New York Times*. It had all started the year before, with Irving Harris, the man who had introduced my brother to the Rosses. Harris had connections with *The $64,000 Challenge*, a TV quiz show that was the successor to *The $64,000 Question*, and he arranged for me to go to a kind of audition, really just to see if I had the personality they were looking for. Then I was informed that I was going to do the show and the producers were trying to decide on a category of expertise for me; naturally, I didn't get to volunteer what I thought I'd be good at. In a few days I was told that popular music had been chosen. It could have been anything; they might as well have said Chinese.

The person I dealt with most on the show was a woman named Shirley Bernstein, who was the associate producer and composer/conductor Leonard Bernstein's sister. She was very attractive, an elegant-looking high-class New York lady with a husky voice who was always willing to caress me or pat me on the head when I needed it. We had several meetings the week before each show. At the first one I was told about material "it would be a good idea for you to familiarize yourself with." It was never "This is what you must know," rather, "Maybe you ought to read x or y in *Cashbox* or *Billboard,*" or "You might want to get hold of these ten records." I would also be asked specific questions, things like what label 'Shaboom, Shaboom' was on or what instrument was featured in a particular arrangement. If I answered correctly, they'd let me know I was right and wasn't that good that I was right. If I gave a wrong answer or didn't know, they wouldn't supply the answer but they'd say, "Gee, it might be a good idea for you to study some more in that area." And I'd go tell John Ross what they'd said and we'd go home and study the material furiously.

John Ross was never present at these meetings and I was discouraged from taking notes. Why they didn't want me to write down information I was supposed to know didn't make a lot of sense to me then. What I know now is that they wanted to have deniability in case any of this came out. Which, of course, it did.

By Saturday morning, the day before the show, I would've accumulated an incredible amount of knowledge. And I'd go down to the show's offices, there'd be nobody around but me and Shirley, and she would narrow it down to, say, ten items I was most secure about. Then I would go home again and Ross would just drill me to death, on and on and on until the wee small hours of Sunday morning, when I was bleary-eyed from it all. I was allowed to sleep in after that and late Sunday afternoon, just before the show, I was taken to the studio and Shirley would ask me just four questions. Usually I knew the answers by then, but a couple of times, when I faltered, Shirley got really nervous. And that would finally be the time when she would supply the answers.

By the time the show went on the air, my guts would be in an uproar. Not only was I intimidated by stuff like orchestrations and arrangements, I didn't understand in general why the Rosses had changed their style for this show, why they suddenly didn't want to be present for all meetings and know every single detail. But still I'd go on with Eddie Hodges of *The Music Man*; I'd be adorable, and everybody would go "ooh" and he'd be adorable, and everyone would go "aah."

After a few weeks Eddie and I progressed far enough to

go into the isolation booths, where it had to be 112 degrees. They had a little fan going in one corner and a lot of Wash 'n Dris in front of you; the whole place smelled of Wash 'n Dris. One week, when we were up to $32,000, I almost blew it. My mouth was very dry, so I licked my lips before answering, but I moved too close to the microphone and got a shock. I was very startled and jumped back and when I told Ralph Story, the emcee, he said, "A lot of people have gotten shocks in these booths," which was very funny except that I now couldn't remember what he'd asked me and he wouldn't repeat the question. I really thought, "They're gonna kill me. I can't even get out of this booth and they're gonna kill me." And suddenly, just when I was about to cry, I remembered the question and out came the answer.

Eddie and I both answered all our questions (no surprise here), so the last show ended with us splitting the $64,000. It's difficult to describe how relieved I was when that show was over. The pressure I'd felt was enormous, much worse than anything involved with acting. For one thing, the hype for those high-stakes game shows was pretty hefty then— people didn't leave their homes when they were on—and the award money seemed astronomical to me. My winnings were supposed to go into a trust fund but, like the rest of my earnings, what really happened to them is a mystery.

So while I may have seemed to be a very composed little girl, with pigtails and bows and perfect little dresses, I was actually much too terrified to be anything like excited. I was afraid of the Rosses and their browbeating kind of consequences if I messed up: "You didn't study enough." "You didn't practice hard enough." "You knew that answer, how could you be so stupid?" "If you had done what we told you, you wouldn't be in this mess."

I knew the difference between right and wrong; I'd taken tests in school and knew you weren't supposed to give the answers to anybody. But whom could I tell about what was going on? Whom could I tell about being so afraid? My mother? When I finally told John they were giving me the answers, what he said was, "It's a secret, you mustn't tell anyone." Eventually, though, not only did it come out, but everyone in America knew.

Things began to fall apart in 1959, the year after my appearance, when first the New York district attorney's office and then a grand jury began to investigate both *The $64,000 Challenge* and *Twenty-one*. John Ross said to me, "We've got to go to the district attorney. All the people connected with the show are going to tell the same story, that you were not given the answers, you were only given general areas to study." Later, when the whole thing burst wide open, he said, "Remember, you would come out of the meetings and say that what went on was a secret, that you couldn't tell me." Which, of course, wasn't true, but it was my cue. Now I could see how he expected me to play this game.

By the time I went to see the district attorney in one of those ancient New York municipal buildings, I was seriously scared. His office was stark, with those brown wooden chairs with arms that smell from all the sweaty palms that have been rubbed over them. My feet didn't touch the ground, so I couldn't even feel physically grounded. The meeting was very brief and, as instructed, I lied to him about what went on before the show.

The grand jury was worse. For one thing, they subpoenaed my mother to testify. Now, there was one person who truly knew nothing about the show. She fell apart in the hall, got hysterical and fainted. Next came my turn. I was dressed like Shirley Temple and I carried a little stuffed dog, Scotty, with a Catholic medal pinned to his underside. It was the same kind of chair, the same kind of smell, but I was taken aback by seeing forty people in the room: the only juries I knew about were the small ones I saw on TV.

When a tiny girl walks into a jury room carrying a stuffed dog, everyone starts to sigh. My feet still didn't touch the ground, but I wanted to look relaxed. So I put my elbow on the armrest and placed my chin in my hand, but, of course, the elbow slipped off, and my head went flying. I got a big laugh and I was enough of a show business veteran to know I had a favorable audience, that if I didn't screw up, I'd be okay here. I'd been coached by John not to volunteer anything, so when I was asked a direct question, I gave the shortest possible answer. When they said, "Can you be more specific?" I'd pretend I didn't know what that meant. Once again I gave out the party line, that there had been talk in general areas. I never revealed that I was given any answers.

At the same time, I was again very frightened. I was a year older than when I'd been on the show, and what was right versus what was wrong was even clearer to me. I knew what perjury was and I knew I was committing it. I really felt I was selling my soul to stay out of trouble with the Rosses. Also, I had all these gothic fantasies going. I thought I'd committed a crime and I'd end up like a kid in one of those old movies who gets shipped off to reform school and has to live on bread and water. No one ever explained to me the legal consequences of what I'd done; I didn't know that it was not a crime, that it was immoral but not illegal. I don't remember the questions I was asked or the answers I gave anymore; I just know that I was told to lie and I did.

The worst terror of all, however, was still to come. In November, 1959, I had to fly down to Washington, D.C., to testify before the House Special Subcommittee on Legislative Oversight. By now the hearings had been on television, Xavier Cugat was there with his dogs—it was like a Barnum & Bailey production. John Ross told me one more time, "This is what everybody's doing. You have to do it, too, or else everyone will be in trouble." I was filled with feelings of having been betrayed, of terrible remorse and humiliation at having to perform again in front of all these people.

Because of my age—which I revealed under oath to be twelve, two years older than the Rosses had been saying, leading the press to joke about how much I'd aged in front of the House—the subcommittee decided to hear my testimony in executive session. Though I didn't know it, they'd already pretty much figured out what had happened and wanted my testimony largely for corroboration. I remember the room as being huge, with lots of microphones, but since it had just been cleared, it looked strangely empty. The initial questioning was very similar to the grand jury's, aimed at determining whether I knew the difference between right and wrong. Direct question: "Did I know the questions ahead of time?" "No, I did not."

Then there was a lull and the congressman in charge, Oren Harris of Arkansas, very sweetly said in his Southern

accent, "Now, Anna Marie"—I'd told them my real name—
"are you sure you've told us the truth?" And I don't remember any time passing between the moment he said "truth"
and my saying, "No sir, I have not."

Why did I finally break down? Partly because I think I'd
guessed, from the nature of their questions, that someone
else had already told the truth. But more than that, something told me that enough was enough; the basic honesty of
this child had been violated for too long and she cracked.
The fear of how the Rosses would retaliate no longer mattered
in the face of this real need to be relieved of that burden.

Then the questioning started again, to establish not
only that these people had perpetrated a hoax on the public,
but that they'd gone so far as to use children to do it. The
Washington Post editorialized the next day: "What they did to
Patty Duke amounted, in the real sense of the phrase, to a
corruption of innocence." And one of the congressmen let
John Ross have it, saying he shared "a very heavy part of the
responsibility" and noting that Patty Duke seemed to be
"exploited at the moment very profitably by quite a number
of people, and not with the test as to what is for her own best
interests." If he only knew.

As for me and John Ross, I was in a no-win situation. I
remember leaving the room and not being able to look at
him. Although I had freed my conscience, I had betrayed
him and the other people who were supposedly hanging
tough together. On the ride to the airport and the flight
back, there was a lot of heavy whispering between John and
the lawyer, who had also been lied to and was afraid he was
going to be disbarred. What I did was never mentioned again.
It was the unspoken judgment that was awful. In my heart I
knew I had done what was right, yet I felt dreadful. Not only
because of the public humiliation, which was certainly punishment enough for my crime—if I'd committed one—but
because it didn't seem to matter that I'd done right; I'd still
done wrong. It was a bleak and confusing time.

EIGHT

Early in 1958 John Ross clipped a small article out of *Backstage*, the theatrical newspaper. It talked about a search that was going to be mounted for a nonprofessional actress to play the young Helen Keller on Broadway. John commented that there was no way they were going to be able to make that work and he taped the article to a long fluorescent light over his desk.

I had never heard of Helen Keller, though I later discovered that there'd already been a *Playhouse 90* version of her story on TV. Our work began with Helen Keller's autobiography, *The Story of My Life*, plus a couple of other books. John Ross had an interesting philosophy: he didn't want me to have more information than I needed, so he instructed me to read only the portions of the books that dealt with her childhood. He put bookmarks in each volume and I wasn't allowed to go past the point he had marked. And I didn't peek either; that's the kind of kid I was. So I didn't realize that Helen Keller grew up to be a famous writer and social activist, a much-loved world figure, just that as a small child she'd suffered an illness that left her unable to hear, see, or speak.

John's approach was to work separately on the deprivation of each sense. The first was blindness. That meant spending a specified amount of time every day going about my regular routine—putting my schoolbooks away, or cleaning up my area of the foyer, or washing the dishes—but doing it all with my eyes closed. Once I got good at that, the Rosses began to rearrange the apartment, which included everything from moving chairs and tables to putting my toothbrush where it wasn't supposed to be to using a couple of cardboard boxes from the supermarket as obstacles. Sometimes they'd move things around while I was asleep, other times they just made me go into another room. Then it became a game—"Uh-uh, we saw you peek. If you hadn't peeked, you would have fallen over that."

The idea, of course, was to see how a person responds when she can't see. You bump into something—what do you do? Do you want to know what it is you hit? Do you bend down and feel it or do you just plow right through? Eventually I actually got too good at all that; the Helen who was wanted for the play was supposed to be clumsier than I was. So once I got the part, I had to regress. But that obstacle-training helped for more than getting used to blindness: it gave me an insight into frustration that I was able to use in other ways in the role.

Dealing with blindness, however, was simpler than what came next: deafness. We never used earplugs or anything like that. It was a matter of my concentrating as the Rosses created disturbing sounds. That was especially hard because when you're twelve years old, you respond easily to stimuli. If I reacted, I got ten demerits. If I didn't, I gained points.

These practice periods lasted one or two hours. Sometimes I'd get hooked and it became fun; we'd all laugh about my response or lack of it. At other times it was real drudgery. Loud, annoying noises were the Rosses' specialty. They'd smash a hammer on the floor, and if I didn't react, that was worth twenty-five Brownie points. They had two phone lines and they'd use one to ring the other. And they'd bang pot covers so close to my ears that they'd ring as well. Another drill was to shoot questions at me. Ethel would ask if I wanted a Coke and I couldn't respond. Direct orders like "Go pick up your socks" presented a real dilemma: Should I do it and get busted for hearing, or not do it and get busted for not picking up my socks? A real judgment call.

All this was undeniably effective, but also a little sadistic because of the intensity of the exercise and the length of time it lasted and because there was no payoff for the kid in me, no reward of, "Okay, now you can go play outside." When we finished we'd start on another role. Sometimes, when I'm working with my own kids, I find myself slipping into some of the old Ross patterns, being overly insistent and not sensitive to the fact that either the kid is tired or he isn't getting it. An adult shouldn't be saying things like "What's the matter with you? It's so simple." If it's that simple, madam, there must be a better way to impart the information.

Another area we worked on was Helen's guttural speech. Many of the girls who are cast in this role choose to play it absolutely silent, and I can see why. Getting the sounds right was very difficult for me; I had to practice them a lot. Not only are they embarrassing, they certainly don't come naturally to a child, whose voice is very thin. John Ross was very helpful with this. He had a remarkable ear and he could create or reproduce sounds well. My work was almost a direct imitation of the sounds he was making.

The most positive effect of all that work with the Rosses was not so much the specific things they wanted to teach me. It doesn't take that long to learn not to look around you and not to react to sound. What took longer but turned out to be more valuable was developing the ability to concentrate. I was eventually able, through trial and error, to put myself in another place mentally, to practice pure concentration bordering on meditation.

While I wasn't eager to do the work involved, I was obedient. If the Rosses said, "Do it," I did it. Boredom was frequent; a year is a long time to be bumping into walls. And I never really entertained the idea of a reward. I often thought, "It's really dumb to be doing all this work without any real promise. What if the show never goes on, or they don't even let me come and audition?"

But to say, "When is this going to be over?" was to incur the Rosses' wrath. That was simply a question you didn't ask, especially since the importance of this particular assignment was apparent from the very beginning. John Ross would often say, "You have to really study, because this can be it. You couldn't play *The Bad Seed* in Long Branch, but this is the one that's going to take you to Broadway." As far as he was concerned, the whole thing was preordained.

Even though the play's qualities made an enormous and lasting impression on me, I don't remember *the* moment of first reading *The Miracle Worker*. Maybe that was because I'd worked on my character so long, the practice blended into the play, or maybe just because I didn't have any words to remember. Dialogue or not, however, once I became familiar with the play I fell in love with it.

The Miracle Worker's first act opens in the Keller family homestead in Tuscumbia, Alabama, in the 1880s. Captain Keller and his new young wife, Kate, are concerned about their daughter, Helen, who's been struck by fever. The doctor says she'll be fine, but Kate, to her horror, discovers that her little girl can now no longer see or hear.

When we first see Helen, she is a violent, unkempt six-and-a-half-year-old who speaks only in crude grunts. A law unto herself, she is the tantrum-throwing terror and despair of the entire Keller household, including her half-brother, James, who thinks she ought to be institutionalized as a mental defective for her own and everyone else's good.

The scene now switches to Boston, where twenty-year-old Annie Sullivan, herself just graduated from a school for the visually impaired, is being prepared for her first governess assignment: young Helen Keller. "She is like a little safe, locked, that no one can open. Perhaps there is a treasure inside," Annie is told. "Maybe it's empty too?" is her response.

Back in Tuscumbia, Annie's youth, inexperience, and handicap combine to make not the best of impressions on Captain Keller, who growls, "Here's a houseful of grown-ups can't cope with the child, how can an inexperienced, half-blind Yankee schoolgirl manage her?" Undaunted, Annie begins to try to teach Helen the manual alphabet, spelling letters into her hand, but Helen responds by furiously swatting Annie with a doll, locking her in an upstairs room, and calmly dropping the key down a well.

Annie Sullivan, herself the product of a terrifying public

asylum where her brother died, is not to be so easily gotten rid of, and the second act finds her contending not only with an obstreperous Helen but the well-meaning obstructionism of her parents, who give in to Helen's whims as the only way to have even a semblance of peace in the house. Finally, Annie confronts the Kellers over Helen's grasping behavior at the breakfast table. "I can't unteach her six years of pity," she said, "if you can't stand up to one tantrum!" She insists the Kellers leave the room and, after a prolonged and furious free-for-all that includes hair-pulling, chair-throwing and Helen spitting a mouthful of water at Annie (who responds by throwing a pitcherful back), Annie is able to report to the Kellers that Helen "ate from her own plate. She ate with a spoon. Herself. And she folded her napkin. . . . The room's a wreck, but her napkin is folded."

Confronting the Kellers, she tells them she's convinced of Helen's innate intelligence. "I don't think Helen's worst handicap is deafness or blindness," she says. "I think it's your love. And pity." Though the captain is of half a mind to fire Annie, just for general sassiness and because Helen now flees from her very presence, a compromise is reached. Annie will have the girl all to herself, with no parental interference, in the garden house on the Keller property for a period of two weeks. "Two weeks. For only one miracle?" Annie asks before agreeing to the deal. "I'll get her to tolerate me."

The Miracle Worker's third and final act begins at the end of those two weeks. Not only does Helen now tolerate Annie, she has learned cleanliness and obedience as well, but though the Kellers are ecstatic, Annie Sullivan is not. Above all else, she wanted to teach Helen the manual alphabet, to give her the gift of knowledge. "One word," she says, "and I can—put the world in your hand." The Kellers, however, insist on having Helen back at the main house. But at the family's first celebratory meal together, Helen once again begins misbehaving and ends by flinging a pitcher of water at Annie, who insists on taking her outside to fill it up again.

As the water at the pump douses Helen's hand, Annie automatically does what she has so many times before: she spells w-a-t-e-r into Helen's free palm. This time, however, the miracle happens. Helen understands, and uncovering what the stage directions call "a baby sound buried under the debris of years of dumbness," actually says the word "wah-wah." In her joy Helen rings the farm bell, tries to be everywhere and identify everything at once. She finds her parents and Annie spells first "mother" and then "papa" for her. When she points to her, Annie spells out "teacher" and then, tentatively at first, the two embrace. As the play ends, Annie spells into the child's hand, "I love Helen. Forever, and—ever."

It was finally determined that they would not use a nonactor for Helen after all, so the call went out for every professional in that age group. And they came in droves, well over one hundred girls, I believe. My turn came around four o'clock in the afternoon at the Booth Theater, a tiny, tiny place, where Anne Bancroft, who'd already been cast as Annie Sullivan, was doing *Two for the Seesaw*. And even though John Ross had given me the traditional "It's your part, all you have to do is go claim it" pep talk, I was extremely nervous when the stage manager led me onto that cold stage.

Out there in the traditional darkness of the theater were Bancroft, director Arthur Penn, writer William Gibson, and producer Fred Coe. I was just cuter than a bug, Little Miss Adorable in a short dress with lots of petticoats. They asked me the obvious questions, name, age, experience, and then Arthur came up on stage with Anne and asked us if we'd do part of the second act fight scene. We went right into the scene, slapping each other and wrestling on the floor. Then there was some laughter, embarrassed comments like "Boy, you're strong!" and "Yeah, so are you!" They thanked me, I thanked them, and I left without even a clue as to how I'd done.

It turned out I had to return twice more. The first time, a couple of weeks later, was almost an exact replay of the previous audition, except the Rosses were called and told, "We really like her, but we're very concerned about her size vis-à-vis Anne. If Patty grows, we're in trouble." This was one of those times when the Rosses' lack of truthfulness worked against them, because everyone thought I was a tall ten-year-old who might spurt further, when in fact I was already twelve. But John Ross must have done a rain dance or something, because he convinced them to look at me again, and this time I came prepared.

I think my height at the time was fifty inches and the worry was what would I look like if I grew two inches more. So John took a pair of my Mary Janes down to the neighborhood shoemaker and asked him to put on a two-inch block heel. The little Italian shoemaker didn't want to do that because he thought it was dangerous for a child, and John had to keep explaining, "She's not going to wear them to walk, she's just going to show somebody how tall she can look." He thought he was convincing, but when he came back to pick the shoes up, the heels were only an inch and a quarter and the shoemaker kept insisting, "You don't understand, more than this and she'll fall down."

Finally John got an exact two inches and I took the shoes with me in a brown bag to the Booth for the third audition. My instructions were that under no circumstances was I to leave that theater without having shown what I looked like in those shoes. There was a little more chitchat this time, just to see what kind of brain I had, if any, and after they said good-bye, I had to pipe up, very embarrassedly, and say, "Excuse me—uh—I really—um—would like to show you, I know you're concerned about—uh—the possibility that I might grow and be too tall and—um—my manager wanted me to show you what I would look like if I were two inches taller." There was some chuckling in the dark and I said, "If you wouldn't mind, it'll only take a minute." So I put the shoes on, walked over and stood next to Anne, and assured everyone that the heels had been measured, they were exactly two inches. More whispering and chuckling out in the house, a warm good-bye from Anne and that was it.

At last the call came to meet with Arthur Penn. I went to his office one evening, we sat down, and he wanted to know what I knew about Helen Keller. Well, the poor man, I just went and told him everything there was to know; I seemed to be this extraordinarily articulate child who knew all about frustrations and psyches and everything. He had no idea how intensively I'd been preparing for that question for nearly a year and a half. He'd ask me, "What would you say if you were Helen Keller?" and I'd come back with, "I wouldn't say anything." Penn was probably thinking, "This kid's been well programmed," but I was thinking, "He's really buying all this." I felt I had scored intellectually with this person. He was warm and charming and I already had a crush on him.

Finally, about a month after the first audition, the phone call came: "Okay, but if she grows another two inches, she's out." When the Rosses told me I'd gotten the part, I broke down. It was partly relief that the training was over, and partly exhilaration at having succeeded in pleasing them. But I was still scared. I'd never been on Broadway before. And the notion of working in front of a theater full of breathing humans was very, very intimidating.

NINE

Rehearsals for *The Miracle Worker* began in the very hot August of 1959 and I immediately felt that something important was happening here. For one thing, all my other work stopped, which was quite a relief. But more than that the experience was like walking into another world. This was "the theah-tah," a sacred, almost magical place which to me had the feeling of uptown, of class. So even though no one intended it, I was initially intimidated. They'd all done this before, they talked a language I didn't understand, things like "stage right" and "stage left," which to this day I have trouble keeping straight. It was a neighborhood I'd never been in before, both literally and figuratively.

Given all that, I remember being surprised at how unglamorous the place was. The Playhouse dated back to 1911 and looked it. The theater where Tennessee Williams's *The Glass Menagerie* had played for more than a year was always dark, with only one worklight. There were dinky little dressing rooms and iron steps that clanked when you stepped on them and everything smelled. Now I feel that as tradition and I love it, but then my reaction was, "This is how a Broadway star lives?" Also, given the nature of the part, with me always crawling on the floor, I ended up being dirty all the time and that hardly seemed glamorous.

We had to deal with two crises just before rehearsals started. One was my falling and breaking my arm while I was roller-skating. Both my mother and I were terrified to tell the Rosses that this had happened. It turned out to be a hairline fracture going straight up the arm, which wasn't really noticeable but meant that I couldn't hold anything. And if someone touched me, it hurt a lot.

The Rosses decided, however, that nothing would go on my arm, no cast or splint or wrapping, because I might lose the job. Ethel had a wrist injury at the same time—I think a toilet seat fell on her hand—and she was busy doing Christian Science on herself, so what they told me was, boom, you're a Christian Scientist. I did all the praying and read my Mary Baker Eddy and decided I had indeed had a healing experience, even though the thing continued to hurt like nobody's business. I got fairly involved in Christian Science because it linked up with my fear of death, but once I didn't have any more broken bones, the Rosses lost interest, and it wasn't until years later that I began to deal with what I came to see as a betrayal of my Roman Catholicism.

The other difficulty was that once I got the part I was told that Helen was to be played with eyes open and a fixed stare, while all my practicing had been done with my eyes closed. My initial reaction to the change was terror: could I learn a different way and could I learn it fast enough? Then it was step-up-the-drill time—I had to get to work on that look. I was able to develop it myself just by practicing staring at something for a long time, until my consciousness went elsewhere. Eventually I was able to keep that fixed stare and not refocus my eyes even when I moved my head. In some ways, the new method was a relief because I'd had some fears about doing the role with my eyes closed; the stage was on different levels, and the fight scene included chairs and plates and forks and knives flying all over the place. In retrospect it was a stupid oversight on our part not to have realized the role would have to be done with the eyes open. It was just too dangerous any other way.

I started the first week of rehearsals carrying my little

doll and wearing my little ankle socks and my little short dress with my little panties showing. I don't recall exactly what phrase Annie Bancroft finally used, but the essence of it was, "What the hell are you doing with that thing? Let's get rid of the doll and get down to work." To me it meant "the jig is up," and I liked that very much. It was the beginning of a sense of camaraderie that was wonderful for me.

On every show I'd worked on, I'd found someone who was my channel of energy and love, and certainly Annie fulfilled that role on this one. She's New York, she's comfortable, she's got that earthy Italian thing, and we became really close. Once we both learned the manual alphabet that Annie Sullivan teaches Helen, we used it to make little jokes to each other and drive Arthur Penn crazy. I really hero-worshipped her, every blink of her eyes mattered to me, and that's a terrible burden to put on somebody. And even though I was very demanding, she had problems of her own, so I had to learn when to back off and not bother her. But she gave me a great deal and always tried to come up to the mark.

The most generous thing Annie did was to allow me to come into her dressing room a half hour before every curtain and just hang around, fiddle with her makeup, and things like that while she was opening her mail and getting dressed. I'd say ninety percent of actors won't let you do that, especially not a kid, but never did she say, "No, you can't come in now." I loved watching her get ready, sitting there in her Merry Widow, putting her braid on and making it a bun, applying what little bit of makeup she wore. Those were treasured moments, like being in the inner sanctum. There's a line in Our Town: "Do we know every minute of every day?" That half hour I knew. The whole feeling of the room, the temperature, the smells, the perfume, the costumes, and her, just her.

What I felt from Annie, the sense that it was truly possible for someone to care about and accept me, to want me to be intelligent and mature, has stood me in good stead ever since. I'd tell her my current woes, talk about my romantic life, which I didn't have, and she'd listen and kid around with me. I was allowed to be twelve, or thirteen, or whatever age I was as the months went by, instead of always having to be ten. She treated me the way she knew a kid that age wanted to be treated.

I also worshipped Patricia Neal, who played my mother, Kate, but it was a different, less needy sort of admiration. She was indeed patrician-looking, stately and tall, yet there was an earth-mother aura about her as well. She had nifty things on her dressing table, antique sterling and expensive brushes. And she wore Femme, a wonderful perfume. There's a scene in which I had to sense my mother's arrival after having been kept from her for a couple of weeks, and she always made it easy for me because I could smell her coming across the stage. And she had a great command of four-letter words, but they sounded like poetry coming from her.

There's a famous story that Pat Neal often told about Torin Thatcher, who played Captain Keller, my father. We'd been running about three months, which is one of the key concentration trouble spots because the bloom is off the rose by then. I don't know where Torin's mind was, but suddenly he couldn't remember a scene he'd never had trouble with before. There were a bunch of us, maybe five people, onstage with him, and instead of asking for help from someone who was sighted and hearing and speaking, he asked little Helen Keller, and all he got out of little Helen was a gurgle. And then he got mad at me and whispered loudly, "What do I say, child? What do I say?" Pat wanted to kill him. "Of all the people to ask, Torin!"

And then there was Caswell Fairweather, who played Percy, a young teenaged servant. He looked just like Muhammad Ali, but because he was the only guy among the backstage gang of half a dozen or so kids, he hated us all. We made his life miserable, I know we did. We would tease him terribly and do awful little-girl things behind his back and get him in trouble. If we did something wrong or something got broken, we just said, "Caswell did it." And who's not going to believe four little blind girls and two little black girls and a little star? The play called for me to beat up on him sometimes, and he spent the whole run convinced I was going to kill him right there onstage.

One person I really couldn't figure out was Fred Coe, the producer. He was big and overweight and "suth'n," with a great lap to sit on. But he was a complete mystery to me as a kid. I had no idea what producers do and it seemed to me he just sat around all the time. He was usually quiet and easygoing, but occasionally, on a technical rehearsal night when it would be approaching two o'clock in the morning and things like lighting and sound cues weren't getting finished, he would lose his temper and it was something to behold. Much later on, in 1968, Fred became a very good friend to me when I really needed one.

Now, Arthur Penn. Arthur was something else. I just thought he was the *most* handsome, the *most* sexy man ever. I even loved the clothes he wore, khaki pants and a white shirt, and the way he stood in his white tennis shoes, with one foot turned a little bit in. He'd walk by and my little heart would absolutely flutter. I was very inarticulate around him after that first meeting; isn't it funny what a twelve-year-old girl's psyche will do when she's smitten? I even used to screw things up just so he'd come talk to me and give me more direction.

Arthur Penn never spoke above a whisper. He knew that it's easier to penetrate someone's private area by being really quiet and gentle. Then the person would let you right in, which is what I did. And he'd always say to me, "Duke! You're all right—for a girl." I wasn't sure I knew what that meant, but I loved it because whatever it meant, it was obviously a compliment.

If a director's supposed to be a father, Arthur was a good, fair father. I don't ever remember feeling I'd been talked down to or treated as if I didn't have the same intellect as the rest of the cast. Being talked down to, being talked around, or having people discuss me as if I weren't there, as in "What would she like for lunch?" were situations I resented more and more as I got to be a teenager. I also don't remember being treated as if I were any better than anybody else, or even feeling that Annie, the star of the piece, was getting preferential direction or concessions. It was a working situation and everybody worked together.

Arthur was also a director who'd let you go your own

way a long time without his interrupting to intellectualize. He was a fine-tuner, and when he gave directions, they were very simple, very basic. One particular time, when he helped me to say "wah-wah," the otherworldly sound Helen makes that signifies the miracle, it was the single most embarrassing direction I've ever received, before or since.

We'd been at it a few weeks, working on this critical sound, and I just wasn't getting it. Arthur must have been very frustrated, because he stopped everything, trotted from the back of the darkened theater, and hopped up onstage. Very dramatically, with an intensity that indicated that he'd found the miracle. He came over, bent down, and whispered into my ear, "I want you to make this sound as if you're very constipated and you've been constipated for a long time."

Well, I thought I would die. This was a twelve-year-old girl in 1959, and nobody, least of all a grown man, said "constipated" out loud. My face, I'm sure, was purple, because I could feel the heat. I was grateful that the directions hadn't been said out loud but at the same time I felt that everyone knew what he'd said. But when we began again, his advice worked, it really worked. Arthur's gift is that he truly keeps it simple. I can't think of any other way to get a child to understand that sound.

More than anything else, Arthur respected the process that actors go through, and respected that I happened to be a kid who went through the same process as everyone else. He talked to me very quietly and sensitively, telling me about how Helen didn't want to be taken away from her mother and asking me, "Have you ever been separated from your mother?" He didn't know he was asking the sixty-four-dollar question. He talked to me as if I were a grown-up; he could have told me to walk off the top of the second story and I would have done it.

We rehearsed *The Miracle Worker* in New York into September, then had a two-week tryout in Philadelphia followed by two weeks in Boston, the traditional pre-Broadway route. The parts of Annie Sullivan and Helen Keller were fine as written; what needed to be wrestled with were the other family members, especially James, Helen's wishy-washy half-brother, a role which by now has gone through twenty-five years worth of changes without anyone being able to solve the problem. Maybe the two principal parts are so dynamic that the rest of the play is bound to feel like filler.

For Annie Bancroft and me, *The Miracle Worker* was as exhausting physically as it was emotionally. The heart of the play, both for us and for the audience, is the big fight scene in the second act, when Annie Sullivan stands up to one of Helen's more impressive dinnertime tantrums. The battle lasts a full ten minutes onstage and although it's realistic enough to scare the life out of you, it was as intricately choreographed as a ballet. Little movements might get altered a bit depending on where the plates or spoons or food might fly, but every single moment in it was written by Bill Gibson.

Each movement had a thought behind it; nobody went anywhere on that stage without a reason. The printed directions alone take up more than four full pages. There were a few things that had to be done by count, such as how many times I tried to get out of my chair, how many times I bolted for the door, or how many times Annie chased me around the table, but mostly what the scene required was keeping track of its logic, remembering where it was going, and that your goal was the next step. That may sound complicated, but after a month of doing the scene, it made perfect sense; we knew exactly where we belonged.

Some aspects of our fights, like my pulling Annie's hair, did require special techniques. I ended up really just holding her head but making it look as if I were gripping her hair. Then she'd put her hands on top of my wrists as she sank to the stage, supposedly in pain. What she was doing, actually, was pushing my hands away as she was going down, but if it worked properly, it looked as if I was tearing her hair out. Nobody told us how to do that, it's something that just evolved because after the first two times I pulled she said, "Look, figure out something because that hurt! There must be a better way."

A similar kind of cooperation was essential for the scene where I smack Annie with my doll. We used a doll with a soft head, but still, if you're coming around with a haymaker, it's crucial to have the timing just so. Still, if you do seven hundred and some performances, even though I knew it was critical not to hit her in the ears or eyes, you're gonna miss once in a while. And it was always devastating to me to hurt her.

We took whatever measures we could to minimize the fight damage. We found that using real eggs on the plates was too slippery—you couldn't get them off the bottoms of your shoes—so we used bread crumbled up to look like scrambled eggs. Also to avoid slipping, we used a particular kind of rubber with a particular kind of waffle weave on the bottoms of our shoes. I wore shin guards, knee pads, and hip pads, plus a chest protector when I started to develop. All the padding had a plastic backing, so when the water hit my clothes, the padding wouldn't get totally wet and could dry between shows. But that plastic made the padding very hot, and in the summer I'd start sweating and couldn't stop.

Even things that may not have looked that awful, like Annie shoving spoons into my hands when she's trying to teach me table manners, gave me painful blood blisters. And I had continual bruises on the backs of my legs from slamming into a chair or the chair slamming into me. In fact I got so black and blue that the Rosses made me wear knee socks and long sleeves even in the summer because they were afraid some authority might come in and put a halt to this child abuse.

The two of us did get physically fit during the play; we used to make jokes about having real muscles in our arms like Popeye. Still, accidents did happen. Once during rehearsals Annie ran into an upturned chair with such force that she was seriously injured. She got a lump the size of a goose egg on her instep and she had to rehearse sitting down for several days. Those poor chairs took a lot of punishment as well: even though we would brace and reinforce them, we'd break an average of one each performance. I'd be holding on to the chair and Annie would pick me up and swing both me and it from side to side to build up momentum, and once I let go, the chair would hit the table, which was solid as a rock, and either smash or splinter apart.

The one part of the fights that always had to be done for real, and was always horrible, was the slapping. From the acting point of view the most difficult thing for both of us was concentrating hard enough so we didn't flinch even though we knew we were going to take a whack right in the face. That never got any easier, and neither did the actual fact of getting hit. We were as good at it as anybody could be, we had gotten it down to a science, but even so, we were human; accidents happen. One person's face isn't exactly where it should be and you hit it where you shouldn't. I have a cap in my mouth because one night I committed the ultimate sin: I gritted my teeth because I knew Annie's slap was going to hurt and my jaw slid across and knocked off half a tooth. There really were moments when I felt, "How many times do we have to go through this? I give! I give!"

Close to a year into the run, we experienced a bad time when both Annie and I became a little paranoid and each thought the other was hitting to hurt. I don't think either one of us knew how it began, or where, or why, but that suspicion kept building and building and then, out of the paranoia, we really began to be mean to each other: if you think someone is doing it to you, you're going to do it back. Slaps got a little harder each time. When I pulled her chair out from the dinner table, I'd be rougher than I had to be, so that Annie would really fall on her ass.

Finally I reached the point of almost becoming phobic. I grew convinced that somehow or other she was going to literally kill me, and so I was afraid even to go to the theater. Of course, when Annie heard this she was extremely upset. She asked to come and see me and we hugged and kissed and cried. I couldn't tell her what the hell was the matter with me. I didn't know. I just knew that I was afraid. And she recognized that these kinds of feelings had been present on both sides, that it was just a series of insecurities on both our parts that had gotten us there. I went to work with her that night, we got through the fight scene, and it was a catharsis for both of us.

Although it was a connection I didn't make intellectually until much later on, those scenes with Annie were in many ways a saving grace, a needed release for me as a kid. I think one of the reasons I survived all those years with the Rosses was that I was able to get onstage every night, beat

the bejesus out of an adult, and have people applaud and
think I was brilliant. I certainly didn't recognize it then—
"Here, let me smack Annie because I really want to smack
Ethel"—but there was horror happening at home and this
was a way to get rid of it. Being able to get that stuff out of
my system on a daily basis had to be helpful. Undoubtedly,
one of the things that made my audition and my portrayal of
Helen so different from other actresses' was that I had so
much anger in the first place and that it was so accessible. I
guess I never got enough out, however, because there was so
much left—and no place to get rid of it—that it all got
turned in on me and eventually became self-destructive.

An example of what I was dealing with came in Philadelphia during our tryout there. I was alone with my mother
most of the time, and she was very, very depressed. Not
unusual for her, but this was one of the worst times. Ethel
came down from New York at one point and had given my
mother her usual persnickety instructions about doing the
laundry just so. Ethel came back to the hotel after having
had a couple of drinks, and when my mother told her that
she'd done the laundry but hadn't done the socks yet, all hell
broke loose.

Ethel called my mother a lazy bitch, said she never did
anything to pull her own weight: here was everybody else
working so hard and what was she doing? All she'd been
asked to do was wash some socks, her own daughter's white
socks. She was tired of doing my mother's job for her and on
and on and on. Ethel continued to drink during this diatribe.
She finally decided that my mother had ruined everything
and she called John and announced that she was going home
to New York, she wasn't going to take this crap from my
mother anymore.

I watched this scene like a nightmare unfolding. I remember feeling really confused about where my loyalties
should be. Was Ethel right? Was my mother right? I was
furious at my mother, guilty at being angry with her, sorry
that this other person was talking to her this way. And I
strongly suspected that my mother really had ruined everything, and that now I was going to be stuck with her. And
she was no fun. Not that Ethel was a barrel of laughs either,

but by now my mother was completely emotionless, so depressed she simply did not communicate. It all seemed so hopeless.

As far as the play itself was concerned, nobody had a clue about what the opening-night reaction in Philadelphia was going to be. There were still lingering doubts as to whether anyone would pay $9.60 to see a story about a blind deaf-mute. And because this was a huge show to mount, with an extraordinary number of light and set cues, almost like a musical, we were all there until four or five A.M. the morning before the opening, trying to solve all the technical problems.

Our advance ticket sales were not very good, including opening night, and then we got a most unusual break. Across town in another theater Melvyn Douglas was appearing in a play, and because he was a huge star they were doing a land-office business. But it was ungodly hot in Philadelphia that week and on the day of our opening, Douglas collapsed from the heat. They had to cancel that night's performance, and when the audience showed up, they were given tickets to our show.

So our opening-night crowd was larger than it would have been, but it was far from a stacked house. It was, in fact, a theater full of people who were very disgruntled and even somewhat hostile. That play wasn't where they wanted to be, but they'd already paid the baby-sitter so they took a chance. After the final curtain, however, they went bananas. I mean, I'd heard "Author, author" only in the movies, but they yelled "Director," "Producer." They called for everybody but the cleaning crew. There were eighteen curtain calls, and since I'd never been in front of an audience before, I sort of assumed this was what being onstage was like.

After it was over, Kathleen Comegys, a wonderful old woman who played Aunt Ev, set me straight. She and I went up those long, seemingly endless flights of iron stairs to the top of the theater where we had our dressing rooms. Kathleen was just behind me and she said very quietly, "Well, my little dear, I want you to take a moment and really remember this, because it doesn't happen very often." Which was *the* understatement. It didn't take me too many years to find out that not many plays get eighteen curtain calls on the opening night of a tryout.

It really wasn't until that opening night that I realized my importance to *The Miracle Worker*. Up to then I'd felt like a kid; now I felt part of a team. All my previous work had been on TV, and whatever praise I'd gotten was from co-workers or, if it came from the Rosses, was always tempered with "But in the third act, you could have done such-and-such." I'd never experienced the exhilaration of real live human beings I didn't know screaming, "Bravo! Bravo! Bravo!" for all those curtain calls. It was the best moment of my life and I started to feel tears that came from I don't know where. They weren't little-girl tears, they were tears of real revelation, of relief, of true joy at receiving that kind of acceptance. John Ross wasn't up there, Ethel Ross wasn't up there, I was up there. I didn't have the words then and I don't have them now for what it felt like to stand there on that stage amid all the pandemonium. Staggering, astounding, astonishing—it was certainly all of that. I don't know when my feet touched the floor again.

TEN

If there was ever any chance of my head being turned, that night in Philadelphia was the time. It didn't happen because the Rosses were always just around the corner. They redoubled their efforts; in fact they cornered me that very night and said, "Well, they may all think you're great, but we know the truth." I was very hurt by that, and also confused. Should I believe the Rosses—or all those people screaming their admiration? I think that was the first time I allowed myself to hold a thought that was contrary to theirs. If I'd known the phrase, I might have said, "Don't rain on my parade." And when my own kids win awards these days, I'm very careful to allow them to wallow in it, as well they should.

Back then, however, I knew I had to go on living with the Rosses, so I said, "They were applauding only because I did what you told me to do," and everything was fine. These were very frightened people, and a success beyond even their imaginings had just occurred. They first felt, "My God, if she's this successful, where are we going to be?" and then, "Quick, lash out, keep her in tow." They knew our relationship was built on sand, so they were always sandbagging in every sense of the word.

Because we had done so well out of town, we knew

there was a lot of excitement surrounding *The Miracle Worker* as the October 19th New York opening neared, which gave that night a different kind of dynamic from the Philadelphia opening. We weren't unknown anymore, so we experienced a different kind of insecurity, the "Oh my God, they may be expecting more than we're about to deliver" variety. The day that preceded opening night was endless, and we breathed a heightened, rarefied air. Our dressing rooms were all filled with flowers, like a gangster's funeral. It seemed we would never get to the moment when that curtain would go up.

Once we got started, the audience was so responsive right off the bat that their reaction kicked us into another gear. At one point I threw a pitcher of water at Annie and I nailed Rosalind Russell, who was sitting in the front row. People nearby tried to help her, but she was so enthralled she wouldn't let anyone interrupt what was going on onstage, she just sat there drenched, with water dripping off the hat she was wearing. She also got spoons thrown at her, and at one point, concerned that we'd run out of them, she very gently reached up and put one back on the stage.

We got thirteen curtain calls that night, which was the talk of Broadway, unheard-of for a straight play, but after the eighteen in Philadelphia it was a *real* disappointment to me. The party afterward across the street at the Absinthe House was fun, I may even have sat on Mel Brooks's lap, but by the Rosses' usual orders I wasn't allowed to listen to the reviews.

The Rosses, however, could shield me only so far, and as *The Miracle Worker* became the play of the year, they couldn't stop people from recognizing me in restaurants or on the street and coming up to offer congratulations. I did have some sense of myself as the darling of Broadway, which I loved and took great pride in. But I had to hide that pride, it had to be very secret in me. I had to seem rigorously humble and willing—not to say eager—to instantly pass all kudos along to the Rosses or Arthur or Annie. If I didn't, I risked Ethel's coming down hard on me for being egocentric or having a big head or any one of the forty phrases she'd pop up with that said the same thing. I felt like a "poor little rich girl," on top of the world but not really free to enjoy it.

As soon as the play got established on Broadway, so did my routine. I'd have my coffee in the morning, spend three hours in school, and then immediately call the Rosses to check in. I'd get to the Playhouse about two, it would be just me and my mom in this darkened theater. I'd do my school-work, eat an early dinner, take a nap, and then get ready for my half hour with Annie and the show.

Matinee days, though, were hell, and it's only now that I realize that because Annie was an adult and I was twelve, it must have been physically even harder for her than for me. I dreaded those days from the moment I got up. If I missed my nap between shows, I would feel as if I were going to die out there. The only pleasure to be found in matinee days was the battle scars, the being able to say, "Well, we did it twice today."

Once I nearly missed a scheduled performance, and that was on a matinee day. It was a Wednesday, when the after-noon show starts earlier than on Saturday, but because I'd gotten the day off from school I was in a Saturday mode in my head. So Mom and I, thinking we were early, were taking our time getting to the theater, just sauntering along Sixth Avenue and looking into windows. I saw a clock and was about to say to my mother, "Gee, we still have a lot of time, we could go for an ice cream or something," when it hit me: *this was Wednesday*.

I said, "Oh my God! It's Wednesday!" and took off running down the street, leaving my mother in the dust. I ran the eight blocks to the theater nonstop, and sure enough my understudy was standing at the stage door, wearing my clothes and shoes and ready to go on. I said, "Thank you! Thank you!" and started literally ripping the clothes off her. I dressed onstage, in the dark, while the first scene was going on, trying not to huff and puff too loudly. That poor girl, standing there in her undies; Jack the Ripper had come along and stolen her clothes. By the time my mother showed up, I was already playing the scene. It was like *All About Eve:* There was no way anybody was going onstage for me if I had any control over it.

In fact my insecurity was so great that I took only one week off during the entire seven-hundred-performance run and I spent that whole time being worried that my understudy was better than me. The Rosses and I went to the Virgin Islands. It was our "Three Musketeers" period, when I was young enough not to miss having a friend along. Since I had no friends anyway, it didn't really matter. We went boating, ate tropical food, sat on a balcony overlooking the Caribbean; it all suited me okay and it set the pattern for vacations we'd take throughout our relationship. The Rosses did know how to take vacations, they traveled very well, albeit on my money. This was not the tropics on five dollars a day—three hundred dollars a day was more like it.

Those times, the water-skiing and boating, were fun, but as I grew older I missed having someone my own age along for the ride. A kid wants to do what a kid wants to do, and that does not include four-hour très continental candlelit dinners for three that went on till one in the morning. The talk was always the same, because as far as the Rosses were concerned, show business was my life as well as theirs. Anything else, say, national politics or social issues, was unimportant, or, worse than that, a distraction. The TV didn't go on until Johnny Carson (or Jack Parr before him), and if any political references were made, I didn't get them. The same thing would happen when I heard actors talking during rehearsals; a topic like blacklisting would come up and I wouldn't have a clue what it meant. We lived in a vacuum; no one so much as read a newspaper. There really wasn't an outside world for us; it was that simple and that stupid.

The best time for me, clearly, was when I was onstage. I felt transported in that role, it came to be almost like a religious experience to play Helen. I think I could count on the fingers of one hand the times when Annie and I weren't completely emotionally involved in that play. There was never a night when there weren't tears—I can't imagine playing the end of that show, when Annie Sullivan finally reaches Helen, and not crying. A real chord was struck at each performance.

The audience was very involved in the play as well,

particularly during the big fight scene. They would become very vocal, you'd hear a lot of "Oooh, uuuhhh, ooh, uuuhhh!" And when kids came on Saturday afternoons, it was a regular hoot 'n' holler matinee. Oh, how they would root—for *me*. When I hit the teacher, they just went bananas.

And then pieces of furniture or plates or spoons or eggs or who knows what would fly out into the audience. I'm sure a lot of people in the first few rows watched the fight scene with their hands over their faces because they were really getting it. One night a woman up front took more than her share of abuse. A chair landed in her lap, a spoon hit her, food got spit on her, the works. Finally, toward the end of the fight scene, she stood up and said, "That's it! I've had it!" And we thought, "Oh, boy, she's going to start throwing things back at us." But she just sat down again and didn't say or do another thing. She just had to vent her annoyance, that's all.

Another night, a man put his hat, a gray fedora, on the stage and left it there. Before the curtain went up, that area looked like part of the apron, so he might not have immediately realized what he'd done. But all during the first act and the second act the hat remained there and it drove Annie crazy. There's a moment at the end of the second act when her character feels she'd had a victory and walks proudly downstage, blesses herself, and turns around to look back at the garden house. As Annie marched downstage, she put first her right foot and then her left foot on that hat, then she smushed and smushed and smushed it before she finally turned around and got off. The man was still there for the third act, but his hat was gone.

Some of the things I liked best about the play were bits almost no one knew I did. I played the offstage voice of Jimmie, Annie Sullivan's lost brother. And near the end of the second act, when as Helen I'm supposedly lying in my bed asleep and Annie picks up my doll, I make the "ma-ma" sound for the doll. I'd keep one eye open under the covers so I'd see just when Annie would pick it up. You can't know how much I looked forward to that "ma-ma" every night. It was such a relief to say something.

Despite all our planning and timing, there were nights when things did go wrong. During the second act fight scene, Helen gropes her way first to the front door and then to the rear one and finds them both locked. Every once in a while, though, one of the doors would be accidentally left open and I'd have no choice but to go out through it. Annie wouldn't know I was gone, she'd be distracted picking up a plate or something, then she'd get up and find she was playing the scene by herself. I'd be backstage, laughing, trying not to pee in my pants. She'd come after me, cursing out loud backstage, "I'll kill you, you son of a bitch!" Once I got so hysterical I did wet my pants and had to go back onstage that way.

Another time we had just the opposite problem. The door that we were supposed to leave through at the end of the scene had been locked with a key as well as bolted and wouldn't open. Annie, of course, was trying to find the right key on the ring of six she carried and was being very profane, saying, "Goddamn son of a bitch" under her breath while I made my guttural sounds very loudly because I was afraid the audience was going to hear her. Finally she just said, "Screw it." She picked me up, walked to the window and, in full view of everybody, pushed me out and dove out right behind. So much for the romance of live theater.

The most unnerving mishap we experienced was an incident that actors still ask me about. They'll come up and say, "I heard a story about you in *The Miracle Worker* that just flabbergasted me. Is it true?" This time it happens it is.

The incident took place one night in the third act, the scene in which, instead of spelling to Annie Sullivan, I'm spelling to the family dog, one of those white-with-dark-spots English setters. All of a sudden a cable let go and a row of lights crashed to the stage to the side of us. It made, as you can imagine, a very startling sound and everyone, I mean everyone, reacted. I did not. At least I did not have the normal reaction of jumping or being startled by an obviously dangerous noise. I was as terrified as anyone else would be but what I did for release was something that nobody saw. I squeezed the poor dog's flank, and he screeched bloody blue murder and ran away. But the impression was that I had done nothing and people were astounded at that kind of concentration.

After the final curtain, a whole stream of visitors would come to our dressing rooms, whoever was really popular at the time. Often visitors would say, "How do you remember all those lines?" when in truth I didn't have any. Elizabeth Taylor and Eddie Fisher made a big impression, mostly because she wore a mink-lined raincoat. And Cary Grant—we were all truly beside ourselves about his visit—when everyone in the place was going, "There he is!" He signed my autograph dog (it was a clear, simple signature, very forthright) and I just stared at him, amazed at how gorgeous he was, even better in person than he was in the movies. I kept saying, "Thank you" and thinking, "Can I live with you forever?" He spent a little more time with Patricia Neal and I hung around her doorway, listening to their conversation, just wanting to be in his pocket.

By this point I had been groomed so well by the Rosses to be the next Princess Grace that I didn't need instructions about receiving my visitors, I knew exactly the appropriate behavior. "How do you do. . . . It's very nice to meet you. . . . You're very kind to come back and tell me that," always in the form of the startlingly gracious child. I was invariably very humble as well; if the conversation went on at any length, I would start referring the compliments to whoever was handiest. I think I was genuinely well trained by the Rosses—I have no resentment about learning basic manners—but some things were carried to ridiculous extremes. Part of what I did, the hugging and kissing of visitors, was my own. I just can't help that, it's how I am. I really like people, and there's something about embracing them that feels good to me.

Easily the most memorable visit to result from *The Miracle Worker* took place outside of the theater, and that was my meeting with Helen Keller in the spring of 1960. Katharine Cornell, the great actress, was a neighbor and friend of hers at Aachen Ridge, Connecticut. Katharine Cornell came backstage one night after the play and asked if I would like to meet Helen Keller. What a question! She said that Helen had been rather reclusive since Polly Thompson, her companion after Annie Sullivan, had died, but that she would set it up. I thought it was just going to be a private meeting, but of course the Rosses got involved and all of a sudden the visit wound up as a big *Life* magazine piece. Everyone was there except, of course, my mother, who as usual had not been invited.

When I first saw Helen walking down the stairs, she looked almost regal. She was wearing a blue dress, pearls, and what I found out were her favorite red shoes. She was close to eighty years old by then, but she carried herself very straight. She had alabaster skin, very thin white hair, almost like an angel's hair, and was very buxom with small hips and great-looking legs. And a terrific smile. And she was so jolly, like a jolly grandma. I'd expected serious or sweet, but not jolly. Not someone who was so much fun. Not someone who loved to laugh, and about everything, even the fact that we'd come before she'd had a chance to take her bras—rather large bras, I might add—in off the laundry line.

Helen hugged me and I hugged her and she told me that she'd heard from some friends how wonderful I was as her. Occasionally she would spell to me, just to be gracious and indulge me because I wanted her to, but mostly she would talk out loud. Her voice was very hard to understand, like a computer talking; she said she'd never been happy with the way it sounded. To understand me, she would put her thumb on my lips and her fingers on different vibration points. She didn't miss a thing.

She introduced me to her dogs, labradors and golden retrievers, and we went for a walk in her gardens. They were fairly extensive, with railings all around, but very nicely done: nothing screamed "A blind person lives here!" She told me the name of every tree and bush and flower and talked about how at one she felt with nature. And she told me about her martinis. The doctor had told her that she shouldn't have her martinis anymore, and she told the doctor that at her age, if she enjoyed a martini, she was going to have one. I loved that. I mean there she was, nearly eighty years old, deaf and blind, what the hell else could go wrong.

I saw Helen Keller only one more time, at an official eightieth birthday reception for her in New York. I have a picture from that meeting in which it looks as if I'm staring at God. I would write to her occasionally and get a handwritten note back. And then, several months after she died, one day a package showed up with a lovely jade bottle she had specified she wanted me to have. I would have loved to have known her better. She radiated a large, good spirit: just to be in the woman's presence felt wonderful.

ELEVEN

Given the kind of schedule I had, even the Rosses knew I couldn't do any other work while I was appearing on Broadway. But just once as I was starting *The Miracle Worker* stage run and just once as I was ending it, I appeared in prestigious TV productions that were too glamorous for John and Ethel to resist.

"One Red Rose For Christmas," a *U.S. Steel Hour* I did with Helen Hayes, was a terrific tearjerker about a cranky nun and this one belligerent orphan in a sea of sad little waifs. The nun is mean to the troublesome tyke, who ends up accidentally setting fire to the orphanage, starting a blaze in which a sweet cherubic nun, who just happens to be the bad nun's sister, dies. Finally, in whatever part of the place is left standing, Helen Hayes is on her knees praying to God for forgiveness because her hatred of me had led to this tragedy. Hating is bad if you're a nun, I guess. She asks for a sign and, on Christmas Eve no less, I bring her one red rose. The show was such a hit in the fall of 1958 that we did it again a year later.

In 1961, toward the end of *The Miracle Worker*'s run, I appeared in the David Susskind production of Graham Greene's novel *The Power and the Glory* along with Julie Harris, George C. Scott, Keenan Wynn, and, most exciting of all, Laurence

Olivier. It was just a brief scene (Olivier's on the run and I bring him food) that they wrote in because Susskind, who liked to work with me, wanted the two of us in a scene together. I rehearsed during the week, performed on Broadway at night, and taped *The Power and the Glory* on a Sunday, my only day off.

I'd heard of Laurence Olivier, I knew this was a great actor, but I was just a kid and I'd never seen him in anything. The only image I had was a newspaper picture of him as Hamlet or somebody, looking very Shakespearean. We always rehearsed our live shows at Central Plaza, an all-purpose hall on Second Avenue right over Ratner's Dairy Restaurant; it also hosted bar mitzvahs and wedding receptions. I showed up before anyone else on the first day of rehearsals and I was alternately looking at my script and looking at my schoolbooks, when the elevator door opened and this nondescript man got out. We nodded hello to each other and he went and sat at the end of the table.

More people started to arrive, chatting and taking their little coffee cups out of paper bags. There's an inner room where people started rehearsing—a certain number of people would go in, a certain number would remain outside, and the whole time I was looking around wondering, "Where's this Sir Laurence Olivier?" Finally I was called to rehearse my scene with him and there's this little old man who was the first one out of the elevator. And I thought, "Gee, that's not what I thought he would look like, but if they say this is him, okay."

We rehearsed that day and a few more, then on Sunday we went to Brooklyn to do the taping. I was waiting on the set when someone called for Sir Laurence and suddenly here was this amazing man, all dressed up in Mexican getup, with two pieces of rubber on his nose, a piece on his lip that made it fuller, little pieces of something on his eyelids to make them fuller, and suddenly I saw Sir Laurence Olivier. Here he was, he just came in pieces!

Even to a kid, Olivier was charming and lovely to work with, so comfortable and secure. In some ways, though, he had the same actor's foibles that I did: we started the scene talking at a normal level, but every time he lowered his voice, I went lower still, each of us trying to underplay the other until the director had to come in over the loudspeaker and say, "Excuse us, the scene's going beautifully, it's just that none of us can hear what you're saying."

I've met Olivier only once since, at an event at the Motion Picture Academy while I was married to John Astin. I'm very shy about approaching people, even if I've worked with them, but I really wanted John to meet him, so I swallowed my reluctance and went right up. He was extremely gracious but he had a terrible problem with his hands, really painful arthritis, so when John naturally extended his own hand, Olivier said, "I'm so ashamed, I can't shake your hand. But would you mind if I just touched you." So John put out his hand and Olivier touched him lightly, because he couldn't move his fingers. It was quite a moment.

Though professionally I was having enviable success across the board, that only created more problems with the Rosses. The more famous I got, the more neurotic they got. Perfectly nice people can do some pretty bizarre things when they're mixing pills and booze, which is what the Rosses did. I've often tried to figure out why they couldn't relax and enjoy my success, and the only thing that makes sense to me is that they felt guilty, and when you base your behavior on guilt, that means you're afraid. The fear of losing me had to come from the fear that they had done something to drive me away, which, of course, they had.

Although John Ross was a heavy drinker and went through periods when he was sauced every night, he was able to quit from time to time. Or he'd parcel the liquor out for himself, sometimes just drinking beer in a small brandy snifter. Ethel, by contrast, drank more and more and more, to an incredible capacity, as the years went by. She was an Olympic-class drinker who preferred vodka martinis with a lemon twist; fifths of vodka would go in two days. From about age eleven, I was their bartender. I was given very strict instructions about how dry the mix should be; sometimes I used an atomizer for spraying the vermouth so it would be truly dry. To this day, I make a great martini.

Ethel was also cross-addicted. She took tons of pills— not a day went by without some barbiturate or other—and she sometimes spent the entire day in bed recovering. She would get boxes of all kinds of narcotics from a friend of hers in Detroit who was a nurse, things like phenobarbital, Stelazine, and Thorazine. She took Percodan, a heavy-duty, very addictive painkiller, eight or ten times a week for migraine headaches. Ethel was not in the best of shape.

Gradually, during the course of *The Miracle Worker*, when I was thirteen or fourteen, the Rosses involved me in their habits. They'd take me to Atlantic City, they'd be drinking, and they'd give me a little brandy snifter of my own with something innocuous in it at first, then later booze. Or they'd mix Bloody Marys and make a Virgin Mary for me, eventually adding vodka to it. Finally, they started giving me full-out drinks. I felt guilty at first, and then I didn't care. These adults were giving it to me, after all. And whatever little buzz I got from it felt good.

The same kind of pattern developed with drugs. Early on, whenever there was even a hint of my being sick, if I sneezed or complained of a sore throat, they took me to a doctor who gave me shots. The Rosses claimed they were Vitamin B_{12} shots and maybe they were, but still it's unusual to take a kid practically every week for injections to keep her healthy. They were also very quick to shoot me up with penicillin, which turned out to be unfortunate for me. At first it did its job, then I built up a tolerance, and finally an allergy, so I can't take it at all anymore.

Eventually the Rosses started giving me Thorazine and Stelazine, both antipsychotic medications, as well as phenobarbital and Percodan. Ethel would say to me, "Okay, you have to take your happy pill now, because you've got to go to sleep so you'll be bright-eyed and bushy-tailed in the morning." It wasn't a nightly event, it came in spurts over a period of about six years. Though I was never given enough to become addicted, it certainly wasn't a healthy practice. I think the Rosses simply thought I was keyed up, or, given that I had trouble sleeping, wanted to insure that I had a good night's rest. No one was educated then about how dangerous that stuff could be, so they probably weren't acting from malice, just a combination of ignorance, greed, and bad judgment. It's odd that even now I feel nervous about revealing this aspect of their behavior. I feel like I'm betraying them.

I didn't find out specifically what kinds of pills they'd been giving me until years later, in 1965, when I was hospitalized in Los Angeles and given Stelazine and Thorazine in a little white cup. I thought those pills looked familiar, and then it hit me. I wondered if that stuff had somehow damaged me, if the depression I often felt came from those pills. And years later, when I learned I was manic-depressive, I wondered if the Thorazine and Stelazine had triggered those episodes in the first place. Although you're born with the potential for manic-depressive behavior, many people go a whole lifetime without it's being set off.

Though I tried not to show it, I was depressed and insecure a lot of the time during The Miracle Worker's run. But the facade, like the show, had to go on. In fact the Rosses used to tell what they thought was an adorable story about how everyone in The Miracle Worker cast was seeing psychiatrists and how I had come home once and asked, "How old do you have to be to be in analysis?" Their answer was, "You'll never need a shrink. People who are in analysis just don't feel loved. And you always have all the love you need."

Perhaps coincidentally, but probably not, this was the time in my life when my weight first became a problem. Annie at one point complained that I was getting too heavy for her to lift, and the Rosses, of course, decided I was too fat. They pretended not to notice that a year had gone by, and I might simply be growing, which was actually what had happened. It wasn't a thrill at thirteen to be told to cut out ice cream and candy and eat grapefruit and cottage cheese, especially when I wasn't overweight. Ethel invented what she called the lettuce sandwich, which was baloney on lettuce with mustard. Whenever I could, I'd go to the nearest candy stand on the subway platform and fill up on Hershey bars. I was starving!

That was the beginning of life-long dieting and self-consciousness about weight. My weight has fluctuated as much as forty pounds from time to time, which on my frame makes a major difference. I really peaked in 1979. I went to the market one day, probably for more garbage to eat, and a woman standing behind me at the checkout counter very sweetly asked, "And when is your baby due?" I came home and I really had to face the truth. I couldn't pretend any longer by wearing bigger clothes, not looking in the mirror, not getting on the scale. By coincidence my next project was a TV movie about a woman who was fat and got skinny. I lost those forty pounds and I've never been that overweight again.

Contributing to my state of mind was the continuing unhappy situation with my parents. My mother was backstage with me all the time, staring at the walls in utter misery. She'd read the papers and doze; she rarely watched the show—I think it made her nervous. I was always anxious when people came backstage, in case she might make a scene. She always had an angry face and I was always trying to do something to make that face, or the mean face, or the sad face, go away. Always checking with her, "Is this okay, Mom? Is that okay?" and almost never getting an answer.

We took a cab after the theater. Usually my mother would drop me off at the Rosses' but sometimes we'd go home to Queens. We'd have fun for a few minutes during the ride. I'd stop for ice cream and she'd stop for pig's knuckles, really gross, and we'd have a little bit of a lighthearted time. But once we'd get home, she'd retreat to that miserable place in her mind, wherever it was, and I'd fiddle around, trying to get geared down to go to bed.

The incident I remember most clearly from that period was the one time the Rosses gave my mother permission to take me away for a long weekend. We went to a lake in New Jersey, with little cabins around it. I wasn't a very strong swimmer to begin with, and one day, for some reason, I got into trouble out on the lake. My mother, who can't swim at all, remembers this thought going through her head as she watched me start to go under: "Oh, my God, what am I going to tell the Rosses?"

With my father, the situation was more complicated, though I didn't know it at the time. The last time I'd seen him was when I was about eight. He was in a hospital and had all these scary-looking tubes in him. I remember I brought him rice pudding, which may not have been too practical—the guy had tubes everywhere, how's he going to eat rice pudding?—but I knew my daddy liked rice pudding without raisins, which, of course, I love to this day, so I had to bring him some.

After the Rosses took control of my life, they told me in so many words that my father just didn't exist. "We don't know where he is" was the exact quote, which turned out to be a lie, because my father would surface periodically, sometimes to get fifty dollars or so from the Rosses, sometimes just to talk. He wasn't, after all, forbidden by law to see me, even though that might have been his perception. I think it was a combination of his own embarrassment, his own feelings of inadequacy, and the Rosses' callous manipulation of those feelings that kept him away: "If you love her, Mr. Duke, if you're a responsible person, you'll stay away from her. If you want things to remain as comfortable as they are now, you'll just let sleeping dogs lie." That's the way I'm able to sort out in my head what the Rosses did. Certainly they were capable of such behavior. In 1961 my sister wanted to bring her future husband to meet my father, and the Rosses, who'd been told this by my mother, made a big to-do and in their paranoia refused to allow it; they were afraid my father might be encouraged to rock the boat. Momma begged Carol, "Please, please, you'll make trouble," so Carol didn't push. The Rosses had the whole family that firmly under their thumbs.

In 1968 a woman came up to me at the Improv in New York and asked how my father was. I told her he'd been dead for five years, asked how she knew him, and she told me a story that really wiped me out. Apparently she ran a luncheonette where my father washed dishes. He'd go on periodic benders, wouldn't show up for a while, but because everyone in the place was crazy about him, they'd go out and find him, help him pull himself together or send him to his sister's house in New Jersey until he straightened out enough to come back to work.

Suddenly, my father didn't take a drop, went on the wagon, and stayed on for several months. Everyone kidded him about what he was doing with his money now that he wasn't spending it on booze, but he never answered them. Finally he told this woman, "I got a kid in this play on Broadway. Three or four times a week, I go there and stand in the back." He told her that if this was as close as he could get to his kid, then that's what he was going to do. He never came backstage. He never made himself known. I never knew he was there. Just like my mother, he was insecure, he didn't know what to do, so, with the purest of motives, he broke his own heart.

As *The Miracle Worker* entered its second year on Broadway, I began to have some concentration problems. Not in the tantrums—something was always new and vital there, plus the physical danger meant we had to maintain a keen awareness. But for no reason at all, during other scenes it would be tough not to laugh. Sometimes I simply did it—Helen's behavior was a little erratic anyway—but I'd make sure I was turned upstage just in case.

The worst scene for setting me off was the last one before the miracle. Everyone is sitting around the table and Captain Keller is cutting the ham. We used a wax ham and wax ham slices and every once in a while they would fall on the plate a certain way that looked like the funniest thing I ever saw. It might have been mildly amusing, but not grounds for the absolute hysteria that would follow. My shoulders would start to shake, Annie would poke me, then she'd start to laugh and her shoulders would shake. Everyone else would be trying to do the scene while these two crazy girls were falling apart.

Two major *Miracle Worker* events took place in my fourteenth year and I had strong feelings about both of them. The first, on March 7, 1960, was the raising of my name above the title of the play. Even though there were ego-reducing admonitions that this was just a good business move and didn't change anything, the Rosses fought for it, they wanted me to be a star. They wanted me to be, in fact, the youngest child ever to have starred on Broadway. That would be another little P.R. phrase to throw into the hat.

I felt very good about that. Having star billing was quite a big deal. It was important to me to be equal; I felt I was doing an equal job and I didn't want to be treated differently because I was thirteen. What I hated was that the Rosses made me go up and pretend to paint my name on the marquee for a publicity picture. I didn't see anybody else up there painting their names on marquees while flashbulbs went off. I'd just wanted to be like everyone else, and there I was, the youngest and littlest again. I still hate that picture, it wasn't dignified. But I didn't get to tell anybody that. I just kept smiling and saying, "Oh, isn't this nice."

Much worse than that, in fact, the worst thing that I could imagine, was that Anne Bancroft was planning to leave the play the following December. I was so upset about it that the waiting time while she decided whether to extend or not was excruciating. She finally agreed to stay on until the spring of 1961, and I put the problem right out of my head. Then the last month arrived and I lobbied strongly for her to stay even longer, I straight out begged her, "Don't go, please don't go." As the time got closer she'd just say, "I have to, I have to do other things." I knew realistically that it was time for her to move on—a year and a half is a long time to do a play—but I was distraught. I'd hinted to the Rosses that I wanted to get out, too, but there was just no way. And yet I didn't want to be there without her. Once she left, the play was over.

At Annie's final performance, I don't know who was acting for me, because I was very busy being hysterical. During the last scene I was out of control, sobbing and sobbing and sobbing, but not so anyone could hear, "Please, please don't go." When they brought the curtain down, I thought I'd die. And when it was our turn to take our final bow together, it was some of the worst pain I've ever felt. I cried and I kept crying. It was a wrenching experience.

Annie's replacement was Suzanne Pleshette, but given the way I felt, Suzie's performance could have been the second coming of Christ and it wouldn't have been good enough. I tried to be very nice to her on the surface, but my sense of rejection and resentment—"Where's my Annie?" —wasn't far underneath. We had very little rehearsal time together, Suzie was frail and not in training, and by that time I was a very strong little person. As a result, there were a couple of times when I pushed her in a scene, forgot to compensate for the weight difference, and she lost her footing and went through one of those false walls. I think Suzie believed I'd done it on purpose, but there was definitely no thought-out viciousness on my part. There was the resentment of a child, which means I may not have gone out of my way to make her comfortable the way I normally would with another actress, but I certainly didn't go out of my way to do her in either.

One area where we genuinely had a problem was Suzie's nails. She was a flashy, very glamorous young woman, with great hairdos, lots of makeup, and *long* fingernails. Now, obviously she knew she couldn't play Annie Sullivan with long red fingernails, so off came the polish and down came the nails. But not far enough down, because her nails not only scratched me, they were dangerous and they really hurt. For weeks, night after night, I would go to the stage manager and say, "Her nails are not short enough." Probably if I had gone directly to her, we could have solved this at once, but I still wasn't used to the fact that someone else was occupying Annie's dressing room.

The problem was, she could have avoided hurting me only by cutting her nails so short they would be positively unattractive. Now that I have fingernails myself, I understand the great import of having them. I'm sure she wanted to go out on dates and wear jewelry and that's a drag—jewelry doesn't look right with short fingernails. I don't think she meant to be obstinate about this or anything else—she thought she had done enough; it was hard for her to believe her nails had to be *that* short. Eventually we settled the matter. She was convinced, and the little war ended.

Suzie used her glamour as an avenue to reach me. She had things like brocade-lined mink coats and six-inch-high heels that she let me try on; it was real dress-up time, and that was a lot of fun. And, though there was something cute and very disarming about the way she did it, Suzie was into real profanity. Whew! If Helen Keller could have heard her, Suzie could have *cursed* her into the miracle. She was a tough cookie but a good soul, and awfully sweet to me. I had a lot of laughs with Suzie, and I got to love her, but in a very different way than I loved Annie.

I did about three months of *The Miracle Worker* with Suzie, and by the time my last performance came around, I was tired and relieved. Most of the original cast had left before me, but there were still lots of tears and gifts. I'd lived intimately with those people for a long time, during a very remarkable period of my life, and even though I was ready to leave, it was hard to go.

At that moment I didn't at all realize the importance *The Miracle Worker* was going to have in my life. As for the future, I didn't think much further than "Well, I'm sure I'll get another job because this has gone so well." And I kept wondering, deep down inside, "Why am I successful? Is it them or is it me? Am I nothing without them? Could I have the acting without the rest of the bad stuff?" Because what I had realized with absolute certainty during *The Miracle Worker*'s run was that I would never give acting up, ever.

TWELVE

Though there were always rumblings about turning *The Miracle Worker* into a film, it wasn't until a couple of months before I left the play that it became official: the movie was the main reason, in fact, that the Rosses were willing to let me leave at all. The filming and especially being reunited with Annie sounded exciting, almost like reliving the experience from the beginning, only better, because we'd already gotten through a lot of the hard parts.

Even after the film was set, it wasn't clear whether or not I was going to be in it. There were negotiations similar to the ones before the play opened: "She looks too old, she's too tall, she's this, she's that, shall we take a chance?" Finally someone said, "Who are we kidding? If we're going with Annie Bancroft, we've got to go with the kid." If another actress had played Helen Keller, I would have been devastated. Not so much about missing out on a movie but because I felt the part as well as that ensemble experience was mine. The idea that I might become a movie star was nowhere in my thinking.

The filming began in the summer of 1961. The interiors were done at a studio on West Twenty-ninth Street in Manhattan, and the Rosses let me travel there by myself. I took a cab down the West Side Highway to the studio every morning, and you have no idea how much that meant to me. It was early in the day, the air was fresh, and the feeling of freedom, just being able to go from the apartment to the cab door alone, was best of all. I kept wondering, "How come I'm being allowed to do this?" The answer was that filming schedules begin a lot earlier in the day than theatrical schedules, and the Rosses didn't want to get up at that hour.

The exteriors, shot over ten days in Middletown, New Jersey, were also fun. I spent most of my off time just hanging around in the back of a nearby apple orchard. There was an old black lady who lived there in a little shack up on cinder blocks. She must have had upward of sixty cats; she called them her "chirruns."

This woman lived in one room—I'd never met anybody that poor before—and on the walls were nothing but pictures of people in caskets. Just the way you or I would hang pictures of our children or our friends, she was hanging them, too, but in caskets. It was spooky to me, because there was also no light in this place and it smelled funny from all those cats. But I loved this lady and every day, when I'd come to see her, she'd call out, "Chirruns, chirruns, chirruns, come on! Little girl's here to play with you! Chirruns!" And these sixty cats would come from everywhere. She wanted to give me a kitty, but the Rosses, of course, wouldn't allow it.

After doing the play all that time onstage, we hardly needed any preparation before shooting started. Though there were some trims made, including some lines of Annie's that I was in love with, the basic text is the same for the two versions. And because almost everyone involved had done films before, Arthur Penn didn't have to dwell on the difference in technique involved. Occasionally he'd step in with a comment like "You know, we have to bring it down for the camera," but that was it.

As the filming progressed, people began to worry for real that I was getting too tall. I think a lot of blocking choices were made with that in mind, for example, placing me next to Inga Swenson, who played my mother, because she was taller than Annie. And even though I spent a number of scenes all scrunched up, there were still some shots in which my legs look suspiciously lanky for someone who's supposed to be seven.

Our cinematographer was a Cuban with a thick accent named Ernesto Caparos. He was terribly charming, very dedicated to his work, but although he adored Arthur, they fought constantly because Arthur wanted a very particular dark, moody look. I'm sure he explained that to Ernesto but after a point there is something in a cinematographer, unless he works for Ingmar Bergman, that says, "I can't stand these shadows anymore, I gotta see the people."

So they'd go out on location, Ernesto would walk around making disapproving noises, and Arthur would finally say, "Do you have a problem, Ernie?"

"Chados, Arthur, there's too many chados. All the time she's in the chade."

And Arthur would generally laugh and walk away and get what he wanted. But occasionally they would square off toe-to-toe. Ernie would be screaming, "Too many chados!" and, "She's in the chade!" and Arthur would be yelling right back, complete with the accent, "I want the chade! The chados are the whole point!"

One thing that characterized the look of *The Miracle Worker* was a lack of closeups. There was criticism at the time that this made the movie look too much like the play, but I don't agree. As I see it, Arthur concentrated on telling the story instead of punching it up every two minutes. Both as an actor and part of the audience, I never missed the closeups at all. There's so much action that to cut in is distracting. Also, there's so much going on psychologically between these two people that when you cut away to one or the other, you lose something of the dynamic. And boy, does it ever work when one of those rare closeups appears. You're so startled by it, you almost gasp.

One closeup I had my own reasons for enjoying is the scene in which, mimicking Annie, I do first a good girl's face and then a bad girl's. Audiences in the theater always loved that, but since I made the bad girl face by rolling my eyes back in my head, there was never any way, not even by looking in the mirror, to see what everyone thought was so funny. So it was great for me the first time I saw the movie to be able to say, "Oh, *that's* what they're laughing at." It is pretty funny.

The tantrum scenes were the most complex to film. The major one in the second act was shot over four consecutive days, working mornings only. I was in great shape and at an age when you can usually refuel in five minutes anyhow, so when I think about how tired I got, Annie must have felt fifty times worse. I was very quick, and God bless her, she kept up with me. There is one particular moment when I'm going hellbent for election around that table and Annie cuts me off. Now, she had longer legs, but just the breathing power to do that is not easy to come by.

And it wasn't just the actors who needed to rest, there were guys with cameras on their shoulders who were as physically involved as we were. A lot of the film was shot with hand-held equipment, with the operators sitting in wheelchairs because they were small and mobile enough to get into corners. Often we'd get half or three-quarters of the way through a complicated take and have to start all over again because one of us didn't hit a position we thought we were going to hit or the wheelchairs missed their marks or the camera tilted or was jolted in some way. That scene was just exhausting for everyone.

The most complicated camera move, however, comes not in the fight scene but in the one in which Helen first enters the garden house and circles it wildly like a caged bird. The camera is in the center, following the flight around and around. Then suddenly I charge the camera, fall to the floor, and the camera follows me in one unbroken shot so you see my face all the way down to the ground. You accept it, you're expecting to see the girl's face, but it took some very clever planning for that to work. The camera was placed on a platform, and as I fell to the floor a trapdoor slowly opened, the cameraman stepped out of the wheelchair, bent his knees, and got down to the floor level with me. It's an extremely effective shot because it doesn't jump off the screen at you as a camera trick; you don't even notice it.

A couple of times in the film, if you look closely, you can see accidents that were left in. In the fight scene, Annie starts laughing from sheer exhaustion, something that was not in the script. It was decided, rightly I think, that it was entirely possible that that would have happened, and it also shows that the character has a sense of humor. In one of the outdoor scenes, Annie says "shit" when she accidentally falls into a stream of extremely icy water. We didn't have microphones on and the scene was used with a voice-over, so you really have to look to see it. I love looking, of course, and I giggle every time.

One of the strongest moments in the film is also the result of an accident. It happens right after the miracle, when Annie spells "teacher" into Helen's hand and Helen understands. It was a tough day for shooting; the sun was going in and out of very fluffy clouds, forcing a lot of retakes. It was getting cold and dark, there was time pressure because we would soon lose the light, and this scene was unbelievably emotional for me. Not only was it one of my strongest scenes, but I knew that pretty soon Arthur was going to say, "Cut, print" and that would be the last time I'd ever play it. My eyes were out of focus, I couldn't really see anything, but just as Annie finished spelling "teacher" I suddenly felt an amazing light and warmth on my face. Call it serendipity, God, you name it, but the blessing of having the sun move out from behind a cloud at just that moment really got me by the throat. And one tear, which was also definitely not planned, fell to my cheek. The cloud moved, the light hit the tear, the tear glistened. It was such a dog and pony show, who could believe it all happened by chance.

As the last day of shooting approached, something I'd been dreading for quite some time, I was working my way up to a real fit. The end of the film was a very painful, very lonely time, and an even bigger loss than when Annie left the play because there was no getting around the fact that this was truly final. Even though everyone's intentions are always to see each other and get together and la-di-da, even by that age I'd learned that that didn't work out too often, especially when you're living with Mr. and Mrs. Jack the Ripper.

When the last day came, I tried to be professional but it was very hard. In fact I can pinpoint the scene of the chick being hatched in my hand as being shot at that time because

I can see how swollen my eyes were. The heightened emotion of watching something being born, which I'd never seen before, coupled with the impending grief of being separated, made for two really beautiful faces on the screen. I don't think Annie and I look as vulnerable anywhere else in the movie as we do there.

Later that same day, I'd recovered enough to at least attend a poolside wrap party. John Ross used to tell the story that when I came out in this little leopard-patterned bathing suit, Arthur Penn supposedly said, "Whoo, we just made it!" I looked like a teenager—small, but a teenager nonetheless.

If anything bothers me about the film version of *The Miracle Worker* as opposed to the play, it's what they did to the very last scene. It upset me then and it upsets me now. In the play, everything happens at once, a kind of whirling dervish of excitement: Helen says "wah-wah," she spells half a dozen objects, the parents are called out, Annie screams, "She knows!" and the bow is all tied up with teacher's, "I love Helen, forever and ever." The crisis and the catharsis are happening right there for the audience.

In the movie what they did was break it up. The miracle happens, the crescendo builds, and suddenly the family takes the child away. Though it may be dramatically accurate that her mother and father are excited and want Helen to themselves for a while, somehow it cuts everything off and there isn't the chance to gear up again. You just go right into a nighttime scene, Annie's sitting on the porch looking much older than the Annie we've seen all through the movie. Then this perfectly well-behaved child comes out, kisses her on the cheek, and Annie says, as she spells it, "I love you, Helen." She doesn't even say "forever and ever," even the poetry of that moment is missing. They may have done that because the movie was short and they wanted an additional scene, because of a misguided desire to put a button on the thing, or because it's more historically accurate, but if dramatic license is ever permissible, it certainly is there. The whole intensity of that scene is simply gone.

Still, I get very emotionally involved with that film whenever I watch it; it's almost like a potion for me. If people talk while we're viewing it, I get annoyed, and none of my other roles affects me that way. Moreover, if I ever have to enter a scene crying, I will very often repeat to myself Annie's speech at the end, where she says to Helen, "Reach, reach, I wanted to teach you everything the earth is full of," and it's like turning a key and unlocking something inside me—the tears always come. Part of that is the identification I've always had with the desperation of this woman who's done everything she can think of—it's almost there but it's not and it never will be. That's very painful to me, but beautiful also, because she won't give up, and won't let Helen give up. Most of all, I connect with that desire to enlighten and to be enlightened before you die, so that you leave something behind.

Over the years I've gotten a lot of compliments about my role as Helen Keller, but I think the one that means the most was what my son Mack said after he saw the film when he was very little, maybe three or four.

"Mom," he wanted to know, "when did you get over being blind?"

Never, Mack. I'm still searching.

THIRTEEN

As *The Miracle Worker* filming progressed, the Rosses began drinking even more heavily than usual. Mornings were impossible for them because they were so hung over, but sometimes in the afternoon they'd wander out to the set and talk more to me about my behavior on the set than my behavior in front of the camera. "Why are you running around like that?" "Don't play with those cats!" "Go sit over there!" Never anything positive, except their standard phrase, "Love ya!" which I heard all the time. Alcohol always made Ethel abusive, while John by contrast got really mellow and faded into the woodwork. The only problem was, when John drank, he would get increasingly sexual with me.

What happened to me was minor compared to the real horror stories some kids have gone through. But the trauma was the same; I was about as molested as I ever want a little girl to get. It's always been very difficult for me to discuss these "incestuous" attempts, which is what they felt like; it's very disturbing to me still. In fact I spent years in therapy without even remembering them—I had totally blocked them out. Nothing came back to me until John Astin and I were watching television one night. He was flipping the channels and stopped at a discussion of incest and I freaked out. I screamed, "Change the channel! Change the channel!" I got really frantic, and John kept saying, "It's okay, it's okay. What's the matter? Why does this bother you so much?" I felt ashamed and embarrassed and all of a sudden I remembered why.

It started comparatively innocently, usually after nights of drinking. John would wear these short pajamas that were very revealing, I would be standing at the sink or getting something out of the closet, and he would accidentally on purpose brush up against me for just those few seconds too long for it to be an accident. There had to be something off-center about these incidents for me to catch what was going on, because I wasn't sophisticated enough sexually to make up something like that.

The first real incident that's clear in my mind took place while we were in New Jersey on *The Miracle Worker* location. The rest of the crew was in one hotel and the Rosses and I were in another. It was a broiling hot Sunday and we were sitting around the pool, reading the papers and chitchatting. They started making banana daiquiries, which I liked because they were sweet, and all of us got pretty well plotzed. And sunburned. So much so that Ethel finally noticed and said, "Boy, you better go in and put Sea 'n' Ski on. Take a shower first and use a lot of soap, that'll take the sting out." She had theories about everything.

Whenever we traveled we all stayed in one room, John and Ethel on two big beds and me on a cot. The shower helped a little, I put on the Sea 'n' Ski, but because of all that alcohol I was feeling pretty sick to my stomach. I got in bed and turned out the lights because they were hurting my eyes. The smell of rum and suntan oil was heavy in the air, and I felt close to vomiting.

I heard the door open and when they came in I pretended to be asleep, because if I had to talk to them, I'd throw up for sure. The room was really flying now. I was desperately trying to regulate my breathing, anything to make this sensation go away. John came out of the shower and they began to bicker. She said something like "I don't care, I'm taking a nap" and got into bed with me. Then he came around and got in bed on the other side.

They were both lying very close to me, and I made some noises to indicate discomfort but nobody changed positions. Then he began to fondle me, and he got an erection, which was up against my rear end. My whole body felt very hot, not just from my sunburn but from the inside, as if all the capillaries were bursting. I was terrified, I didn't know what to do. Meanwhile Ethel was making similar moves on her side. I made another noise, as if I were asleep but uncomfortable, but he pursued and put his leg over me. And I sat bolt upright and threw up all over him. Thank God for a weak stomach.

Not a word was ever mentioned, then or later, about what happened between us. I never said anything to either of them. I allowed them to believe I had been asleep; we pretended that I'd simply been sick and thrown up. If I hadn't done that, I've never wanted to think what might have happened. And there was another incident, about a year later in Palm Springs, when John left their bed in the middle of the night and got into mine. At first I kept hoping he was going to go away and when he didn't I just gave him a real kick. He got the message.

On the one hand, it seems impossible that John would have pursued things far enough to really rape me in either situation, because the potential consequences were too dangerous, but that first time it's entirely possible he was too drunk to care. I really don't know. I don't use Sea 'n' Ski anymore; that smell brings it back to me. And for years banana daiquiris were one drink I just couldn't touch.

I think Arthur Penn and Annie and a few people who had contact with me on a steady basis probably surmised that there was trouble in paradise, but they were hard-pressed to do anything about it. People have said to me through the years, "Why the hell didn't somebody try to help you?" but when you think about it, on a practical level, what were they going to do? No one witnessed any actual abuse, that was certainly well guarded, even by me. If anybody had made an accusation against the Rosses to me, I would have denied it or been very defensive. Because I had the classic reaction: guilt. "I know this is wrong, but it must be my fault, so I

better not tell anybody." So what was anybody going to do?
They'd open up a can of worms they'd have no control over.

Ever since *The Miracle Worker* ended, the Rosses had
been searching for a stage role of equal impact, and in 1962
they thought they'd found it. I'm not sure how *Isle of Children*,
written by Robert L. Joseph, came to their attention, but I
wasn't given any choice as to whether I would do the play.
Their treatment of me was a briskly patronizing "This is what
we're doing today," like a nurse saying, "How are we today?
Do we have our blue eyes open?"

The play was about a well-to-do couple and their cher-
ished only child who was dying of some unknown disease.
Unwilling to admit, as the girl does, that this is happening,
her parents schlepp her around the world, searching for a
cure. The mother especially is tilting at windmills, and the
marriage is not going well because of that and because the
girl adores her father and leaves poor mom out in the cold.

The part of Deirdre Striden, the little girl, was a tour de
force role. It was a wonderful opportunity for any kid, but
especially for this one, because it dealt with death, which
was *the* topic for me, and I was able to hear it explored and
discussed in ways that I did not hear in the house I lived in.
But more than that, Deirdre was the perfect child you dream
about. She was pretty, she was smart, she danced, she told
jokes, she did accents and imitated baseball players. I mean,
the loss of this child would be felt by every human being in
the whole world because she was just this mystical being who
could do it all.

Deirdre had a charming scene, beautifully written, that
made people terribly uncomfortable. She invites a boy up to
her bedroom and asks him to lie down next to her because
she's not going to live long enough to get married and have
sex and she wants an idea of what the experience feels like.
Deirdre's emotions went from A to Z and back again in that
play, so I got to do all kinds of things and show many
different sides of myself, and that was part of what was
wrong. It was really a one-woman show more than a play;
there was nothing for anyone else to do.

The other problem with *Isle of Children* was that if there

were fifty people involved with the play, there were fifty different opinions on what the play was about, and so many different versions of the ending I have trouble remembering them myself. Although I was still too terrified to have an opinion of my own, even as a fifteen-year-old I sensed that the piece was too scattered and didn't have the courage of its convictions.

The solution that everyone came up with during our pre-Broadway tryout in Wilmington was to introduce a Chinese play within a play for Deirdre's birthday. To this day I don't understand why they did that. All of a sudden there's a bunch of people, the mother, the father, and the maid, all running around in Chinese outfits. The girl had never spoken about anything Chinese, she didn't even talk about Chinese food! I was playing it and I didn't know what the hell it was about. I thought I was hallucinating, it was that bizarre.

One of the worst experiences I've ever had onstage came during the Wilmington tryout. The play was in such chaos we had new pages and scenes every day. Since I had an excellent memory as a kid, my burden usually was to put all the new material in that same night. One new scene involved Norma Crane, who played my mother. She had to say things like "Yes, dear" and "We'll see" and I had two pages of dialogue, so much that I wanted to wait until the next day to put it in. Norma, however, strongly wanted it in that night and I agreed to try, with a fail-safe system. If I suddenly lost my place, I would scratch my ear and we'd go back to a prearranged spot in the previous version.

Naturally, once we're onstage, all of a sudden I'm gone. I give the signal, and she doesn't take it. I give it again, she still doesn't take it. I could feel the heat coming up in my body and the blood rush to my face. I look to the stage manager in the wings, and either he hasn't been given the scene or he's lost it somewhere in his book, but at any rate there are pages flying everywhere and I'm dead. I was so flustered—the silence lasted for what felt like an eternity but was probably only a couple of minutes—before I came up with a way to begin a monologue that ended the scene.

When I got offstage I was furious. I was too young to

swear much but the air turned as blue as I could make it, it was one of the few times in my childhood when I was enraged at the unfairness of a situation and actually spoke up. I complained to the Rosses, the stage manager, even to the director, Jules Dassin, and to a person they all thought it was the funniest thing they'd ever seen, which made me feel even worse. Never again did I agree to take a scene and put it in the same day. I never wanted to have to go through that embarrassment again.

After four weeks of rehearsal and four weeks out of town, *Isle of Children* opened in New York at the Cort Theater on March 16, 1962, and lasted only eleven performances. I got some great notices, including one from Walter Kerr in *The New York Times* that said a theater ought to be named after me, but I didn't read that until more than ten years later, when I was coming home from a lunch with John Astin: when I told him I'd never seen the review he immediately headed for the Beverly Hills library to show it to me on microfilm. Despite that, the overall word of mouth on the play was horrible; nobody wanted to see a one-teenager show and the audience stayed away in droves. Believe me, it's humiliating to perform a play to maybe an eighth of a house. Arthur Penn came one night and handed me a folded leaflet someone had given him on the street. I opened it up and it said, "What to do about the Bomb!" I didn't know whether to laugh or cry.

Still, I was stunned when *Isle of Children* closed, crushed is the only way I can describe it. Remember, I'm the one who thought eighteen curtain calls was normal. So this was a *major* shock. For the first time the sense of loss came not from the thought, "Gee, I won't see these people anymore" but rather, "Hey, wait a minute, we didn't finish with this yet." I really wanted to keep playing that role. Plus I was out of a job, which meant the whole rigmarole had to start all over again.

It was only a few months later, though, that *The Miracle Worker* film was released. It was a very small opening—a few interviews but really no hoopla at all—but it was a picture that really snuck up on people. The first inkling of its considerable success came when I won the Hollywood Foreign Press Association's Golden Globe for Most Promising Future Star. It was exciting to be out on "the Coast" at last, exciting to wear a strapless dress and high heels for the first time, exciting to experience all the affirmation, all the adoration that comes with winning. You're *the* darling, and if you're someone who wants to be liked, it's hog heaven.

But there's something else going on inside of you that gives any award a double edge. In those final moments, when they're reading off the nominees, you can't help yourself—you really want it. It's a sad state of affairs for the human spirit when you're seduced into feeling an award matters that much, but that's what happens. And once you start to be that needy and that greedy, you begin to lose respect for yourself.

Although I was conscious of those feelings even then, I was a long way from being able to articulate them, and when I learned I'd been nominated for an Oscar in the best supporting actress category for *The Miracle Worker*, I had other things on my mind. For one thing, the news was delivered to me along with the flat statement, "Your mother's not going." My assumption by then, based on experience, was that at any kind of occasion she would invariably be excluded. The Rosses felt she was an obstructionist and a constant problem. Coming from the Lower East Side, depressed all the time—she did not present a pretty picture. And just as I had no ally against the Rosses' decisions, neither did my mother, not even in me. I'm sure she knew people who would've said, "Hey, you have a perfect right to go to the Academy Awards with your daughter," but she was too petrified to talk to anyone else and I, out of embarrassment and fear, said nothing. And not only didn't she get to go, but Bambi the dog did go, wearing a dress and a mink stole and being carried in a pyramid-shaped black leather bag. I'm not kidding; I wish I were. That Oscar situation, the fact that I couldn't be a nobler person and stand up for my mother, has caused me great distress for a long, long time.

I was also upset by what I'd been told I had to wear. Ethel made me a hideous-looking mint-green dress. The bottom of it actually had a quite pretty overlay of voile, and the top was supposed to be the same, but when Ethel saw the bodice she liked it so well she decided it didn't need to be finished. It looked as if I were wearing the lining of a jacket. The hairdo she arranged for made me look like my mother's mother, as if I were trying to play Annie Sullivan already. Remember, those elements that sound so trite and silly were very real to a sixteen-year-old kid in 1963. I would hint around, saying, "Couldn't we do this," or "Couldn't we do that," but since there was no way for me to say "I don't like this dress," I knew the bottom line was that I was going to wear it and I was going to be embarrassed and humiliated, and I was. I remember standing in the lobby of the Santa Monica Civic Auditorium being photographed with everyone else for a fashion layout, smiling and being little Miss Goody Two-Shoes but just wanting to die. Every time I see a picture of the dress, I cringe when I remember that I actually paraded around in front of people at that auspicious occasion looking like that.

Inside the auditorium on the night of April 8, I nodded to people, but there was no chatting. I felt like a little bitty lost person; I didn't know what to do, so I figured the best thing was to sit down and shut up. But when the overture started, and all that glitz got going, it was impossible not to get excited. My category came up early, and since Angela Lansbury had been touted very heavily in the trade papers to be the winner for *The Manchurian Candidate*, I was sure I was going to lose. So when George Chakiris, the presenter of the best supporting actress award, was introduced and the nervousness, the heightened adrenaline rush, started up, all I wanted was to be able to maintain a "good sport" face when she won.

George started reading the names—Angela's, mine, Mary Badham for *To Kill a Mockingbird*, Shirley Knight for *Sweet Bird of Youth*, Thelma Ritter for *Birdman of Alcatraz*—and for the first time I knew I really wanted it. Didn't know why, didn't give a damn, I just wanted it. And when George said my name, I hesitated to get up because I thought I'd been wishing so hard I'd made someone else's name sound like mine. I was in a kind of dream state. That's when John Ross leaned over to me and said, "They're not gonna bring it to you, honey, you better go get it." Well, as any actor knows, there are many ways to read that line, and the way he afterward related it to reporters was *not* the way he said it. The true reading was hardly avuncular, more like "If you don't get up there, I'm gonna kick you."

Of the rest, I have very little recollection. It was as if I'd gone into another dimension, never-never land. I know that "Thank you" was all I said because "Thank you" was all I had been instructed to say when I'd asked John Ross earlier that day, "Suppose a crazy thing happens and I win? I don't want to say anything you're not going to like." I asked if I should say something about Arthur Penn or Annie Bancroft or Fred Coe, and he said no, just thank you. One of the nicest things that happened after that was that the card that said "The winner is . . ." had been left on the podium and Frank Sinatra, who was the master of ceremonies that night, made sure somebody got it to me. I had not met him at that point but he was to figure in my future.

The Miracle Worker had gotten four other nominations, for best actress, direction, screenplay, and costume design, but the only other winner was Annie Bancroft, who was in New York doing a play so Joan Crawford accepted for her. The ball afterward was a loud blur, a lot of handshaking and picture-taking and no eating. I remember seeing Arthur Penn and feeling uncomfortable because he'd lost and I'd won. I kept the Oscar with me the whole time, and because of all the commotion and chaos, for those hours at least the Rosses had no shot at "keeping me humble."

Although I didn't know it until years later, my father was able to watch the Oscars on TV. I was at the funeral of another relative and asked, "Do any of you know if Daddy ever knew that I won the Academy Award?" And my uncle Tommy said, "Yes, he was with us at our house." He was in failing health—it turned out to be the last year of his life— but when I won he got very excited. He used his favorite nickname for me and said to Tommy, "That's my Ree-Ree!"

I called my mother as soon as I could after the award, and it was not a good call because she was not where she belonged, out in California with me. I could tell that she was happy but she was also very tense, and no wonder. For me, it was the usual public/private phone call, monitored by the

Rosses, with layer upon layer of coverup, so I couldn't say, "God, I wish you were here! Why aren't you here?" Throughout that evening there were fleeting moments of wishing my parents were there, of wishing that anybody were there but the Rosses. I'm not sure I missed them specifically as much as I missed feeling the warmth and support of a family around me. Here's a major achievement, the youngest person ever to win an Academy Award, the biggest A plus I ever got, and I had only the Gestapo and the dog to share it with. And if the truth be known, I would have preferred a date!

FOURTEEN

Preparations for what was to become *The Patty Duke Show* began well before the Oscars. Because I was a popular young performer, ABC wanted to do a series with me even though no one at the network had the slightest idea what it ought to be about. The Rosses didn't have a concept either, but they were taken with the idea of my becoming the youngest person in television history to have a prime time series named after her. The only person who wasn't excited, as well as the only person who wasn't given any choice, was me. I was never sure that the right thing was being done, that I shouldn't have stayed with the movies instead of being committed to a TV series. But the Rosses were the experts and I still believed they knew what was best for my career.

Once the deal was made, Sidney Sheldon, a TV writer before he became a best-selling novelist, was called in to do the pilot. The Rosses sent me out to Los Angeles to spend time with Sidney, his wife, Jorga, and their daughter, Mary, in the hope that my presence would spark an idea. A very gracious household, such nice people. And though he tells it jokingly, I think it's pretty much true that Sidney based the series on the me he got to know in those few days: he felt I was schizoid and that's how he came up with the concept.

There was the perky me and the corporate executive me and rarely the twain shall meet.

On the show I ended up playing identical cousins. There was Patty Lane, a bubbly American teenager who was the comic despair of her elders, and Cathy Lane, her demure, intellectual Scottish double. As Patty I had typical sitcom parents, a combative younger brother, and a loyal boyfriend. And I'm sure, though details don't come to mind, that Cathy and Patty got into trouble a whole lot.

The show was shot in New York, and not just because the Rosses lived there. The production would save money because there were no child labor laws in New York, so I could be worked harder, often from seven A.M. to seven P.M., than I could in California, where a child can be used for only four hours a day. Even so, doing the first shows took forever. For one thing, there was a lot of technical stuff, split screen and all that, that had to be worked out. And then there was Bill Asher.

Bill was the director, full of piss and vinegar, someone who actually used, as part of normal everyday speech, expressions like "chickie-baby." Bill ended up marrying Elizabeth Montgomery and doing *Bewitched*, but at the time he had a very complicated personal life, and there were days when we didn't accomplish as much as we wanted to. Still, I had a great time with Bill; he made everything light and funny and nobody was finding a cure for cancer. For some reason, though, Bill had to leave the show on very short notice, so someone else was brought in to replace him, which I thought would make me very unhappy.

The new director (and producer) was Stanley Praeger. I absolutely adored him, he was one of the funniest people I've ever met in my life; he could look at me and I would just burst out laughing. This was a man I was nuts about, but my fear of the Rosses was so great that when the chips were down I had no loyalty to him. Because not only did the Rosses have him fired, they made me do it. It's among the ugliest things I've ever done.

The Rosses had Stanley fired because he was getting too close to me. They didn't like him because I adored him; they were afraid if he really got too close he might find out our setup was a house of cards. So the Rosses set up a very formal suits-and-ties meeting with a bunch of guys from William Morris and a bunch of guys from United Artists. Ethel, of course, wasn't there, but I had my orders from her about what I was to do. I went in and told everybody that I couldn't stand to work with Stanley Praeger, that he made me nervous and very unhappy, and that I'd like him removed as both producer and director, or at least as director so he couldn't come on the set anymore. And that's what happened.

Stanley, who wasn't there to defend himself, was, of course, in shock when he got the news. He'd been seeing this little girl who kissed him good-bye and laughed at his last joke and now this. It was dreadful. Even worse, as producer he would pass me in the building every day and I didn't even say hi. We'd just look at each other, look down and walk on. A few years later, after I broke with the Rosses, I told him what I'd done and why I'd done it. I said I didn't feel my fear excused my actions, but I wanted him to know that I was sorry. He was extremely gracious and forgiving, but I know it must have hurt.

Although the directors may have changed frequently, the cast remained steady, and I felt close to all of them, especially Jean Byron, who played my mother and will tell you at the drop of a hat that I'm the only daughter she's ever had. She was a real grande dame, bawdy, outrageous, swore like a trooper, really my first experience with a woman who was able to maintain her grace and dignity and still be one of the guys.

I've since abused the privilege, but it was from Jean that I first learned the many uses of certain four-letter words. Much more important, Jean would talk with me about her intimate relationships, something I certainly didn't get from my mother or Ethel. I vicariously enjoyed the excitement of romance and also learned about the down side, the weeks and weeks of agony when a relationship is breaking up. She was very generous in allowing a teenage kid in on that, treating me like an adult but also knowing that she was instructing me at the same time. I may have been sixteen or seventeen chronologically, but in terms of emotional experience I'd been frozen at age twelve.

William Schallert, who played the father and who now works with me on the Screen Actors Guild board, was another one of those daddy role models, very warm and cerebral, the wise old owl. I'd confide in him occasionally, but mostly I would just hang around or literally hang on him. There are similarities between Bill and John Astin, whom I later married; if you ask them what time it is, they start with the invention of the sun dial. Now you're getting a good deal of information, and it's all very interesting, but in the meantime you're twenty-five minutes late for wherever you're going. Both those men can waste an hour of my time, and I'll be absolutely fascinated, while at the same time I'm thinking, "Son of a bitch—get to the point!"

Bill did something else that drove me absolutely berserk and that was to pretend he was a monkey. He's basically a dignified person but he had this way of lengthening his arms and making screeching noises. And, of course, the minute he got a rise out of me, which was always, he was gone. He would chase me up and down three flights of stairs, all over the building and onto the roof. I'd run into the ladies' room and he'd bang on the door, all the time doing this hideous monkey screech. Finally the assistant director and everybody else would say, "Bill, stop it now! We're trying to get some control here!" Oh, God, I hated it. I'd try to figure out what I was doing to trigger that monkey act, but I never did. In fact, he's still doing it to me at the Guild and I'm still screaming, *Stop it!*

When it came to casting my boyfriend, Richard, I was initially very disappointed that Tommy Rettig, the guy from *Lassie*, didn't get the part. Whew! He looked terrific and I figured I could just instantly have a crush on him and it'd be a built-in romance. Instead, they chose Eddie Applegate, who turned out to be very sweet and wonderful to work with. But although he had a Dorian Grey ability not to look it, he was a good ten years older than me and married. Eddie really looked like the typical dumb blond of that era and he behaved off-camera exactly the way he did on-camera, really goofy and ditso. I'll bet his agent said to him, "Hey, don't start acting your age around the set or you'll get canned." He got divorced during the last season, and we teased the hell out of him because he'd discovered partying on the Sunset Strip.

Then there was Paul O'Keefe, who played my brother, Ross, a name I tried to avoid saying. That poor kid, he worked all the time, worse than me. If you didn't see him on the set, he was off making a commercial somewhere. I remember yelling at him because his ears were dirty, and someone said, "This kid doesn't have time to take a shower. He's got another gig!" He was always late, always looked half-asleep or all-asleep, and we were always teasing him to wake up. Or about his complexion. "You look like a bottle a' milk! Go to makeup! You look like a bottle a' milk!"

It was a true sibling relationship between me and Paul, because I loved him and I hated him. He could be a pain-in-the-ass little brother; every time I'd try to have a conversation on an adult level, there he'd be. But he was also a midget Einstein, very bright, playing chess with some of the guys on the set to amuse himself. He wore glasses and was very disappointed when he found out that pilots have to have twenty-twenty vision. He'd often show up in a leather flight jacket and one of those old-fashioned helmets with the earflaps that come out. He wanted to be a pilot in the worst way.

Occasionally it was nice to be just warm and loving with Paul, but we didn't let people see that too often. A couple of times we had shows in which we had to go at each other physically, and whatever it was we were feeling for each other came out. Once we were told to kick, and I'm telling you our shins were bloody when it was over. I'd say, "Stop kicking so hard!" And he'd say, "I'm not!" Then I'd kick him even harder and he'd kick me even harder back and say, "You're supposed to be the older one!" Poor kid.

At first *The Patty Duke Show* was exciting to do because those guys were fun people to be with, and I was out of the house. And the Rosses were rarely around. But because of what I felt were the inherent limitations of the roles, I got bored very quickly. And the longer it went on, the more I began to hate it. I hated being less intelligent than I was, I hated pretending I was younger than I was, I hated not being consulted about anything, having no choice in how I looked or what I wore, I hated being trapped. As opposed to *The Miracle Worker*, which felt so true I never stopped learning new lessons from it, *The Patty Duke Show* had no connection to any reality I'd experienced or even heard about. I didn't want the series to be canceled—I had a sense of loyalty to the other people involved and enough ego investment not to want to be in a flop show that had my name on it—but it felt like a trap.

The show ended up running for 104 episodes, all the way through 1966. It was one of the most popular series of its day, so much so that parents apparently used it as a weapon (as in "You better do your homework or you're not going to watch *The Patty Duke Show*") but I never had an idea of the size of its audience. More than that, I honest to God don't remember any of the episodes, largely because to prevent my head from being turned I was never allowed to watch it. That was a flat-out edict from the Rosses, who'd send me to my room, where I could hear but not see what was going on. Except for watching ten minutes of it in Japanese when I went to Japan on a publicity tour, I never saw any of the shows until just a few years ago.

The story that I did a lot of work to prepare for my dual role is true, but it turned out to be useless research. I wrote lengthy bios for each girl, but they were more silly than anything else. I went to the Scottish Rites Organization's dances and socials, learned the sword dance and the Highland fling from Ethel, even practiced the bagpipes—that was a trip. It turns out no one ever gets good at the bagpipes, you have to be born a Blackwatch or forget it. All that went into the dumper after the pilot. The same thing with my accent. I learned a true Scottish burr, and then everyone got nervous that the viewers wouldn't like or understand it so they decided on a general European nothing accent, a kind of "anyplace but America" speech. That always bothered me, I didn't feel it was professional to be doing an accent like that. I mean, Cathy should be from someplace. That's one of the reasons I tend to think of my work in that show the same way I do the split screens we used, as part of the trick as opposed to genuine performance.

Actually it was the Patty role, for which I did no

research, that proved to be the more difficult for me. As glib as I was for a person my age, I was really not that outgoing, and certainly not about teenage pursuits. I didn't know how sixteen-year-olds danced. How would I know? I Never went to a dance. I listened to rock music only when I visited my mother; with the Rosses it was almost never allowed. I wasn't a teenager of my era, I was too busy talking with forty-year-olds. If I was anything, I was a teenager of John and Ethel's era. I had no more idea than the middle-aged screenwriters what someone my age should say, so what I was speaking was a Writers Guild idea of teenage talk. It had nothing to do with kids of my generation.

So the Cathy character, which everyone thought was the more difficult because she was so polished and la-di-da, that was the easier one. I liked Cathy better because she was more sedate, seemed older and was less silly. She was kind of boring, but at least she wasn't called upon to do things that I felt were demeaning and scatterbrained.

The same thing went for the clothes I wore. Frankly, I preferred Cathy's because they were more conservative in color and style. Others might think they were boring, but that was less offensive than skirts that were too short and too wide, things that were in general stiff and unreal. To me they were trick clothes, an extension of the trick photography and my trick accent. None of it had anything to do with the way a human being of that age really moves or thinks or chooses clothing. Not only did I hate those clothes, but they put my name on some and successfully merchandized them, so a lot of other poor girls were walking around with the same ugly clothes I was. But that's because they saw them on television, like one of my kids taking a diamond earring of mine because he wanted to look like Mr. T. Kids will imitate, but that doesn't necessarily mean they think what they're copying is any good.

Aside from the clothing and the accents, I separated the characters by examining my own mannerisms and then figuring out which ones I would be able to give up in order to animate the other character. One takes longer strides and when she sits down, she doesn't necessarily cross her legs. The other wouldn't dream of sitting down without crossing her legs at the ankles. One has very erect posture, the other slumps. One is very vivacious, the other looks more cerebral. One is going to talk louder and be left-handed, the other the reverse.

It was an interesting acting exercise in some respects, but it was also baloney; the technique could be boiled down to playing it faster and funnier for one and slower and quieter for the other. It was also annoying not to be able to perform either character fully because of the restraint of keeping them separate, having to eliminate certain things I might have done for one character because it belonged to the other one. No human being is either that perky or not perky. Although Sidney Sheldon had developed the roles as a device to use all parts of me, I felt as if I didn't get to use any. It was like asking a ballet dancer to dance only from the waist down.

Much of the strain of the dual role, however, was strictly physical. For one thing, as a public relations gimmick, I had to use two separate dressing rooms, one for Patty and one for Cathy. It was really a pain, because I was always leaving in one room something that I needed in the other. I kept begging the people in charge to knock down the cardboard wall between them so I could have one room and be comfortable, but the answer was always no.

Also, because of the use of a split screen, I did a lot of responding to myself, which was hard, and we had to film each scene at least twice and often a number of times. Sometimes I ended up changing twelve or fifteen times a day. That actually turned into one of the more entertaining parts of the shooting; when you're in the army, you make a game out of anything to survive. I would drive the poor hairdresser crazy, saying, "Quick, quick, put in the pins," trying to get the changing time down to under a minute and a half. I didn't care what I looked like—I never got to see the show anyway. There was a mirror in my dressing room, which was surprising, because usually they were forbidden to me by the Rosses as self-indulgent. The only one I had access to at their apartment was on the medicine chest in the bathroom, but I was allowed in there for only ten minutes at a time. As a result, I rarely used the one on the set and to this day I don't use a mirror much because it's not a habit I ever developed. There were no mirrors, so I didn't look.

One of the most positive things to come out of the show was my increased involvement with the Muscular Dystrophy Association. I became National Youth Chairman the first year of the series, the idea being to pay attention to this incredible force of teenagers who were doing something right and to help mobilize more of them. Though I think my participation was initially a public relations idea on the part of the Rosses, a way to keep my name before the public when I was between roles, it rapidly became very important to me and today, twenty-three years later, I'm still involved.

My job may have sounded honorary, but it was really a lot of work. I'd finish with the show on a Friday night and I'd fly to Detroit or Chicago or New Orleans or wherever. I'd be interviewed all morning, do a luncheon speech, more interviews in the afternoon, then usually make an appearance at a sock hop or something like that at night. You're continually on the ball, you've got to give the right answer, you can't offend anyone, you're never allowed to be tired. Appearances like that are the hardest part of this business. Acting's easy by comparison.

For someone my age, who had not been trained to deal with seriously ill people, that contact was initially traumatic. It takes an enormous toll to see these exquisite-looking, bright children who are withered and tortured in their little bodies. You might be bright and cheery in front of them, but inside it hurts and you're enraged. You're saying to yourself, "What the hell is life about? Where's this just God I keep hearing about?" It's tough stuff to wrestle with, especially when all the Rosses would give me were trite answers to serious questions. Maybe there are no answers, but at least respect the fact that I have the questions.

Through a combination of the Muscular Dystrophy national office and the fact that Peter Lawford was one of the producers of my show, I was invited to accompany the Whittakers, a family with two children with dystrophy, to meet President Kennedy in the White House. Talk about auras. With him, you really knew you'd met up with a special essence, so much so that I don't remember a thing about visiting Washington or how I got to the White House, I just remember *the* moment in the Oval Office.

We were in that office less than a minute before a hidden door, one that looks like a curved part of the wall, opened and in he came. He wore a dark suit, a red tie with a PT boat tie clip, and a smile. The moment he walked in, I started crying, and I cried the whole time, sniffing and wiping my eyes and with a real lump in my throat. I was shaking, there was a ringing in my ears, I'm frankly surprised I didn't pass out.

He was very relaxed and casual and charming and I felt like a sniveling fool. He gave me a bracelet that had a PT boat medallion on it and he kept making cute little remarks, just charming things to make me feel good. I gave him a kiss on the cheek when it was time to go, and he said something about it that made everybody laugh, but I had no idea what it was; it was as if I went deaf in there, deaf and all aflutter. God, was he spellbinding, the sexiest man ever.

Aside from that meeting and an off-season trip I took to Japan with the Rosses—where, as much because the Japanese deify Helen Keller as anything else, I was mobbed by thousands of weeping little Japanese girls and boys with cameras—I never really had any sense of the impact of the show. In fact, I'm still amazed at how many people I meet who can sing me the entire "Cousins, They're Identical Cousins" theme song. My son Mack can tell you exactly what his *The Facts of Life* ratings are, but I never knew about numbers and audience share. I was just doing my job and my life was very restricted. I was in the apartment, I was in the studio, we ate in the same two or three restaurants every night, and I never went anyplace else; there was no such thing as walking down the street or going to Bloomingdale's to browse. Plus I had no real friends, no telephone conversations with anyone—I got all my information from the other people on the set, and they probably assumed I knew how the show was doing. I did know the show must be somewhat popular because people recognized me more and more, but getting through the daily stuff was so all-consuming, I never even gave a thought to things like that. Tunnel vision is what it was.

Looking back now, I do have some theories as to why

The Patty Duke Show struck a chord. For one thing, I'd like to think a part of me, either the vulnerability or the zest for life, shone through. Also, those years were the beginning of the mounting number of divorces in this country, and the breakdown of the *Father Knows Best* type of family. Even with the absolute unreality of identical cousins, the family unit on our show was very strong. The kids could do outrageous things, much more preposterous than the kids watching ever would, but in the end everything was okay, the love was obvious, everybody was still together and strong. There was a security in that family, and that was wish fulfillment of a sort for the kids who sat with their TV trays and watched at home.

It may seem as if the money I made during all these years should be some sort of consolation for what I went through with the Rosses, but it doesn't work that way. For one thing, I still don't know what my income was during all those years with the Rosses. I've heard various figures for various jobs, but as for the total of what I actually made over the whole period of our relationship, I have no idea. I was never told and I never asked for an accounting. Because there was no freedom to spend money, no such thing as going shopping with my girlfriends, it wasn't on my mind at the time.

An educated guess is that I earned three thousand dollars a week for *The Patty Duke Show*, which means with over one hundred episodes I made three hundred thousand dollars. Plus the money from *The $64,000 Challenge*, my other work, the merchandising, and the one record I had that was a big hit. It probably added up to between half a million and a million dollars, a lot of which was supposed to be put into trust funds, but that turned out to be a sham.

Not only don't I know how much money I made while I was a minor, I don't have more than a clue about what happened to most of it. When I turned eighteen and went to collect on those trust funds, there was eighty-four thousand dollars in savings bonds. I was dead set against contacting the Rosses for an explanation, a quest I knew would be futile. It wasn't like them to sock money away somewhere; I never expected to find hundreds of thousands hidden in coffee cans under their potted palm. With their continual dining out in the best places, their frequent exotic vacations, and all the rest, they were very big spenders and I was the cash cow. Without either myself or my parents' having any kind of say in the matter, my earnings supported a decade's worth of very expensive living.

While many people will be appalled that my money was ripped off, the curious thing is that doesn't mean one iota to me. My *life* was ripped off. I was not allowed to grow and learn at my own pace, the pace of a child. If you don't get to have opinions, don't interact with people your own age, you never learn how. Precious years, *years*, of my life were taken that I can't have back. It's not that I wouldn't like to have the half a million right now, but really that's meaningless to me. You can't give me half a million, or even twice that amount, and call us even. No way.

FIFTEEN

While the appeal of *The Patty Duke Show* is not hard to understand, I still don't have a handle on the success of the six albums I made for United Artists. One single, "Don't Just Stand There," was actually a big hit, number three on the charts with a bullet. With a bullet! I wanted to sing so much, but when I hear what I did, it sounds awful. Even the covers still give me a pain in the stomach. I look like a forty-year-old pygmy on one, on another I have white hair with black roots, like an early punker, well ahead of my time. Sometimes I'll be eating spaghetti or something in a restaurant and someone will come up to me out of nowhere with one of those awful things, saying, "Oh, guess what I found? Would you sign this for me?" There goes my appetite.

Singing, it should come as no surprise, was also the Rosses' idea. They noticed that other little girls were singing bubble-gum music and making money at it, so why shouldn't I? That was the beginning of the years of singing lessons with Mr. Polanski, who ate bananas and cream-cheese-on-raisin-bread sandwiches and drank buttermilk and left a map on the glass. He was very nice but was he ever gross—I'd have to look out the window while I sang. I'd be stuck singing the scales for forty-five minutes, they were so boring and I was so bad at it. He was always saying, "No, no, no. Meee-eee-eee-eee."

Mr. Polanski's other obsession was this smelly thing he was always concocting in a pressure cooker the size of a small valise in a kitchen the size of a broom closet. Whew, it stunk! He was forever going into the kitchen to take care of whatever that strange beast was. I swear to God, it blew up one day while I was singing, all over that tiny closet of a kitchen. I finally got to sing a song, and the thing blew up!

It wasn't until *The Patty Duke Show* in 1964, when the trend had been established for a TV series star to make a record, that I started actually recording. The idea was that the acting and the recording would reinforce each other, each area would help you become popular in the other. Whether you could actually sing or not didn't matter; the technology was getting so good that if you could get out three notes in a row, the record people could splice a performance together. And, note by note, that's exactly what they did with me.

You have to understand that even though I'd hated my lessons, I really loved to sing and I didn't know that I couldn't. I mean, it sounded okay to me. Nobody taught me any better, not even the guy with the raisin bread. So I was very excited about all this. I'd learn the songs, though they had to be very careful when they taught them to me, because if they didn't immediately catch that I was singing the wrong note, that was the way it stayed. Forever. Then they had all these musicians come into a studio, and an arranger would come in, too, tap the stand with his little baton, and everybody would look up and start to play, and that was *my* song! It was so thrilling, I could hardly stand it.

The excitement lasted until someone said, "Now you have to go over there and put on earphones, count eight bars, and sing along." I can't read music, never could, probably never will. I don't know from bars, that's where my father was! Nobody told me when to come in, when to get out, when to be quiet, when to speak, and I became absolutely petrified about the entire experience. I knew I didn't know what I was doing, but I didn't have the confidence to reveal that until the situation reached crisis proportions. Then I'd start sobbing and saying, "I don't *know*, tap me on the shoulder when I'm supposed to sing and I'll sing." And that's what literally had to be done. They must have suffered so, those poor record producers. They all kept saying, "But you really can do this. You really can sing." And something that had been joyful to me became an absolute nightmare. Each one of those "sides," as they say, was a painful extraction from my psyche as well as from my body.

My so-called formal education was as problematical as my singing lessons, and it's also been the source of real frustration and shame. If I was in a group of people later in life and it was apparent that they'd been to college, I became intimidated and less a participant in the conversation. How could I possibly talk to these people? Gradually, though, I realized that either I ought to go to college or else become better informed on my own. I became a voracious reader of all kinds of things, and I also became a better listener. The real breakthrough was getting past the fear of asking a question because of the worry that I'd sound stupid. I found clever ways to phrase things, so it didn't look like I was ill educated or illiterate, but I asked questions and got answers.

Once the Rosses got hold of me, my little Sacred Heart of Jesus and Mary school didn't suit their needs. The compromise they reached with my mother was to send me to the Notre Dame Convent School on Seventy-ninth Street and Columbus Avenue; it was still a Catholic school (obviously!) but I would supposedly be allowed ample time off for work. That turned out to be not true enough for the Rosses, who quickly yanked me out. I was glad to leave Notre Dame; lots of rich kids went there and I felt very out of place. And we're talking heavy-duty Catholic—the nuns spoke French. And, as opposed to the group at Sacred Heart, the nuns there were mean. At least they looked mean, even if they weren't, because of the scary-looking "bat wing" habits they wore.

So I spent my last two elementary school years at Willard Mace, which I liked a lot even though I didn't always fit in. It was a professional children's school and although I was working, I felt very isolated from the other show biz kids. I didn't know all the agents in town or what auditions were happening or what had been written in *Backstage*, and these kids did. They were like midget adults and I quickly became a quasi-midget to fit in. One of the ways I did, both there and in high school, was to become the class clown, which was partly a reaction to my shortness. I made a lot of jokes about being small so I could say it before somebody else did. I still occasionally make the jokes today, but it's now just leftover patter, I don't feel the same kind of defensiveness I did then.

My high school was the Quintano School for Young Professionals, and the truth is that it was a high school out of a musical comedy. It was located in a narrow brownstone building on West Fifty-sixth Street, around the corner from Carnegie Hall—two big rooms with folding chairs and rickety folding tables that wiggled all the time. It still functioned as a part-time ballet school, with wall-to-wall floor-to-ceiling mirrors. How many teenagers, especially performers, do you think were concentrating on their work in that environment? The joke around school was that I was the only one who carried books. One of my teachers was always borrowing my geometry book and spitting all over the pages while he talked. And he didn't talk about math, he talked about Richard Burton and Elizabeth Taylor.

I wasn't that much different from other kids my age. I was becoming more and more interested in boys and romance, but I had nowhere to go with those feelings. I was attending school with girls who looked twenty-five and I had to fight the Rosses to get out of pinafores and into skirts and sweaters. Finally getting to wear knee socks was a big achievement; stockings took even longer. I never got to wear makeup until after I was married. The dress I wore to my prom showed my underpants, and not in the best way either—kind of like a Chatty Cathy doll. I was still "one of the guys" and the other girls were all the sex objects we now claim we don't want to be. I loved school and I hated school, but for different reasons than most kids. I disliked being with my classmates, where I didn't feel I belonged, and I wanted to see the teachers. It was a really confusing time.

Making things worse was that the Rosses refused to let me have any social life with any of the kids in that school. I had a telephone, a new Princess model, so that if anyone came to take pictures or interview me, my bedroom would look like a typical teenager's, but for a long time the phone wasn't even connected. Then, finally, they connected it but I wasn't allowed to give out the number. I was not allowed to have a recess—I had to take another class. I was not allowed a lunch hour—I had to take another class and eat when I got home. I wasn't allowed to hang out the way kids hang around with each other, and if I did it for even five minutes after school, I'd be very guilt-ridden and have to come up with an excuse why I was late in calling the Rosses, which I was supposed to do the instant I got out. Of course, I would sneak a few minutes here and a few minutes there, but I never really developed a full-out relationship with anybody in the school.

I did, however, manage to get my first real kiss. I was nearly fourteen when I developed a crush on a guy named Steve Curry—very curly hair, great eyes, a sweet, nice guy. He was in *Stop the World, I Want to Get Off* on Broadway, and when we rode the bus down to our respective theaters, I managed to reveal my crush and, man of the world that he was, he kissed me. I'd seen a lot of movies, but I didn't know people opened their mouths when they kissed till I met Steve Curry. He was in a Broadway show with a bunch of chorus girls and he knew. After that, Steve found one of the models in school to go out with and oh, was I mortified. I thought that kiss meant we were going to get married.

My first real romance, and it certainly was a curious one, was with Frank Sinatra, Jr. I met him in 1964, when I was seventeen. It was during the second season of *The Patty Duke Show*, when we were using all Peter Lawford's friends to punch up our appeal. It was quote-unquote love at first sight; though I'm tempted to say I liked him because he was male and interested in me, there's a real sweetness in Frank, and a kindness that's been in all the men I've fallen in love with. But although our relationship has lasted twenty-two years, it's always been platonic, in the neighborhood of romance but never getting there. Maybe it's because when we first met I was still under age and he got used to treating me that way.

And though I don't remember any discussions of marriage, it wasn't a frivolous relationship either. It's been almost the madonna kind of thing, and not the "Material Girl" Madonna either.

After the first time we met, he sent me a letter telling me how wonderful I was and a gift of a little charm with an angel on it that said, "You are my angel. Frank." And he left and went on the road. Frank is a very gifted composer but what he does for a living is play a lot of one-nighters as a band singer backed up with huge arrangements. So then the relationship became a telephone romance, because Frank Sinatra, Jr., was *the* reason the Rosses finally agreed to connect the telephone in my room.

Remember, the Rosses had patterned me after Grace Kelly; they were always waiting for the ruler of some principality, or certainly some major mogul, to come calling. I think the reason they didn't object to Frank was that he was *Frank Sinatra, Jr.*! In that way, the Rosses were as naive as people who had absolutely nothing to do with the business. They didn't know he didn't have any money, they didn't know he probably didn't have the kind of career his father had. To them, he was part of show biz royalty and that was okay, while some kid from Queens was not. So Frank would call me from Japan and places like that, he gave me the first stereo I ever had, sent me things he wanted me to listen to, like Respighi's "Pines of Rome" and lots of his father's stuff. I'd see him sporadically, whenever he was back on the East Coast, but mostly it was a long distance relationship.

I don't know that I was boy crazy during that period, but I was certainly sexually alert. My knowledge about sex, however, was sketchy at best. I knew that sex existed, I knew that men and women did things, but the mechanics, exactly *what* they did, I didn't learn until I actually went to bed with a man. There wasn't any sex education in school, my mother certainly wasn't going to talk about it, and as for the Rosses, they didn't volunteer and I didn't ask.

Although they considered themselves very free thinkers in that area, what the Rosses did in practice was something else again. The story of my first period is an example. Oh, that was a doozy. Initially, however, their attitude was fine.

When I was packing for the Golden Globe Awards in California, Ethel said she needed to talk to me. We went into the kitchen and she said, "Girls your age begin menstruating and John and I have been talking about it, and we figure that the time must be coming pretty soon, so I wanted you to be prepared." She had bought me some Kotex, which I'd seen in machines and been sent to buy as a little kid, with a note to the druggist. But it was a secret thing. Nobody had told me what you *did* with it.

That talk was very considerate on Ethel's part; if I got my first period in California, I wouldn't have to go get the supplies. But I was late in developing, all the girls in school had had their periods before me, and it didn't happen on the trip to California. I completely forgot about the whole thing, and as a result I wasn't prepared on a daily basis.

It was several months later, on a bus trip coming down to join the Rosses at a hotel they frequented in Atlantic City, that I got my first period. It was not a bus equipped with a bathroom, it did not make any stops, and by the time we got to Atlantic City I was close to hemorrhaging. And what would I be wearing but a white dress. And a blue sweater, which I tried to tie around my waist. Because I had nothing with me.

I didn't get too worried when the bleeding started, because I thought, "Oh, well, nobody will see." But once it became what it eventually became, I was frantic. It's bad enough for something like that to happen when you're anonymous, but some people on the bus had recognized me. So I could imagine the "I saw Patty Duke today and . . ." stories. I didn't have the presence of mind to go to one of the women who'd spoken to me and ask for help; that didn't even occur to me. When I arrived, there I was, in front of a busload of passengers, the driver, and all the people in the Atlantic City terminal, mortified, sobbing uncontrollably, and bleeding all over the place.

I got off the bus, and I saw the Rosses waiting by the car. Ethel said, "What are you crying ab—" and then she saw. And they laughed. I swear to you, they laughed. There was a beach towel in the car which I wrapped around me (they wouldn't let me go to the bathroom in the bus station) and they laughed all the way to the hotel. I didn't come out of the room the whole time we were there. I didn't want to come out of any room ever again. And I was filled with hatred for them. Now, maybe they thought making light of the incident was the best thing to do, but they weren't just making light: they laughed and laughed and laughed. And it was probably, if not the absolute beginning of our break, then certainly the most obvious moment when the bitterness against the Rosses began. It was truly the straw breaking the camel's back.

As the years of *The Patty Duke Show* went on, I was in a constant haze of anger and depression, the same kind that I'd witnessed in my mother except that I was functional and my mother was on the borderline of not being. I went and did my job, but I felt lonely and hopeless, and I was becoming less facile at the charade. If you're covering up, one layer won't do after a while, more and more layers are needed, and that's very wearing. Plus there was the strain of playing both sides of the street, of being duplicitous and telling the Rosses how much I loved them and missed them. I knew it was what they wanted to hear, so I played along; all I cared about was getting through it.

Consequently, there was a real sense of unrest in the Park Avenue apartment. Occasionally the Rosses would chalk it up to "a phase," and I'd hear about how I was not allowed to have phases, but never before had my anger been so apparent or so steady. The only hope I had was that if I were lucky, I'd get to be eighteen someday. But then what was I going to do? I didn't know any way out.

It was about this time that a habit I'd gotten into when *The Miracle Worker* ended reached full force. My situation at the Rosses' apartment felt so unbearable that I would escape by sleeping all weekend, from the moment I got home on Friday until it was time to go to work on Monday. No food, no nothing. Occasionally I got up to go to the toilet, but rarely. My whole body just shut down; when I got up on Monday I felt as if I were coming out of a coma. This went on for two years. It wasn't like some wondrous and refreshing yoga feat, it was classic emotional exhaustion and escape, the only running away I could do. And I knew, even though the Rosses never questioned it, that there was something seriously wrong with that kind of behavior. Healthy people don't sleep for forty-eight hours and more.

Although I wasn't informed, it was about this time, late in 1962 and near the end of his life, that my father reappeared on the scene. Contact had been reestablished, not between my father and my mother but between my father and the Rosses. My mother, in fact, was so dominated by the Rosses that even though she would occasionally recognize his voice on the phone, she never said, "John Patrick, this is Frances," or tried to have a conversation. "Oh, no, no," was her feeling, "I couldn't do that." Apparently the Rosses had begun giving him something like fifty dollars a month; suddenly, after all these years, they decided he should be bought off.

I didn't find out what the Rosses probably had in mind until a few months later, when they announced they wanted a lifetime contract with me. Most of the time I was feeling so hopeless I was still saying, "Sure, anything you want." They got in touch with a Wall Street lawyer named Bill Marrin, who did work for the Kennedys from time to time and had probably been suggested by Peter Lawford. Marrin insisted on meeting with me alone and that really bothered Ethel. I think she expected me to say that I wouldn't go without her and John, but I didn't and she had to agree.

Bill Marrin, it turned out, was outraged by the whole concept of this contract. I don't think he wanted to betray the Rosses' confidence, but he also felt a responsibility to someone who was still a minor and he urged me to look deeply into what was going on. I kept insisting everything was okay, but finally I agreed to hold off. So I went home and told the Rosses I wasn't signing it and everything hit the fan; it turned into another one of Ethel's crazy, marauding nights.

Ethel didn't stoop to profanity, but she had a wicked tongue. She went straight for the most vulnerable, insecure parts of you and just chewed them up. She told me what a little tramp I had become, how ungrateful I was—how could

I have come so far with them and not realize who the real talent was? John, as usual, sort of wandered around, blending into the background as much as possible. Occasionally he'd look at me and raise his eyes to the heavens, as if to say, "Well, we're just putting up with another Ethel tantrum." But he wouldn't challenge her. Ever.

What I finally figured out, with the help of Bill Marrin's hints, was that paying off my father was the groundwork the Rosses were laying for trying to adopt me. They wanted him to agree to a legal separation from my mother, which would get him out of the picture once and for all and give my mother custody. Then they would have my mother declared incompetent, commit her to a sanitarium, and boom, they would have legal guardianship of me. It was crazy, when you consider that I was getting close to being legally of age, but that was their plan.

It turns out that the Rosses needn't have been so concerned about my father, because he died on February 2, 1963. The date of record is February 7, because that's when his body was found. He died alone in a rooming house in the old neighborhood, but the only next-of-kin identification he had in his room, besides a signed picture of me, was a letter from my brother, Ray. Ray was in the service in Germany, but he was brought back to identify the body. There was a single shot missing from a new bottle of rye, and Ray figures that that was the last drink my father had before he died. Someone may have been kind and written *coronary thrombosis* on his death certificate, but I don't care what it says there. What he died of was alcoholism.

Within twenty-four hours or so of Ray's return I was told the news. It was evening, I was in the kitchen, and the telephone rang. John answered it, and when he hung up, he looked very grim. He said, "We have to tell you something. We just got word that your father died." There was very little emotion on my part, not then, not in front of them. They told me that arrangements for a wake were being made at Skelly & Larney's. The neighborhood wasn't there anymore, but Skelly & Larney's still was.

Although I didn't fully realize it at the time, the Rosses choreographed both the wake and my father's funeral just for my entrances and exits. First of all, they wanted me to go to the wake after work, when fewer people would be there. The funeral home was in a New York brownstone, narrow, close, the history of thousands upon thousands of flowers reeking in the woodwork. People always passed out in there, and now I knew why.

I went in and knelt by my father's casket. It was closed, with a flag draped over it. I cried and I felt hypocritical for crying, because it had been ten or eleven years and I hadn't made any effort to see him; I didn't even know who that was in there. Sure, I had fleeting, really nice memories of being Daddy's little girl, but I had no real knowledge of this man, nor he of me, and now it was too late.

I sort of looked at people whose faces were vaguely familiar and they turned out to be relatives I hadn't been allowed to see since my involvement with the Rosses. I said hello to my mother and my sister, who was pregnant at the time, and then it was time to go. I wasn't supposed to return the next night, but I begged, so the same scene was repeated, though this time they made sure the room was cleared out when I went in and a few minutes later I was gone. There wasn't the usual wake thing of sitting there talking about the dead person. No feeling of family or mourning. Everything was staged to accommodate the comings and goings of the little TV star.

The day of the funeral was much the same. I was instructed to go to the studio very early to be fully made up, costumed, and wigged, and then I was driven by limousine the three blocks to the funeral home. I fell in line with my brother in the procession into the church. It was the first time I'd seen him in uniform and, because the Rosses hadn't wanted us to communicate, the first time I'd seen him at all in three years. After the typical Catholic mass, and the recessional, everyone else went on to the cemetery but I said good-bye and went to work. I begged to go to the cemetery and the Rosses said no. The show couldn't afford the time.

Even if I could have fully played out the drama, how-ever, even if I could have gone to mourn and heard taps played at his graveside, it wouldn't have filled the void left by all those years of separation. In the time between then and now, I've had to deal with my resentment toward my father. I was busy blaming everyone else for not letting me see my dad, but he was a grown-up. He could have done whatever a father does to make contact with his kid. For a long time that was just too hard for me to accept.

In the aftermath of my father's death a fan magazine ran a contest culminating in a series of articles with the theme "Find Patty Duke's father; she wants to be reunited with him." The payoff was a picture of the rooming house where he died and his grave. When I first heard about it, I was embarrassed and my mother was upset. I was especially ashamed because of the last article, which said he'd died alone and that he didn't even have a television on which to watch his famous daughter. That last part wasn't true, I know, because a few years before, as kind of a hometown-girl-makes-good stunt, I went back to the local Madison Square Boys Club, where my brother was discovered, and drew raffle tickets. And the ticket that won a color TV set had my father's name on it and the address of a bar on Third Avenue. He wasn't there to accept, but I made sure they got the set to him. He may have hocked it, but he had a television.

Later that same year, I almost lost John Ross as well. He and Ethel had a huge fight that lasted an entire weekend. I wasn't privy to all that much of it because I was in my sleeping mode, but still it was unusual to witness a dispute between them; usually I was sent someplace else if there was going to be a major scene. I woke up for a few hours late on Sunday and he wasn't there. Ethel tried to make light of it, but she admitted she wasn't exactly sure where he was. Monday came and went and he still didn't show up. I finally did the unheard-of, I asked what was going on, but she still wouldn't tell me.

Then, on Tuesday after work, John Ross's secretary, John Phillips, picked me up and said we were going to meet Ethel in Newark, New Jersey. He told me that J.R., as I called him then, was in the hospital, but he didn't go into any detail. The hospital looked like Bellevue, very stark with bars on the windows. I waited in a room by myself for a long time and then Ethel came in. She told me that John had gone to a motel in Newark and attempted suicide and that he wasn't expected to live. He had taken phenobarbital, Nembutal, Seconal, Stelazine, Thorazine, and, I believe, Valium, all the pills she was getting from her friend the nurse, any batch of which could kill a person. This was not a cry for help; he took everything in the place—he meant to die. Why the man lived, no one knows.

Later that day, John Phillips told me that before J.R. took the pills, he had written several letters—one to Ethel, one to the police, one to an accountant, and one to me— and he told me their contents. The letter to the accountant talked about how they had played fast and loose with the money earned by Billy McNally, my little friend the Rosses had discovered outside the Metropole in Times Square. The letter to me was basically an apology for not allowing me to grow up, for keeping me from being a normal child, for not being stronger in allying himself with me against Ethel and her restrictions. I never got to see that letter; it and all the others were destroyed by Ethel. She covered it all up; money changed hands to keep the incident off the police blotter and to keep it quiet around the hospital. News of the attempt never came out.

John remained in that hospital for three days and started to rally. I was never allowed to see him, and after that first night I was never allowed to return. Ethel was afraid I'd be spotted. From there John was transferred to Gracie Square Hospital, one of the top places in the city, very expensive. He was there for six weeks and given God knows how many shock treatments.

The last week before John came back I started to get instructions from Ethel about what my behavior was to be once he arrived home. Contrary to any kind of therapy I know of, there was to be no discussion of any suicide attempt. I was *never* to mention it or the hospitalization—we were all to pretend that none of this had ever taken place. Which we did. And to the best of my knowledge, the man never had any follow-up psychiatric care, not a single session, until a number of years later when they were living in California and he apparently had another breakdown. And irony of ironies, although I never saw him, I've heard from several sources that at the time I was hospitalized in Los

Angeles under psychiatric care, he was an outpatient under-
going schock treatment at the same hospital.

Something even more emotionally significant for me,
and much more wrenching, than John's suicide attempt happened right about that time, in the summer of 1963. It
involved a woman I felt extremely close to, Ethel's mother,
Gramma Howe. Whenever the Rosses didn't like my behavior, they'd ship me off to Gramma Howe's in Detroit. It was
supposed to be a punishment, like the honor farm, but what
they didn't know was that Gramma would let me have all the
things I wasn't supposed to. The Rosses never wanted me to
eat anything fattening, but Gramma made me stuffed pork
chops and apple pie every day. Or she would invite boys over
and we'd have a cookout on the tiny hibachi, in her living
room no less. She was very domineering and very opinionated, much like Ethel in a lot of ways, but she also knew that
most of what was going on in my upbringing was nonsense.
Gramma Howe was the only person I knew who wasn't afraid
to ignore the Rosses' orders, the only person I could count on
to love me unconditionally. There was an unspoken pact
between us: "Don't tell."

Every week for months the Rosses would take me to a
weird doctor in New Jersey who looked like Sam Jaffe and
offered a procedure that was right out of a demented science
fiction movie. The treatment rooms in his office had regular
examining tables with the addition of metal coils on the top.
You would lie on these coils, a switch would be turned on,
they'd start to roll, and the combination of friction and body
heat would make you sweat like a pig. The whole thing made
me very crazy, because not only were you strapped to the
table while this was happening but all the lights were turned
out. I learned how to wiggle my hand out of the straps, listen
if anybody was coming, and turn the machine off. I know
this sounds nuts, but it's the truth. If I asked questions about
the treatments, I was told, "They're supposed to make you
better." I said, "I'm not sick in the first place," but nobody
was listening.

One cold, rainy day in September, Ethel's mother, my
friend and ally Gramma Howe, who was seventy-one, drove
out to visit from Detroit and she went to this place with us.

She and I were put in the same room, me on the table and Gramma in something that looked like an electric chair. She was strapped in as if she were going to be executed, and when the so-called doctor went out, she looked at me and said, "What . . . is . . . going . . . on here? Are they [meaning John and Ethel] completely out of their minds?" I laughed and said, "Oh, Gramma, I have to do this all the time." And she said, "Get me *out* of this thing."

I unhooked her, but the machine had been on long enough to make her very sweaty. It was still cold and rainy when we left in the Rosses' Lark convertible and, as usual, the Bloody Marys were popped open. By the time we got back to the apartment, Ethel was blind drunk and Gramma Howe was already having chills. Within an hour both John and Ethel were passed out and Gramma was vomiting and running a high fever. She was lying on the couch in the living room, getting sicker and sicker. I couldn't wake up Ethel, so I went to John and said, "You have to call the doctor. Something's very wrong with Gramma." He roused Ethel and she said, "Oh, there's nothing wrong with her, she always does this to me," and passed out again.

Gramma's temperature was 105, she was sweaty and clammy. But even though I was almost seventeen, I didn't feel I had the authority to call the doctor on my own. Then Gramma started to get delirious. I tried to wake up Ethel again—I said, "She's calling for her mother, she's talking nonsense"—and Ethel said, "Oh, she always does that. It's just to get my attention. Don't listen to her." At which point I took a deep breath and called the doctor myself. He came over and said Gramma had the flu. He advised giving her little sips of Coca-Cola and keeping a cold cloth on her head, which I did.

Then, at eleven-thirty, Ethel came out of the bedroom and said, "*What are you doing?*"

And I said, "I'm sitting here with Gramma."

"You're supposed to be in bed! You have to work tomorrow."

"But Gramma's really sick, and I'm sitting here with her."

"YOU'RE *NOT* SITTING HERE WITH GRAMMA!
YOU'RE GOING TO BED *RIGHT NOW!*"

"Are you going to take care of her, then? Are you going
to sit here?"

"I'LL DECIDE WHAT I'M GOING TO DO! YOU'RE
GOING TO BED, *NOW!*"

So I kissed Gramma and went to bed. But what Ethel
didn't know was that right before she came out, Gramma had
spoken. Her head had cleared and she'd told me, "You've *got*
to get away from these people." I said, "Gramma, that's not
possible. Where would I go?" She said, "I don't care where
you go, you've *got* to get away from these people. They are
crazy." It was like the last words of wisdom from a guru
before the spirit leaves the body. She was the one authority
figure who told me that I wasn't hallucinating, I wasn't nuts.
I knew then that my desire to get away from the Rosses was
an intelligent one. Up to that point, no matter how much I
disliked the Rosses, my loyalty had always been to them. All
that was going to change.

I slept especially soundly that night, but at three A.M.
Gramma Howe had a heart attack and died there at the
apartment. The doctor was called again, a fire department
emergency crew tromped through the apartment, and I slept
through all of it. In the morning, I sensed someone in my
room and woke up. It was John, leaning down to pick up my
alarm clock, which was on the floor next to my bed. Ethel
stood in the doorway.

"What are you doing?" I said. "I have to get up!"

"No, you can sleep in. You don't have to go to work
today."

I looked at Ethel, and she said softly, "I'm sorry."

"You killed her," I said very quietly. "She's dead because you killed her. You get out of my way, you get out of
my room."

I went in to see where Gramma was but the body had
been moved, and now I began screaming, "Where is she?
Where is she? Where is she?" And they kept saying, "Calm
down." Finally I just screamed, "FUCK YOU!" First time
ever.

They told me then she was at the morgue at Bellevue,

where my father had been taken, the hospital where I was born. And I said, "Then get the *fuck* out of my way." Once I used the word, it started to come very naturally. And I got dressed and went to work. Never again did the Rosses have the kind of hold on me they used to. It took me another six or eight months to accomplish getting away from them, but with Gramma Howe's voice ringing in my ears, it suddenly became inevitable.

SIXTEEN

It happened in the early days of *The Patty Duke Show*. I glanced in the mirror one morning and said to Nancy Littlefield (then a second assistant director but now New York City's Film Commissioner), "Who's that guy with the blue eyes?" She said, "That's Harry Falk. He's here to see about the first assistant director's job." And I said, "I'm going to marry him." Never mind that he was fourteen years older than me and already taken. I was determined. It may have taken me a while, but I did it.

Harry was spectacularly good-looking, six foot one with big blue eyes, the kind of guy who turned heads. He was great in terms of what we called "attitude"—just the way he stood was very sexy. And he knew it; he had that aura of quiet confidence that comes with being aware of the power of one's own masculinity. Yet I think he partly resented that; he felt, "Okay, I know I'm good at this, but I want to be good at other things." Harry was very quiet and painfully shy, which made him seem mysterious. And he had this giant dog, an Irish wolfhound named Finn, that weighed about 185 pounds and stood over six feet tall on his hind legs.

Even though I probably now subscribe to the "search-for-the-father" explanation for why I got involved with Harry, part of the reason was simply that no boys were hanging around the show. Men were hanging around. That was the field in which my sexual appetite was whetted. It was a real animal magnetism attraction for me with Harry, and, of course, having had no experience at all with the opposite sex, Steve Curry's kiss notwithstanding, I had no idea how to go about this conquest. I'm sure I acted like a lovesick puppy for the whole season.

No matter where Harry went on the set, I always knew where he was, always. I could be acting in a three-minute scene, and I knew exactly where he was standing, whether it was in the light or in the dark. When we weren't shooting, I always managed to be in the vicinity of where he was, sort of following him around, trying to think of subjects to engage him in conversation. Stanley Praeger was directing the show then, so we had his jokes and one-liners going for us; laughing and enjoying them was something we could have in common.

More than that I dared not do. I thought I had been so quiet and clever that no one had guessed what was on my mind. We had the summer off, and when I showed up for the first day of the second season, I found out Harry wasn't coming back. He had left us to work on a more intellectual series called *East Side, West Side*. It also meant more money and was a one-hour show, but I, of course, thought he'd made the switch because he hated me. I was inconsolable, and within an hour I realized that everyone had known all along that I had this crush on Harry. People kept coming up to me and saying, "Don't worry, honey, maybe the show he's on won't work out and he'll be back." And I kept saying very primly, "Who? Who? I don't know what you're talking about!"

It was during the hiatus from Harry that I became involved with Frank Sinatra, Jr. He was so grand and gracious, so smitten and so romantic. The attention was lovely, but while on most levels my thoughts about Harry were "Well, that'll never work out, I don't even know where the man *is*," I really hadn't given up on him. That's where the passion was. And I did manage to find Harry's phone number and call him. I didn't know what the hell to say when he answered the phone, I simply blurted out, "Hi, I just wanted to tell you that we were all sorry you didn't come back." He sounded very guilty.

Then it came time for my seventeenth birthday party at the studio and he was *the* surprise: I just turned around and there he was. My heart skipped several beats, and I did all those teenage things when I saw him. And his face got very red, as it always does when he's embarrassed. I tried to be friendly but ever so cool, yet I must have asked him eighteen different ways how he liked his new show and when was he coming back to ours. I had never looked at ratings before, but suddenly they were of great interest to me. And then his show was canceled, and somehow—it certainly had nothing to do with me—Harry was brought back as our first A.D. and my life was made.

This time I determined to be more aggressive. I became much more conscious of how I looked. I disliked Patty's and Cathy's clothes even more now, because they weren't sophisticated enough and I certainly didn't want to look like a kid in front of Harry. I started wearing black a lot, black turtlenecks and black pants, a very Greenwich Village bohemian look that I remembered Annie Bancroft wearing several years before. I would strike up conversations with Harry in a much more blatantly flirtatious way. I didn't have to deal with hiding my feelings anymore, because everyone had guessed, so I had nothing to lose. Then I started making hints about going out to the movies, and finally, in the most casual way, he invited me to go to dinner. I thought I would die.

Now, of course, came the real problem: I had to find a way to ask the Rosses if I could go out with Harry. It's hard to believe, since they usually knew everything about me, but I don't think they had a clue what was going on in this case. We were up in the little Romper Room on the third floor where the show was shot; they were rarely there. I considered the "a group of us are going out to dinner" kind of lie, but I figured I might as well tell the truth.

I waited a few days and then I said, "You know, Harry Falk invited me to go out to dinner and a movie, and I'd really like to do that. Maybe I could do it next week sometime?" No answer. I chattered on about how really interested he was in foreign films, junk like that, and finally, I have no idea why, they said yes. Maybe they thought Harry was so old (he was thirty-one to my seventeen, and by this time divorced) that he was safe. I was shocked when they agreed, but delighted.

I really agonized over what to wear. All the clothes I had looked like Patty's and Cathy's clothes, except for those black pants and turtlenecks, and I couldn't very well leave the Rosses' place wearing that. So I ended up being much too dressed up: I wore a blue straight skirt and a blue-and-white checked top with a blue tie and a white Peter Pan collar. Phew! By some coincidence, we went to a restaurant on Thirty-first Street and Second Avenue that used to be a bar my father hung out in. We ate paella and I got back home on time.

That date rapidly led to several more. I got bolder and bolder about letting the Rosses know I expected to be allowed to go. It must've become apparent to them that they'd better agree or else the real rebellion was going to start, because they let me go. Harry and I would talk about the age difference on our dates—he'd say, "Get outta here, you're jailbait," which was the first time I heard that phrase. There was a lot of heavy-duty kissing and stuff, we told each other we were in love, and it was apparent where things were going, but we hadn't figured out the logistics yet.

Right in the middle of all this, the show had its vacation hiatus. The Rosses had planned to go to the Virgin Islands, charter a yacht and live aboard, which we had done before. But I said I didn't want to go, which was the first time I'd ever even dreamed of doing such a thing. I told them I'd rather stay in New York and be with Harry. They were very upset and very angry; this was the first real teenage battle, a classic "I don't want to do what you want me to do, I don't even want to be with you" confrontation. And then, all of a sudden, they turned the tables on me by saying, "Hey, we've got a great idea. Why don't you invite Harry to come with us?"

After I picked myself up off the floor, I did just that. Harry didn't know if he wanted to go, it took him a while to make his decision, but he agreed. The Rosses by this time surely knew I had a crush on Harry, and I think their theory was, "All right, we'll play this one out and it'll be over with. I mean, how far is this guy going to go with her? It's ridiculous." I couldn't care less about their theories, I was in heaven. But predictably, that vacation turned out to be a terrible idea.

It's not that the days weren't wonderful. We spent them water-skiing and scuba diving and frolicking on the beach and all that. There were solitary walks and stolen moments. But the Rosses never closed their door at night, so Harry and I couldn't even fool around, much less sleep together. There was some heavy-duty chemistry happening, though, and the Rosses would have had to be out to lunch not to notice what was going on.

The night after we got back from that frustrating trip— two people locked up on a boat for ten days who can't touch each other—was the first time we made love. It was less than two months after we'd starting going out. We went to The Sign of the Dove, a very hotsy-totsy restaurant on Third Avenue, where we had a terrific dinner, we drank wine, we drank Black Russians, and I have no idea what the man said. Finally, he asked me, "Do you really want to go to a movie?" And I laughed.

We went back to his apartment, and even though I didn't have a clue about what I was doing, one of the things that I'm ever grateful to Harry for is that my first sexual experience was all the nice things it's supposed to be. There was all the nervousness you read about in romantic novels— How do you take your clothes off? Where do you put them? And *now* what do you do?—but Harry was just wonderful, he never made me feel any more self-conscious than I was making myself feel. And the experience was lovely, it was really lovely.

Then, of course, came the problem of how to get dressed gracefully and the panicky awareness that I should have been home two hours ago. So Harry got out *Cue* magazine and we picked out a movie to make believe we'd been to. We read the synopsis and then picked out a second one, because unless we'd gone to two movies I was in deep trouble about where I'd been. I didn't realize that since it would have been so out of character for me to be deceitful with the Rosses, I needn't have worried. I went home on cloud nine, the happiest I'd ever been.

Although Harry never talked about it and, much as I was dying to scream it from the rooftops, neither did I, it was soon very apparent to everyone that there had been a change in our relationship. And it wasn't that long before we started talking about marriage, though in very casual ways, kind of testing the waters. When he'd bring up the age difference, I told him it didn't matter to me, and he eventually said it didn't matter to him either. His best friend initially said, "Oh, my God! What are you doing?" But once we'd met and spent time together, the friend admitted, "This is not exactly the average seventeen-year-old."

Which, of course, was true, but in some ways the friend had been absolutely right in his first reaction, as was everyone else who said, "Don't do this." I don't think I was being contrary—it wasn't as if the more they said no the more I said yes—but I do remember being very defiant and very defensive. I'd seen the man in the mirror, I'd said I was going to marry him, and that was it as far as I was concerned.

The Rosses, not surprisingly, got very nervous. They said, "You're not going to see him anymore," and I said, "Yes, I am." They said, "No, you're not," and I said, "Yes, I am." If I'd thought about it, I would have been surprised at my assertiveness, but I had such tunnel vision when it came to Harry that no consequences mattered anymore. All I could think was, "This is not going to be taken away from me. This is not going to be destroyed by them."

Arguments with the Rosses followed, and then came threats. They were going to talk to Harry. Inside, that terrified me, but outside, I said, "Go right ahead. He feels the same way I do." And, of course, I had the clock on my side, so my real answer to their threats was, "I'm almost eighteen. You can stop me now, but you can't stop me in six months, in three months, in two months." And eventually they just gave up. I thought.

The first thing the Rosses did to counterattack was to take me out to Los Angeles during the summer of 1964, between the second and third seasons of the show, to do *Billie*, a quickie movie musical adapted from a play called

Time Out for Ginger. The film version is about a father, played by Jim Backus, who'd always wanted a son, and his daughter, who wants to run track with the guys. She has a method for running, she uses a particular beat in her head that she moves to, and because of that and because she's so strongly motivated, she's able to beat the boys which, until she relents and reveals her secret, thoroughly alienates them. It teaches a moral to everyone, especially to the father, who learns he should have been glad to accept the girl, and for the girl, who learns that the teenage years are awful for everybody!

A fifteen-day schedule for a musical was a little crazy, and we ended up cutting a lot of corners. There were a couple of jazz/ballet dance routines; I was taught just enough to get through the opening and closing of the number and some closeups. For publicity purposes I was being tutored in track and field by Rafer Johnson, the gold-medal-winning Olympic decathlon star, but he was there just long enough to be photographed supposedly teaching me about the high jump. The attitude was, if she can stand on her feet on the track, that's all we need. I did maybe half a dozen jumps over hurdles, enough to get medium shots, and then doubles did the rest.

One of my doubles was the best pole vaulter they had at L.A.'s University High, where we did the shooting. They made him shave his legs, put him in falsies and a wig, dressed him up in short shorts like me, and had him do my vaulting. Poor kid, I don't think he ever lived it down. I got a letter from University High a few years ago. They were holding the twentieth reunion of that class, and they wanted me to come because they expected that this young man, whose life had been made utterly miserable by me, was going to be there. Twenty years later and it was still his claim to fame.

The worst thing for me, except for the continued agony of having to sing on the soundtrack, was what they did to my hair. It was bleached absolutely white but my eyebrows were inexplicably left dark. It was a very peculiar look, kind of like racing stripes, and I got sores on my scalp from having to bleach my hair every other day. Why my hair had to look that way, I'll never know. While it might have been someone's concept that athletes have lighter hair, what it felt like was just another case of powerlessness. I thought this was the kind of thing Ethel should object to, but what I didn't realize was how intimidated she and John were by producers and directors. The two of them seemed to be calling all the shots, but that was hardly the case.

The night of the last day of filming, the Rosses and I had a huge blowup that effectively ended everything between us. I had just found out about the second phase of their counterattack against Harry: they'd decided to transfer *The Patty Duke Show* to Los Angeles for its third season, banking on the fact that it would be too difficult for Harry to reestablish himself professionally for him to attempt the move. Now the dam had really broken; there was no way to put things back together again, so I let it all out. I was crazed, I was just crazed.

Ethel was on one of her usual rampages that night. She ranted and raved, talked about how they'd given up everything for me and how could I be such an unappreciative little slut. Then, for the first time since it had happened, she brought up John's suicide attempt and claimed it was my fault. She said I'd broken his heart by being disloyal and not working closely enough with him on the show, that I'd made him try and kill himself.

Our voices were very loud for two or three in the morning; John had long since gone to bed, and I was getting even louder on purpose, hoping to rouse him. I did. When he came out I said, "Your wife is accusing me of this and this," and he kept looking at her and shaking his head and then he started to cry. "But worst of all, she said it's my fault you tried to kill yourself." It was clear she wanted to murder me for bringing that up, and he cried harder and said, "No, Ethel, you know that's not true. I wrote you a letter. I wrote you a letter, too, Patty." And I said, "Well, I didn't see your letter; I didn't see anybody's letter."

The hysteria continued on the part of the three of us. Ethel was appalled by my rebellion, but John was a broken man, very guilt-ridden and unwilling to argue anymore. Finally, I just snapped. I told them I hated them, I hated who I was with them, and from now on things were going to be different. I was eighteen and they didn't own me anymore, I was going to live where I wanted to live, with whom I wanted to live, and if they were such goddamn good managers, they could manage to get me an apartment, and a car, and a plane reservation back to New York. Just hostile, hostile, hostile, all the way down the line. The worm had finally turned. My exit line, "I'm going to Fire Island, and I'm going to sleep with Harry," was the first time I'd admitted that in so many words. I walked out, slammed the door, and that was the end of everything. I never returned to the Rosses again.

SEVENTEEN

After that triumphant exit, I went back to New York for the remainder of the summer. I was theoretically based at my mother's apartment, but I spent most of my time with Harry in the city or at his place on Fire Island. When the summer ended, I went into town to get some of my clothes out of the Rosses' Park Avenue apartment and that's when I found out they'd moved. All the locks had been changed and I had to con the doorman into letting me in. All the furniture was gone and my clothes were in a heap on the floor of my room. The Rosses hadn't necessarily wanted to be mysterious (they eventually called my mother and told her where they were), they just wanted the dramatic effect.

I'd had lots of thoughts about not returning to the show, but I knew that I couldn't do that. I kept saying to Harry, "Please come, please come. They have assistant directors out there, you know." Of course, he knew better than I how difficult that switch is, and he learned the hard way later on that he was right. I think Harry was both relieved and heartbroken about my leaving. He promised to come out and visit me, and as it turned out, absence did indeed make both our hearts grow fonder.

When I got to L.A., I moved into an apartment in the

Doheny Towers, *the* luxury building of its time, located right at the foot of the Sunset Strip. Suzie Pleshette had told me about it, I told the Rosses to "manage" me an apartment there, and they did. Of course, I didn't know anything about running a home. Jean Byron even had to help me go to Saks to buy sheets. Only Jean would choose Saks for that. I had four-hundred-dollar sheets on my bed, and that was in 1964. But after the first couple of days of setting up housekeeping in my own cute little dollhouse, living by myself turned into a horror. It was lonely and I'd never learned to be alone.

Making me more miserable was the fact that I was living a life-style that was completely alien to me. I was staying out all night, flying to the East for weekends to see Harry, and trying to do a series during the day. When I was home I left the television on all night and ate mostly junk food; believe me, I did not dine like a sophisticated adult.

The worst time of all was midnight, the panic hour. I couldn't sleep, there was nobody to talk to, it was too late to call anyone. The idea of sitting peacefully reading a book didn't occur to me—there was a motor running inside that wouldn't stop or even slow down. I'd take a walk or drive around and wind up at the beach in the middle of the night. I spent many a night just sitting there, afraid of being alone in my apartment.

This kind of behavior came partly from a sense of release, a feeling of "I'm going to taste it all at once, because somebody might slam the door again." But it also indicated a serious problem: I was panicked at not being prepared to live life. I was fine on the set; I knew how to hit my marks and say my lines—this was where I belonged. But as soon as it was time to go home, I was lost.

It was at this time that I began traveling with the remnants of the Rat Pack. Because Peter Lawford was one of the show's producers, I'd met him early on, but at first he was just a movie star to me, extremely handsome with that studied casualness that is so sexy and appealing—someone who didn't wear socks but did wear velvet slippers with wolves on them. But during the filming of *Billie*, which he had a hand in, and the beginning of the show's third season, I spent more time with him than I ever had. Also, Peter was

My parents, John and Frances Duke, on their wedding day.

The me that my managers, the Rosses, saw—young and eager to please. AP/WIDE WORLD

Proud as I can be at my First Communion, I wore a dress that, to my horror, was later dyed pink by Ethel Ross for an early acting role.

Patty Duke

The four faces of Patty. An early publicity photo with credits, not all of them genuine, listed on the back. © JUSTIN KERR

Travels with Bambi, the dog I couldn't escape: a staged showing of her to my mother, my sister Carol, and my brother Ray, and shopping for an appropriate carrying bag for the beast with Ethel Ross (below). NEW YORK *DAILY NEWS* (above), JACK STAGER/GLOBE PHOTOS (below)

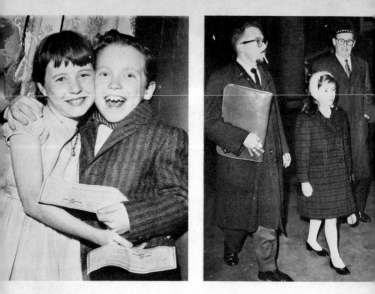

The pleasure of comparing $32,000 checks with cowinner Eddie Hodges (left) was followed by the agony of testifying before Congress when the show we won them on, *The $64,000 Challenge*, was found to be fixed. John Ross is on the right, my lawyer on the left. PICTORIAL PARADE (left), AP/WIDE WORLD

Acting with Helen Hayes in *One Red Rose for Christmas* was a highlight of my television career. The show was so well received we did it twice. AP/WIDE WORLD

Appearing with Anne Bancroft in the Broadway version of
The Miracle Worker was the experience of a lifetime.
AP/WIDE WORLD

Posing with a sign company executive, I officially became a star on Broadway. I was happy for the recognition, but I hated the kind of publicity—like this picture—that made me seem different from the rest of the cast. AP/WIDE WORLD

Anne Bancroft tries to teach me table manners in the film version of *The Miracle Worker*. LOUIS GOLDMAN

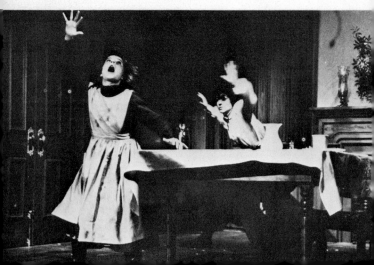

A miracle of another sort takes place as director Arthur Penn places an about-to-hatch chick in my hand LOUIS GOLDMAN

Annie Sullivan spells "Teacher" to Helen Keller for the first time before the sun quite literally broke through the clouds (below). LOUIS GOLDMAN

A dream is fulfilled when I play Annie Sullivan to Melissa Gilbert's Helen Keller on TV. AP/WIDE WORLD

Posing in the dress I hated, with Oscar cowinners Gregory Peck and Ed Begley, and Joan Crawford, who accepted for Anne Bancroft. AP/WIDE WORLD

At the post-awards party, I celebrated with Ethel while John (directly behind me) chatted. I would've rather had a date! AP/WIDE WORLD

I danced with Joey Trent in a photo session designed to make it seem that I had a normal teenager's life. JACK STAGER/GLOBE PHOTOS

"Cousins, identical cousins. . . ." I costarred with myself on *The Patty Duke Show*, playing two halves that equaled less than one as far as I was concerned. PICTORIAL PARADE

Frank Sinatra, Jr., was my first beau and a lifelong friend. His attentions were responsible for the Rosses' finally connecting my phone. AP/WIDE WORLD

I knew I'd marry Harry Falk from the moment I saw him. JOHN R. HAMILTON/GLOBE PHOTOS

Barbara Parkins and Sharon Tate were my costars in *Valley of the Dolls*. TWENTIETH CENTURY FOX

This mournful shot from *Me, Natalie* was taken the morning after I'd attempted suicide. NATIONAL GENERAL-CINEMA CENTER

Acting with Al Freeman in
My Sweet Charlie was a
terrific experience, but
accepting the Emmy I won
turned into a nationally
televised nightmare.
UNIVERSAL (above),
AP/WIDE WORLD (below)

My relationship with Desi Arnaz, Jr., was a romance the tabloids couldn't get enough of. PICTORIAL PARADE

My wedding day with Michael Tell—you can gauge my mental state by my eyes. The marriage lasted thirteen days. AP/WIDE WORLD

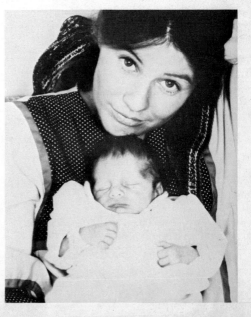

Sean Astin, the answer to my prayers. BARRY BREGMAN/ GLOBE PHOTOS

Sharing a hug and happiness
with John Astin.

Mackenzie at three
weeks. This time John
and I had done it right
and gotten married before
the baby was born.

Sean made his acting debut with me in *Please Don't Hit Me, Mom*. AP/WIDE WORLD

A nun at last, in *September Gun*. CBS

At my regal best as Martha Washington. CBS

With my guys, Sean (left) and Mackenzie.
© PETER KREDENSER

Michael Pearce and I celebrate our first Christmas, in 1985, as he switches uniforms from the Army's to a tuxedo. CRIS COTONE

much more vulnerable by then; Marilyn Monroe had died, J.F.K. had died, his world was crashing.

Carousing with these people was very heady for me; I didn't realize I was palling around with the remnants, I thought this was it. It was dinner at Matteo's every night, occasional visits from the likes of Warren Beatty, Lee Marvin, and Sammy Davis, Jr., lots of show biz and Kennedy stories, much drinking of Jack Daniel's but, oddly enough, no sex. The drinking got so heavy that I was called on the carpet many times for looking hung over during filming, because I was. My not-so-affectionate nickname on the show became the "little shit," as in "get the little shit up here."

During those days I met a woman named Molly Dunn, a friend of Peter's, who was a good twenty years older than me. She became my stand-in on the show, we started hanging around together, and, frankly, Molly became much too involved in my life. She had a place of her own, but she stayed at mine a lot, and slept over so much when we'd go out drinking that she became like a part-time roomie. There was a period when you had to go through Molly to get to me; since I didn't want to be bothered with anyone anyway, I figured, "Let big, bad Molly take care of it." Rumors apparently cropped up, which I didn't hear about until much later, that there was a lesbian relationship going on between us, which was simply not true.

I learned more than just drinking and cavorting with this group. I also started smoking. I'd never so much as sneaked a puff of a cigarette before, so I sat in my car and taught myself how. I threw up, got sick as a dog—for hours I practiced. When I came out, I was a smoker. Sick, but I was a smoker.

The same thing happened with swearing. Except for the night Gramma Howe died, I barely did it at all until I was eighteen, and, until the final blowups, not a single bad word passed my lips during the entire "reign of terror" with the Rosses. I even remember Harry once telling me in a startling statement, "You wouldn't say *shit* if you had a mouthful." But once I started to hang out with him and with the Rat Pack, where I was the smallest and youngest in the crowd, talking like a sailor, the same as smoking and drinking, was a way of saying, "I'm one of the gang. I'm a grown-up, too, even if you are much older than me." One day, only a couple of years later, I was cooking for Harry and I dropped a whole pot of peas on the floor. They rolled all over the kitchen, and I let out with a colorful, cleverly tied together stream of eight- and ten-letter words that would've done justice to the entire Sixth Fleet. And from the dining room Harry says, "Jesus, Pat, you really ought to do something about your language." Go figure it!

By the time I had to go on the set for the beginning of the third season, my determination to get back at the Rosses led me to overkill, and I came out with all kinds of demands, things like having Harry direct half the season. All the resentment that had been pent up for all those years came flying out. I turned down no opportunity to humiliate them or hurt them. If one or the other, usually John, would come on the set to ask me about something, I would refuse to speak to them. If he was standing there, I would turn and speak to someone else, ask that person to answer him. It was that petty, that rude. I eventually had them barred from the set; I said it was too upsetting for me to have them around. I turned into a loud, crass, borderline-manic young lady. It was their worst nightmare come true.

Things got so bad, the Rosses brought my mother out to L.A. at one point to try to talk me into going back with them. They wined and dined her, but it blew up in their faces, because she said, "I'm not doing this anymore, I'm not making her come back. You took her away from me. She wasn't my business for all these years, and she's not my business now." Then I got into a fight with my mother and I put her in some dreadful motel room until I could get her on a plane the next day. People called it rebellion then, but I don't think it was that at all. It was just total rejection of anyone who claimed to have loved me. I didn't believe them for a minute.

All this was politically stupid, of course, because no one who was around the show knew the history that I knew, so it looked as though I were being nothing more than a smart-ass kid. I wasn't trained to do anything but follow orders, but there I was, giving them, and ill equipped to do it. I was a little twerp. And until the last few years, when I made my peace with the reasons for that behavior, I used to be mortified that I'd ever acted like that. Those aren't memories I'm proud of. Yes, I felt justified, it's not as if the Rosses didn't deserve to have to deal with my feelings, but for my own sake as well as theirs, I wish I'd done it some other way. I could, for instance, just as easily have killed them with kindness as overwhelmed them with bile; I could have been more clever instead of being so infantile.

What's strange now is to look back and see that most of my bad behavior was textbook, it wasn't creative at all. The smoking, drinking, swearing, and hostile actions were all attention-getting devices. It didn't matter that it was bad attention I was attracting, it was attention all the same. So I was just running all hours, all directions, wanting to do it all and be the king. It was my turn to be in charge and I wasn't going to let it pass.

In September of 1965, I had a ruptured appendix and, simultaneously, a corpus luteum cyst on my right ovary. Since being diagnosed as a manic-depressive was still nearly two decades away, I had no idea that any kind of a drug, especially an anesthetic, is very dangerous to someone with that condition. So after the surgery I headed into the first major manic episode I can now identify, the first time I exhibited the kinds of off-the-wall behavior that were to plague me until I got a handle on what was wrong with me.

I didn't eat, I didn't sleep, I spent great sums of money, and even though I was still too physically uncomfortable to go running around town, I was on the phone constantly. Bill Schallert, my TV father, came to visit and thought I was behaving strangely. Then Bob Sweeney, the show's producer, came out a few times and didn't like what was going on either. So Bob invited me to come to recuperate at his and his wife Bev's house. Actually, it was more than an invitation, it was "This is what we're gonna do. Period." And a good thing, too, because between their issuing the invitation and their arriving to pick me up, I lost it. Hallucinations, strange mental ramblings and rantings—really out-of-control behavior began.

I stayed with the Sweeneys for six weeks. They were very loving and fun, their house felt like a safe haven to me, and it was a really healthy environment in which to recover. Harry came out for a couple of visits after the surgery, and after the first one we became engaged. He came out again in November, and we got married.

EIGHTEEN

My wedding day was November 26, 1965, a month shy of my nineteenth birthday. The site was the Little Brown Church in the San Fernando Valley, sweet and tiny, the ideal movie set. Not everything else, however, was quite so perfect. For one thing, I realized the morning of the event that I'd forgotten to make arrangements for the bride to be driven to the ceremony. So, furious with myself, I got into my electric blue Mustang convertible with the wire wheels and stormed off, taking myself to my own wedding.

When I pulled up to the church, my *Patty Duke Show* family was there, and the Rosses were too. I toyed with the idea of not inviting them inside but I decided I didn't want to feel guilty later on, and such an obvious slap in the face wouldn't have looked very good in the eyes of anyone who didn't know the whole story.

The person who wasn't there was my mother. Of course I'd asked her, but she'd decided she had to go to my cousin Mary Ann's baby shower or something and couldn't quite make it. Every time she complained about my not calling her or not being an attentive enough daughter, I'd remember she had gone to Mary Ann's baby shower instead of my wedding. Of course, her absence probably had nothing to do with me, she was probably angry at the Rosses. It's one thing to have your parents pick on you, but when you get gypped because your mother's mad at someone else, that's really insulting!

I was wearing a white mink hat and a white silk suit with white stockings and white shoes, all terribly sophisticated. It was a brief ceremony, and I can't remember if anybody gave me away—it certainly wasn't the Rosses! Then we went back to Jean Byron's house for champagne and little sandwiches before Harry and I left on our honeymoon trip to San Francisco.

Almost as soon as we got there, Harry ran into an old buddy and the three of us ended up having drinks together on my wedding night. I remember sitting in that rotating bar at the top of the Fairmont Hotel, kicking him under the table while smiling like the nice, understanding wife I was supposed to be and thinking, "Is this all there is?"

And when we finally did get to bed, we had to call the hotel doctor because I had what I thought was a heart seizure: pains in my chest and arm, inability to breathe, the works. This nice doctor came and kept smiling at the poor little bride. He said it was only an anxiety attack; he told us, "This happens to people sometimes on nights like this." And I kept looking at Harry like, "Doesn't he know that we've been doing it?"

One of the first things Harry and I did after we were married was go down to the Los Angeles county clerk's office and collect the eighty-four thousand dollars in savings bonds that was all that was left from what I'd earned during my childhood. The money had accumulated from the percentage of earnings that minors had to have placed in trust for them under California law. Though I wasn't twenty-one yet, as a married woman I was allowed to take possession. That turned out to be a painful event in itself; there were a lot of photographers, and we were not happy to have our privacy invaded, plus Harry worried "now people will think this is why I married her." A most unpleasant experience, all in all.

Now that Harry and I were officially together, I made a great effort to look the part of someone who could be married to this guy. I still didn't wear much makeup (I'm not good at that, it just looks like I'm playing dress-up) but I did start to wear tighter, more fashionable clothes. Given what Cathy and Patty wore, that wasn't too difficult. Not only was it a great relief to dress like someone my own age, but Harry liked me to look that way, and we began to get less flak over the age difference, something which really got old very fast.

Harry wanted to move from being an A.D. to directing, and I wasn't about to take no for an answer from Bob Sweeney or from any of the other people who ran the series. It was finally agreed that Harry could direct three shows, which turned out to be the last three of the season.

We lived at the time in a tiny little house that I sublet from Jean Byron way out in the San Fernando Valley, really the middle of nowhere. Since it was so far away, I'd gotten into the habit of showing up at work late, and my attitude was: "They're not gonna yell at me, I've got a protector now, my husband will hit them!" Finally, about five months after we were married, the day of Harry's debut arrived, and on that morning we determined that we were definitely not going to be late. After all, this was a man who fancied himself to be in the class of Sidney Lumet, and he's going to do this half-hour sitcom because his wife's the girl. I was going in early to do makeup and hair and, so that we could use one car, he was making the trip with me to look at sets and so on.

We got up early, all excited because today we were going to work together. We had breakfast and he got dressed. You have to understand that it really matters to Harry how he looks. Even as an assistant director he wore just the right color khaki pants, just the right degree of fading in his blue workshirt, just the right everything. All weekend he'd not only been very diligently doing his homework for the show, he'd also taken clothes out and considered various combinations, very carefully deciding what he was going to wear for his debut. I admired what he had on, but it wasn't good enough, and he must have tried on two or three outfits before we left. We got to the car and I said I'd drive so he could make whatever notations he needed to on the script. It was a beautiful morning, and I was just as happy as a pig in slop. I was a married lady, we were working together, this was "Mr. and Mrs. Hollywood."

We came to the stoplight at Ventura Boulevard, and Harry, who'd brought his coffee with him, opened the glove compartment to put the cup on one of the little sections cut out to hold it. I was chatting away, the light changed, I put the pedal to the metal, and Harry was wearing the entire cup of coffee. It may seem funny now, but I certainly couldn't laugh back then. It was totally an accident, because I truly wanted everything on that day to be perfect, but Harry was so angry that he actually called me a cunt.

I hardly knew what to say to him, just "Oh, my God, I'm sorry, I'm sorry, I didn't know, I didn't know" while he was screaming, "That's it! That's it! Turn around! Turn *around*!" And even though we were more than halfway to work, we had to drive back, I let him out to change and we ended up going back in two cars. Can you imagine? The vain man's nightmare. I thought that was the divorce, I really did. Can you get a divorce based on the fact that your wife spilled coffee on you on the way to work? Maybe in California.

Given that kind of a start, our working together was decidedly a mixed bag. Part of the time it was great fun, but it certainly wasn't as wonderful as we'd anticipated, and there were some real rough spots. My youth and my history were not at all conducive to adult behavior in a competitive situation. I felt, "Wait a minute, I thought we were pals here, who are you to be telling me what to do?" I remember a couple of consciously naughty things I did, like not being able to remember my lines for the last scene of the day when the clock was ticking and they were getting ready to pull the plug. I probably wasn't ready to be married to anyone, and I certainly wasn't ready to work with the same person I was married to.

Although the long drive—not to mention the coffee incident—was no fun, Harry and I had other reasons for wanting to move into a bigger house closer to the show business action than our San Fernando cottage. For one thing, we were in general spending money in record proportions. If he wanted a Porsche Targa, he got it. If I wanted a little Mercedes, I got it. We were two young people, with no dependents, we now had total access to my salary, and even though that eighty-four thousand I collected wasn't as much as I should have come into, it came in a big lump of money, which neither one of us was used to.

Also, Harry was a real maniac about antiques—English, some country French, and American. He practically lived at the Parke-Bernet Gallery when he was in New York, and since I wanted to like what he liked, I made the effort to know the difference between a Queen Anne foot and a ball-and-claw foot. We spent a fortune on truly terrific antiques, but they were just overpowering in this tiny place we lived in.

Since I was working, Harry did most of the house hunting. One thing about marital finances that was true then and is still true now is that if I trust this person with the care and feeding of my soul, then I can have no question about whose money is whose. If I need a premarital agreement, then I don't need to get married. And finally Harry found a spectacular place. It cost a lot more than anything else we'd seen, but there was no doubt that this was the house we wanted.

It was a colonial mansion off Benedict Canyon in Beverly Hills, jutting out on its own precipice at the top of the mountain with a twelve-car parking lot, a four-car garage and a 360-degree view of Los Angeles. Its nine rooms were big, bright, and airy, with bay windows and fireplaces everywhere. Everyone who sees the house loves it; Sharon Tate later rented it for a while when she first got pregnant, and she and Roman Polanski wanted to buy it. For Harry and me, two young people supposedly starting out in life, there was great, great excitement about living there.

I was still doing the series when it came time to furnish the house, and that was the beginning of my relationship with a friend of Harry's, a woman who's now a successful novelist, Joanna Barnes. She and Harry had become pals on a Peter Falk series called *Trials of O'Brien*. She was a bright and funny lady and Harry admired her Back Bay kind of background, very stylish and classy. If you're going to go to all the best galleries on Madison Avenue, you might as well go with someone who's dressed to kill.

Because somehow Joanna did everything right. Her hair was the right color, her makeup was perfect, so were her fingernails, her rings were the best, her watch was the most

attractive, her Pucci dresses fit just right because she was
about eleven ounces too skinny, she said "fuck" and "shit"
all at the same time and it sounded wonderful—she just
could do no wrong. Plus she knew where you should buy
everything, the best method of making Hollandaise sauce,
etc., etc., etc.

I had real trouble with that relationship, which I realize
now was probably not that unusual. I was trying to be the
sophisticated good sport, and understand that these two were
just pals—I always wondered if they'd had an affair, but I
really don't think so—but considering how insecure I was to
begin with, their closeness was just deadly for me. And Harry
could be very insensitive about my feelings. If he did notice
how I felt, he didn't seem to care. Instead, Harry asked
Joanna to help him furnish our house because, of course, she
got a decorator's discount. I kept wanting to scream, "Asshole!
Pay retail! Have a happier wife!"

So Joanna became our unofficial decorator. She'd call
from the pay phone at the Beverly Hills Hotel and an-
nounce, "I'm on my way up! Put on the coffee!" Click. It
didn't occur to her that we might be in the middle of making
love or cleaning the toilet bowl or having *the* discussion of
life, she was coming. One day the three of us were sitting
drinking coffee in this cozy lanai setting, his antiques all
around us, and Harry was staring into his coffee cup, which
said on the inside, "Forget Me Not." And he says, "Forget
me not, forget me not, forget me not—who the hell gave me
this?" Of course it was me, and of course I didn't have a good
sense of humor about it. I started bawling, and then I wouldn't
tell them why. The poor woman, never in a million years
would she want to hurt me, but whenever she was around,
something would invariably happen that was guaranteed to
drive me totally nuts.

If one thing summed up my previous bondage to the
Rosses, it was the name they'd stuck me with. On one level I
now disliked it because it was a little girl's name, and it was
very important to me that all diminutive and cute things
vanish from my life. But more than that, because the name
came from the Rosses, because it was given to me as an edict

over which I'd had no control, it symbolized them. That name meant those faces, it meant that helpless, nonperson time in my life, so much so that for many years all the awards I won for acting were very well hidden and packed away because I couldn't stand the name on them.

Once Harry and I were married, the opportunity to reclaim as much of myself as I could by changing my name was too good to pass up. I began fiddling around with various combinations and finally decided that "Pat Falk" was an acceptable name in a way "Pat Duke" was not. Then a real campaign began. People were told, "She wants to be called 'Pat,' " and they were reminded if they forgot. The interesting thing is that, early in our relationship, Harry fleetingly called me Anna Marie. He even used that name when he wrote me letters. It just didn't last, however. Anna Marie really wasn't fully reborn inside me yet, she hadn't the strength to be totally out. That was a resurrection that would have to wait.

NINETEEN

The final episode of *The Patty Duke Show* was filmed in 1966; ABC did not pick us up for another year. The reason wasn't lack of popularity, the network simply wanted all its shows for the next season to be in color, and United Artists, claiming it would cost too much, refused. I think it was a negotiating ploy on United Artists' part; they thought they could stonewall and get another year out of the series in black and white, but they lost.

Part of me was really happy when the series folded. I was having obvious problems staying involved with Patty and Cathy, and until the show ended, I hadn't quite recognized how important acting was to my well-being. I wasn't even smart enough to know that I would have to have a substitute for it in my life. I really felt "I'm married, I'm going to stay home, have babies and wear little white aprons, and, of course, I'll be happy." I didn't realize having a husband is not something you *do* like doing a job, like acting or being a lawyer.

And no matter how much I hated the show and wished with all my might that it would fold so that I could get on with being "Sadie, Sadie, married lady," that didn't matter psychologically. When it fell apart, I got buried by the rubble. Because if you've belonged someplace all your life, unhappy though it may be, that place is home. The feeling of abandonment when it's gone is just as real as your mother giving you up to live with other people.

So at the same time as I was feeling thrilled that the series wasn't picked up and I was free, I felt as if I no longer had an identity. I was no longer associated with the Rosses, so there wasn't anyone telling me what to do. But I hadn't learned how to make dinner, how to make a decision, how to do anything. You can't plan ahead if you've never learned to plan in the first place. And at the back of my mind I was hearing, "You'll never work again. You'll never work without us. You'll be nothing without us." Kissing off the show meant not only kissing off the Rosses, it meant kissing off a lifetime that I'd never gotten to understand.

The upshot of all this was that I went into a major depression after the series folded. Somehow it seemed easier to be crazy. People don't judge you as harshly, you don't hear many mean, vicious things being said about patients in psychiatric hospitals. It's "Oh, that poor thing, she doesn't know." That's easier than having to be responsible for your actions. Saying "I'm nuts, I can't do this, I can't cope" was a new defense mechanism for me. It meant you didn't have to function, and I didn't.

Take going to the market. A good four, five, six hours a day might be taken up with this planned trip. Harry and I would sit down, have coffee, and discuss the shopping list literally for hours. It wasn't really a discussion; he'd give me pep talks and I'd cry. "You can do this," he'd say. "Look, thousands of people do it every day. All you have to do is just walk in. So what if you get the wrong things? Don't worry about it." There were days when he reached his limit, when he'd just say, "The hell with it, don't go to the market," but most of the time he really was a good soul, constantly trying to bring me back to some kind of reality and assuage the fear of whatever these demons were that were raging inside me.

Finally, we'd get the list in order, enough items to make it an acceptable, businesslike list; I wasn't so far gone at this point that two or three items would have seemed like the real thing. Then I'd go upstairs to get dressed. And Harry would come up, sometimes a few minutes later, sometimes hours later, thinking I'd left. And I'd be standing in the closet, or sitting on the floor, the same way I was when I first went up. I wasn't really catatonic; I was aware of what I was doing, and aware that my behavior was an aberration. I just didn't want to go.

With Harry's constant encouragement I eked by. And there were times when I'd come out of this state, when I'd get up of a morning, make a list, and go to the market, just like anyone else. But even as I was performing these acts, I was experiencing constant physical and emotional anxiety. Whenever I was out in public I was always thinking, "Do they know? Can they see?" Plus there was the fact that people were looking at me because I was recognizable, and they were wondering if I might be Patty Duke. If you're paranoid to begin with, and then people do start staring at you, it's much tougher to know what's real and what's not.

Given my mental state, it's not surprising that I didn't work much during those days. Even if I'd wanted to, I don't think I would have been able. I did manage an episode of *The Virginian* (where I was upstaged by a horse) and I remember the triumph I would feel driving off the Universal lot in the evenings, having gotten through another day without letting anyone know that I was crazy as a bedbug.

I also was a presenter at the Academy Awards that spring. I had trouble with the dress rehearsal—Harry had to talk to me for about four hours before I'd leave the house, and when I got there I realized I'd forgotten the shoes that went with my dress, which was critical because I couldn't practice coming down the stairs in my sneakers. So an announcement was made over the P.A. system that Patty Duke didn't have any shoes and could somebody please lend her a pair. And the shoes that were lent to me were Liza Minnelli's. Silly though it may seem, that was a very meaningful gesture to me, because even though no one knew it, I was in a real emotional crisis. So I've always felt a terrific connection with Liza, and every time I hear she's in a crisis of some sort, I keep wishing I could send her whatever she needs as much as I needed those shoes.

By now I was also suffering from anorexia, though in those days we didn't have a name for it. Harry made the mistake one day of saying, "Gee, you're looking a little pudgy there." I weighed about 105 pounds then, but I immediately went on a diet of coffee, cigarettes, and Diet-Rite cola and ended up weighing as little as 76 pounds before I got help. I know now that one of the explanations for anorexia is the refusal to grow up: you starve yourself to get smaller, you attempt to physically match how small you feel mentally, and I think that's what I was doing.

In the summer of 1966, the last summer before my twentieth birthday, we went back East to Fire Island to relax; you can imagine the kind of strain we had been living under. Ironically enough, Harry happened to be reading *Catch-22* at the time, laughing and enjoying it, and I was in hell. He'd bought me a copy of the book so we could share the experience, but I couldn't make sense out of the words on the paper, that's how bad I was.

Occasionally, I'd be able to come out of this state long enough to pick a fight or do something so crazy that he would lose his temper. One day Harry was just sitting out on the deck reading, and I was like a caged lion. I kept sitting down and getting up and sitting down, without any real purpose. I asked him a question and he didn't answer me, he probably didn't even hear me, but I got very hurt and angry. So I yelled at him about his book and he threw it in frustration.

I ran back into the house, into the bathroom, locked the door, and swallowed half a bottle of whatever pills were handy. It was Valium, prescribed for me by a doctor in Los Angeles and not, as I found out later, a good drug for manic-depressives. But I felt as if there were some demonic engine driving me all the time, and the only escape, the only thing that would put me out of my misery for a while, was the peace of a Valium-induced sleep.

If I'd taken all those pills without anyone's knowledge, it would have been a genuine suicide attempt. But Harry could hear me, he knew what I was doing, and I knew that he could hear me and could stop me. I ended up throwing the pills up. Taking these pills was more of a gesture than anything else, an attempt to show what a real crisis I was in. A friend of Harry's who was visiting at the time and had witnessed my behavior over several days suggested that something really had to be done, so we went in to the city on Monday morning to see a shrink.

I had seen psychiatrists a couple of times in L.A. at Harry's suggestion and I'd reacted violently against the experience. And by the time we got into this woman's office, I could easily be diagnosed as catatonic: I was really angry, refusing to talk and allowing them to think that I couldn't. What I was feeling was the culmination of lifelong feelings of rejection, abandonment, mismanagement, and bad parenting. I was completely ill-equipped to be an adult, and the infant in me was just enraged.

This clown of a shrink said to Harry, right in front of me, "This is a very sick girl. She will come out of it and you can get her help from time to time, but this will always be a very, very sick girl." Can you imagine? First of all, no one, I don't care how good a therapist he or she is, can make a diagnosis like that in a half-hour meeting. No one. If they do, shame on them. The finality of that statement had an impact on me that lasted for fifteen years. And you can imagine the impact on Harry, who was not much more sophisticated about psychiatry than I was. The poor guy had married a defective piece of machinery. He was heartbroken.

So arrangements were made for us to return to Los Angeles and for me to be admitted to Mount Sinai (now Cedars-Sinai) Hospital. I fought those plans as much as I could, but I was in a very weakened state physically as well as emotionally; I felt as if I were living all wrapped up in old bubble gum. There was no such thing as having a conversation with me, I was a wreck all the way back on the plane. Harry wanted me to go right from the airport to the hospital, but I begged to go back to the house first. I don't remember what excuse I used, but he acquiesced.

When we got home I started talking a little bit, trying to cajole him into not making me go. And he told me how much he loved me and how important it was to him that I get well. He promised me that the hospital was not going to be a snake pit or anything like that. I would be in a regular hospital room where I would be able to rest, and a doctor would come and talk to me about how to approach my problem. Harry had had several phone conversations with the doctor, and finally he begged me, he just begged me, to go. And as much as I didn't want to, I trusted him and I bought that promise. To this day I trust him. I think he believed what he was told, I don't think he knew.

I remember standing outside the car at Mount Sinai, waiting to go in there, pleading with him not to make me, saying all those terrible "If you love me, you won't do this" emotional blackmail things that people say. He finally convinced me that the shoe was on the other foot now; if I loved him, I would do this.

So we went in and, of course, it was a fully locked, secure ward with cell-like rooms that smelled antiseptic. And when I saw the keys turn in the locks, I just looked at Harry accusingly, as if to say, "How could you do this? You promised, and it was a lie." And his face was like a frightened deer's; he realized, "My God, I promised her this and it's not what I said it was."

The nurses and attendants are always so sweet when you first go in. They introduced themselves and showed us up and down the hall—this was the occupational therapy dayroom, this was the kitchen, if you ever wanted a snack you were certainly welcome to go in. And then the residents came out of the showers, and they looked a lot crazier than I felt. I'd been holding Harry's hand but I let go of it to move out of the way as all these people trooped down the hall. And when I turned around, the attendant was closing the door of the ward and Harry was on the other side. I could just see his face in the little window, and then, obviously distraught, he turned away.

All of a sudden, and to this day I don't know where the strength and the confidence and the sanity came from, there was nothing wrong with me. I decided I had to be very careful and cautious, so as not to seem crazy. I went up to a nurse and I said, "I think there's been a mistake, I'm not sure I really belong here," which is, of course, the classic line. And she gave me a nice, all-knowing smile and replied,

"Things are going to be fine, dear." That's when I realized I really was in serious trouble.

There was a large male attendant at the door, and I went over and stood by him. Somebody with a key was unlocking the door from the outside and as he opened it, I managed to wedge myself halfway out. Then a struggle began with the attendant, and I suspect the guy was half afraid of hurting me since I was so little, because I wound up outside.

All this happened so quickly that Harry was still standing there, waiting for the elevator. I begged him to come back inside so he could see what it was really like. If he insisted I stay there after that, I would. The attendant motioned it would be okay, the unspoken plan being, "You get her back inside and we'll get you out."

But once I got back inside, I began talking with great clarity and sense. I announced that I wanted to speak to my lawyer, that I'd been brought here under what I considered to be false pretenses, etc. All this stuff just started coming out of me, and Harry was in shock. It might have been a year since I'd talked in any kind of adult fashion, weeks since I'd talked at all except to say "Help me," or "Please don't make me," and he was thrilled just to hear me speak.

I got on the phone with David Licht, my lawyer at the time, and very coherently explained the situation. He talked to Harry for a while, and Harry by now had weakened. He wanted out of there too—it was as if some miracle shock treatment had me suddenly behaving normally again. And though they wouldn't let me leave without emphasizing the threat that I'd have to come back if I couldn't pull myself together, I got out of there; I didn't have to spend the night.

And for a few days at least, I really did function okay. But my problems were real, they were all manic-depressive episodes of one form or another, even though no one knew it at the time. So I went right back to the kinds of behavior that got me into Mount Sinai in the first place. I'd find myself in the middle of Wilshire Boulevard, for instance, trying to drive home and not knowing where I was, just sitting in the car with everyone honking at me. It really was like something out of a B movie.

Harry and I limped along with a series of psychiatrists;

they each got three shots at me and that was it. The one I liked best was a kindly, elderly man I thought of as Grandpa. I didn't have to do or say anything, I'd just go there and sob and Grandpa would say, "There, there" and give me some new medication. He didn't give it to me, actually, he gave it to Harry to dole out, because I was too depressed to be trusted. Naturally I resented that; here I was wanting to be an infant and at the same time wanting to control whether or not I took my medicine. But Harry put it away someplace I didn't know about. Or so he thought.

And, of course, some nonsensical argument erupted, provoked by me, I'm sure. I don't mean to paint Harry as a perfect white knight, but he was just not equipped to deal with a lot of this. And he didn't pick fights. I picked fights. After this one I wasn't as obvious about the pills as I had been the last time. I didn't storm out of the room and slam the door to do it. I waited until Harry went to the bathroom, then got the pills from where he'd hidden them, took about thirty five-milligram Valiums, and quickly got into bed. Yet even though I went about it more quietly this time, this episode still wasn't so much a wish to die as a wish simply not to hurt anymore.

Several hours passed and the Valium was on its way to doing its thing before Harry went to get my medication, discovered the pills were missing, and really got crazed.

"Where are they? What have you done with them?"

"I don't know what you're talking about!"

"Where are the pills?"

"What pills?"

But by now I was slurring my speech and it was obvious that I'd taken them, so then the argument about throwing up began.

"No, I'm not throwing up."

"Yes, you are throwing up."

"No, I'm not."

Back and forth and back and forth. He finally did get me to vomit some of them up, but the effect of the pills already in my system lasted for about three days, at which point I awakened to a psychiatric nurse in the house, the idea being to keep the celebrity out of the booby hatch. For, despite advice to the contrary, Harry had insisted: "I'm not going to commit her. I promised her I wouldn't. She's broken her promise to me by doing this, but there must be another way."

Doris was great, kind and gentle but very demanding. She would demand that I get up and take a shower, demand that I get dressed, demand that I eat, because if these things didn't come in the form of demands, I wouldn't respond. I had a kind of love-hate relationship with this woman, and deep respect, but I did it to her too. There was another prescription in the house and I managed to find out where those pills were being kept. And that time was the last straw for Harry. He realized he'd gone as far as he could, he no longer wanted to take responsibility for an awful accident. I pleaded and carried on—to hear me tell it, no one ever listened to me, no one cared—but Harry was very strong; he walked away. So, without a breath of publicity, I was taken to Westwood Psychiatric Hospital and committed.

I spent the first few days in my room, day in and day out, night in and night out, just crying. The first time I ventured into the cafeteria, someone said, "Aren't you Patty Duke?" and that was it, I was back in my room. I would see my friend Grandpa every day, and every day I'd wail. He'd talk a little, try to stimulate some anger or any emotion besides this depression, but to no avail. I never talked to him.

The first progress I made came when Grandpa went on vacation and a rolypoly doctor named Goldman took over for a week and tried a whole new approach. He'd come and talk a little show business, things like opera or Gilbert and Sullivan as well as the movies. Finally, about the third day, he said, very simply, "Why don't you talk to me? I talk to you. How come you don't talk to me?" I just stared at him for a while and then I said, "Okay. Why me? Why is this happening to me?" And he said, "Why not you? Of all the millions of people in the world, why should you be excluded?" I started having conversations with him after that, not dealing in any real depth with what was wrong, but at least I was talking.

Whenever Harry came to visit I'd say, "Please, I want to

go home, I want to go home." When I saw Grandpa again, I'd say, "See, I'm not doing anything bad. I want to go home." Yet in the area of activities, which is one of the ways they measure how you're progressing, I was really antisocial. I kept saying, "I don't want to play with the clay, I don't know how to do things with clay." There was a sense of sameness at the Westwood, nothing changing, every day like the one before.

One of the activities you have to participate in is volleyball. Playing the game with ten people jacked up on Thorazine is really a great way to spend an August afternoon. One poor son of a bitch, a character right out of *One Flew Over the Cuckoo's Nest,* always wore three shirts, a T-shirt, a sweater, and a jacket every time we played. In August!

The attendants, believe it or not, really got off on this so-called game. I guess it was one of the few things they had to look forward to every day. The way a lot of points would end was that someone would spike the ball really hard at this guy with all the shirts and sweater and jacket and then everybody would laugh. It didn't seem to bother him, he just sort of wandered around and stared. But one afternoon, after five weeks in the place, they did it one time too many for me, and I finally freaked out. Out of this sweet little girl who kept whimpering, "I wanna go home, I wanna go home," came "You motherfucking bastards," this veritable torrent of rage.

When you're on the inside, everyone gets involved with everyone else's problems, and it was no secret that my thing was, "She can't get angry." So when that outburst happened, it was like a scene from a movie: everybody (except the guy with the sweater!) stood there applauding because I'd broken through. I started to really function, to demonstrate that I was no longer suicidal, that I was coming out of my depression, and most of all that I was willing to work within the system. A week after that volleyball game I left the Westwood, I hoped for good.

TWENTY

Now that I was out of the Westwood everyone assumed that I was, for all intents and purposes, "cured." Harry and I began a "riding the crest" period. We belonged to all the hot clubs like The Factory and The Daisy, we began developing social acquaintances, playing Monopoly and giving dinner parties: in between bouts with shrinks and hanging around in the closet I'd learned how to set a table and how to cook. I never could make rice, though. I'd go down to Ah Fong's in Beverly Hills and buy enough for sixteen people and everyone thought I made the best rice in town. Things were good for us, the way we thought they would be when we'd first gotten married. What I was experiencing was one of those stable periods that sometimes occurs between untreated manic and depressed moods. I had come out of the tunnel and I thought this was the way it was going to be for the rest of my life.

I wasn't having much luck in my career, though. I had been announced for a play called My Sweet Charlie on Broadway, and I really wanted to do it, but I was in the Westwood when it was rehearsing. The producer, Bob Banner, was very gracious, he hung in and waited for me as long as he could, but finally it was announced that I was "ill" and the role went to Bonnie Bedelia, who'd been my understudy on *Isle of Children*. That was difficult for me, and what made it harder was that I was out of the Westwood by the time the run began and even saw the play the night before it opened. At least I'd shown I was functioning, though, and attending that play gave me a feeling of triumph.

Another role that got away was in *I Never Promised You a Rose Garden*, which was about a young woman with psychiatric problems. The book had initially been sent to me just after the wedding, but I sent it back unread, saying, "Thank you for thinking that I might be interested in this, but I recently married and I'm not planning to work for quite a while." Then I went into the Westwood, and since the book is practically required reading for psychiatric nurses, I saw it around a lot. When I came home I finally bought myself a copy and read it and, of course, I knew exactly who should play that part.

The problem was, I was never able to get my hands on the property again; it always seemed to be tied up. Natalie Wood owned it for a while, and then at one point I was brought to New York to meet one of those fancy-shmancy European directors. We had a warm, fabulous meeting, walked through Central Park together, I told him my experiences at the funny farm, and I thought this was it. Then I came back to L.A. and found that he was not at all interested in me for the part, he had his eye on Liza Minnelli. Then the whole project died, the rights changed hands again and again, and it didn't finally get done until years later with Kathleen Quinlan, who I thought did a fabulous job.

Despite all this, I wasn't worrying that I'd never work again, or, why my career was in the toilet. For one thing, I had become obsessed with the idea of having a baby—that was the main thing on my mind—and I'd worked often enough—that *Virginian* episode and a few variety shows—to have some sense of my career continuing. Harry and I had talked a lot about my getting out of television and the fact that my career had to take a different turn now that I was older. I bought into all of that, which is how I came to be involved in what I think of now as "Valley of the Dreck."

I think it was Joanna Barnes, who was always plugged into whatever was hot, who first started talking about the

Jackie Susann novel and suggested that I play the Judy-Garland-who-wasn't-Judy-Garland part of Neely, the young singer who was a victim of booze and pills. Both Harry and I liked the idea, the book was a big best seller, and we suggested to my representatives at William Morris that "this is the part we should really go after. It'll be so startling, I'll make the transition to adult roles overnight." If we only knew.

I still believe that the novel *Valley of the Dolls*, trash though it may be, was far superior to the film, that it did a real service in its pop psychological approach to exploring what it was in the life-styles of its characters that drew them into addiction. And Neely was the best part in the book. No matter what anyone says, and even though I myself learned very convincingly to proclaim, "No, this is a prototype, this isn't based on anyone real," the part was indeed based on Judy Garland and some of the excitement about the role was reenacting the dynamics of this woman. I don't think we've yet begun to scratch the surface of Judy; there was a wild bunch of cells thrown together in that lady. Playing that, plus figuring out how someone so seemingly stable and bright could get sucked into such a destructive life-style, was instinctively appealing to me.

The first crisis was the announcement that no one would play a role in this piece without having an audition and screen test. Of course there was a great hue and cry of "How dare they! An Academy Award winner . . . if they don't know her ability . . ." Finally my representatives said, "We understand you haven't seen her play this kind of role, and it is someone older, so Patty would be willing to come meet with you and maybe you can convince her to test."

That was as much to soothe me as the production company. The age range in the book is approximately eighteen to fifty and I think one of the reasons my performance suffered so from the critics is that the filmmakers were unwilling to modify the ages. If at age twelve I looked seven, in my twenties I looked fifteen.

However, my screen test was probably better than anything I did in the finished film and it was decided that I was going to play the part. It was also established that I would not do the singing, which was fine with me. I believed a dynamic Judy Garland kind of voice was needed. There was great P.R. excitement about my casting, and I was excited myself. This was going to be my big chance to break into adult roles, to be accepted as an adult, which after years of mandatory infancy was incredibly important to me.

We started shooting with some location work in New York, plus some interiors (though I didn't realize it until he told me years later, Marvin Hamlisch was the skinny piano player in my opening scene) and when I first arrived in the city it really thrilled me—going back to my old haunts as the conquering hero. I had the best part, the best-looking husband, had left *the* home in California to go on location, was driven around in a limousine. . . . I was the Sparkle Plenty little bride who had the world knocked up.

The first thing that went wrong was the appearance of a huge fever blister on the right side of my bottom lip. Ever since my first commercial as a tiny kid, that blister's been with me every time I begin a job, and it can be horrendous, truly a plague. You're dealing with the human beast here, and though as actors our anxiety isn't permitted to show (you could swear there wasn't a nerve in our bodies), the tension comes out in other ways. When I feel one coming on now, I resort to holistic techniques and the miracle is, I don't get a blister on my mouth anymore, I get it on my hands; why I can't get the thing the rest of the way off my body I'll never know. At that time, though, all they could do was try to cover it up with a lot of makeup, but still, one side of the lip was so much more voluptuous than the other, it looked dreadful.

And almost from day one, I was miserable working with Mark Robson, the director. There was a brief grace period when I was the fair-haired girl, "the theater actress," but that went away pretty quickly and he turned into a nasty, unkind man. He was someone who used humiliation for effect, who could be insulting about your physical appearance and who wouldn't hesitate to bite your head off in front of everyone. I'd play a scene and he'd say something unpleasant to me like, "You may have been able to do that when you had your own show, but we're really working here." His mentality was,

"I have to get a performance out of these girls." I don't know about anybody else, but you don't have to get a performance out of me, I'll give it to you. You can help me or you can hinder me, but you certainly don't have to go get it. And even though I wasn't aware of chauvinism or anything else at that point, I happened to notice he did not have that attitude toward the men in the cast.

I don't know if it was the role rubbing off on me or me rubbing off on the role, but the meaner he got, the more frustrated I got. I was too afraid to fight back, however, in anything but little sneaky ways. Like eating. It was almost a joke on the set. If Robson insulted me, you could be sure that within the next two minutes I'd be at the doughnut box—and I didn't even like doughnuts. I gained thirty pounds during that picture. Thirty pounds!

Sharon Tate, however, got it even worse than I did. She was a gentle, gentle creature—you could be mean to her and she would never retaliate. I was crazy about her and I didn't know anyone but our director who wasn't. What's to dislike? She was an exquisitely beautiful girl who was so comfortable with her beauty that you weren't intimidated by it. Robson, however, continually treated her like an imbecile, which she definitely was not, and she was very attuned and sensitive to that treatment.

I did a scene with Sharon one day that ended up going into the night because Robson was so rigid. Not only did he want it played in exactly one minute and eighteen seconds—who knows how he picked that figure—but he instructed her to enter on her right foot and say "Hi," move to her left foot to say "Neely," unbutton her top button for "did," the next one for "you" and so on for ". . . have a nice day?" It was truly demeaning, like the old "Can she walk and chew gum at the same time?" line.

Robson also wanted Sharon's body revealed in a certain way. Well, explain it to the girl, for heaven's sake. She's the one walking around with the body, she knows how to reveal it. All he had to do was say the feeling he wanted; she would have given it to him. But he never took the time even to consider that as a possibility. There were other actors in that scene but he just picked on her. Finally, after hours of this nonsense, Sharon wound up in tears, as would anyone who'd been badgered that way. We were always making faces at Robson and giving him the evil eye behind his back, but he had the last laugh: we were the ones who ended up looking ridiculous.

This was just a prelude to what happened with Judy Garland, who joined the company several weeks into the schedule as the legendary older singer, Helen Lawson. We never spoke about whether or not Neely was based on her, partially because I had my own ambivalent feelings about Judy being in the picture at all. She obviously needed the money, that was why she had accepted, but I thought it was cheap and tawdry to ask her to play the part. And it made me sad that she had reached the point of having to take this stupid role, playing opposite someone who was reputedly playing her. It's tacky, it's degrading, and it's undignified to have to do such a thing, and even though she did a lot of undignified things, she was basically a dignified person.

At this particular time Judy was not in very good shape, to say the least; she was all the insecure things we've read about her. But she was also so sweet, cute, and funny, you just wanted to hug her all the time. She came on the set for three days before she was actually due to shoot in order to get used to the rest of the cast. After all, she was joining a group that had been working together awhile, and that would be a tough position for John Wayne. There was no entourage surrounding her. Her husband, Sid Luft, brought her, but there was no one else.

Possibly because I was playing her, possibly because of sharing a volatile nature and having kindred feelings of insecurity, I felt an immediate affinity for Judy. We hit it off instantly. There was lots of laughter, there was a general feeling of camaraderie and goodwill, and she seemed fine. The last prework day she started telling me how nervous she was and I tried to reassure her. Probably if I'd been older, I would've hugged her, but I was feeling too deferential at that point.

In those days, before mobile homes, stars had quite luxurious permanent standing dressing rooms, and the next day I went over to her room to see how she was doing and wish her luck. The sweetness was completely gone, all there was in this person now was abject terror. We kidded around a little bit, I asked her when they were going to get to her scene, and she said she didn't know, she was waiting for Mr. Robson to come over to see her, and that was the end of that.

Robson was involved on the set and when it was time for Judy's scene, he sent word down through the chain of command to go get her. And the word came back that she wouldn't be ready for another forty-five minutes, which on a movie set is a terrible amount of time to be inactive. He was bugged by that, and even though it was none of my business, I went back to see her again. She was ready, but she wouldn't come out of the room. She said she was waiting for Mr. Robson. I didn't catch on that she was wanting him to show deference, but she later told me there was more than that involved: she was very nervous and she thought if he came for her and escorted her to the set and introduced her to the crew and all of that, it would make her feel better. Maybe she was being a nuisance, but I could see her point. Well, Robson never came and she never did get out of the room that day.

This went on for a couple of days and each day she acted a little stranger; she started slurring her words, for instance. I never saw her drink, I never saw her take pills, but rumor had it that that's what was happening. By the third day, apparently, ultimatums had been issued, and she did indeed come on the set and work. Mark Robson kissed her ass in Macy's window, but everyone could tell she was under the influence of something. I stood behind the set, just cringing, willing each word to come out the way it was supposed to, and it never did. When the dailies were shown, no one was happy and the scene was scheduled to be redone, with a costume change used as the excuse. There was no sense of tragedy on the set, just that this was going to be a long haul.

At lunchtime the next day, I implored her to eat something. No, she wasn't hungry, but if I were a real pal I'd bring her a couple of Hershey bars. I went to the commissary, got my tuna sandwich and my chocolate milk and her Hershey bars—the longest I could have been away was fifteen minutes— but when I knocked on the door, I got no answer. Knocked again, no answer. Went to my room and called, still no answer.

I sort of dozed off and suddenly my phone rang and she was crying on the other end. I couldn't understand a thing she was saying. I kept asking, "What happened? What's the matter? Where are you?" Guessing she was still in her dressing room, I went over there and an enormous racket was going on inside, a lot of crashing and smashing. I pounded on the door, but she wouldn't answer. I ran upstairs to call and again no answer. I couldn't reach anyone else, tried to look in her windows, but no luck. I went back to her room and kept literally kicking at this heavy, old-fashioned door, yelling, "Please let me in! It's me! Please let me in!" I was frantic and frightened.

Finally she opened the door, looking like the wrath of God. She was not physically hurt, but the cloth on the room's antique pool table was torn, the light hanging over it was broken, there was glass everywhere. At this point I did embrace her and hold her. I just said, "What happened? What happened?" And finally I was able to understand: "They fired me. I've been fired. They fired me." I tried to calm her down, tell her everything was going to be okay. Someone from the company arrived and told me I could go, that they would take care of this, but I hung around longer than I was welcome, until Sid showed up to take her home. I kissed Judy good-bye, told her that whatever had happened would work out somehow. And that was the last I saw of her until the following year, when she was appearing at the Palace, in tiptop shape and doing a great show, wearing her costume from Valley of the Dolls.

When Judy was fired like that, it was really the end of the movie for all of us. It was so ugly, so unkind, that even if people had cared before, nobody gave a damn now. The producers may have felt justified in terms of her being unable to work, but, remember, I didn't think they were justified in hiring her in the first place. Also, they were a little too ready

with a replacement. They had gotten their P.R. mileage out
of the situation, the "Judy comeback" stories had created
extraordinary publicity for the film, and now she was
expendable.

Judy's replacement was Susan Hayward, who seemed
tough and very distant; I learned only later that she was
recovering from her husband's death. There was an unfortunate incident between us during the shooting of the scene in
which I steal her wig in a restaurant ladies' room and throw it
down the toilet. She was very humiliated at having to do the
scene in the first place. As written, it was supposed to look as
if she had cancer and was losing her hair, but she refused to
put on a bald cap. She insisted just bleaching her hair white
was going to work.

During the scuffle for the wig I was supposed to push
her, but I pushed too hard and she fell. According to Mark
Robson, she thought I did it on purpose. Did he plant that
seed in her head, or did she actually think that I had? I don't
know. I do know that it was a horror to me that Susan
Hayward would think that I tried to hurt her. She refused to
work for the rest of the afternoon, and I took the rap for
that, as if I had done it on purpose. I apologized to her, I told
her it had come to my attention that she thought I had
pushed her on purpose, and of course I hadn't. So that was
yet another hideous, uncomfortable episode that took place
on that picture. I hated Mark Robson. I truly hated that
man.

Toward the end of the filming, the producers wanted me
to do a nude scene and I refused. It wasn't a moral judgment;
I've taken my clothes off since so that wasn't really the issue.
In this particular scene, however, I saw no point or purpose
in it. I was supposed to strip and then walk outside my house
to find my husband swimming naked with another naked
woman. I was supposedly drunk as well, it was an ugly scene,
and with two naked people in it already, I didn't see that
they needed a third. There was a big argument about it, but
they couldn't force me; nowhere in my deal did it say that I
had to do a nude scene. We were getting toward the last days
of filming and given all that had happened, I was not in-
clined to go the distance for them anymore.

By the close of shooting, everybody hated everybody. War zones had been set up all over the place. On the last night there is traditionally a wrap party. You do the final shot, the chips and dip are already set up, everybody has a drink, and sometimes people hang around until morning. On this picture I had to go around begging grips and electricians to stay so that there could be any kind of celebration at all.

Only a pitiful little group of us stayed for the party, including Mark Robson. He came over and started telling me that he knew I didn't like him but he really loved me and after all he'd gotten a hell of a performance out of me. I told him he was right, I didn't like him—worse than that, I felt considerable animosity toward him, and as far as my performance went, he could have "gotten" a much better one with a different approach. He said, "I just made you mad because I wanted you mad in the scene." And I told him, "Don't you realize that if you're going to hire somebody that you have to provoke, you're not hiring an actor? You hired an actor. Let me play the scene." It was a most unpleasant exchange.

The first hint of what *Valley of the Dolls* was really going to do for my career came in an insulting *Look* magazine article about the filming that portrayed me as a foul-mouthed harridan misbehaving in public. I did indeed swear but not like a sailor on the set, not to the extent that the piece claimed. It was cruel, it was erroneous, and it was bad journalism. I cried when I read it, and I literally did not go out of the house for two weeks, until every one of those issues was off the stands. And afterward, my swearing became worse. I figured, "Okay, I may as well be damned for a lion as for a lamb."

Not long after *Valley* wrapped, I became pregnant, and there was great jubilation about that. It turned out to be an ectopic pregnancy, however, and I had to be hospitalized for the necessary surgery. I needed both an emotional and a physical recovery afterward, and during that period the call came from the studio that the film was ready, and wouldn't it be a perfect shot in the arm for me to see it, my performance was so wonderful, all the usual palaver.

Harry convinced me the screening would be a good

idea, and I was not that hard to persuade. I'd been distracted from my work while I was shooting—I was busy having a war with the director and eating doughnuts and playing an ineffective Florence Nightingale to Judy Garland—and I certainly wasn't aware just how bad the film might be. So with no little effort (it was less than a week after my abdominal surgery) I was gotten dressed and to the car.

It was a small screening—the writer, the producer, probably Mark Robson, and a few other people. Remember, this was one of the first times in my career that I had been allowed to see my work, so I was especially excited. The film started out nicely enough, but then it got to the meat of things, and the pain from my surgery got worse and worse and I thought I would die. I was awful, everything was awful, it was just the pits. I started thinking to myself, "What am I going to do? Should I get sick and leave?" I chickened out and waited until the end of the movie, praying, I suppose, that it would get better somewhere along the line. It didn't. The lights came on and no one said a word—talk about humiliating. I stood up—cautiously—and Harry said, "Gee, the music's beautiful." And that was it.

One of the reasons Twentieth Century Fox had shown me the film was that they wanted me to fly to Miami and join a press junket on a cruise ship going from there to the Bahamas. Well, of course, after I saw it I wasn't going to cross the street to be part of that junket. But then all kinds of pressure was applied from the studio, my P.R. people, my agents, all of them saying, "Hey, it's a cruise! You've never been on a cruise before! It'll be fun!" Finally, I agreed to go. We're such suckers, we actors, we really are.

It was fun to see Sharon and Barbara Parkins and the rest of the cast again, but those of us who'd already seen the film couldn't look one another in the eye because we knew how awful it was. The cruise started, it was enjoyable and romantic, the food was wonderful, and I was indeed forgetting about my recent personal tragedy when it came time to view the movie. They packed us and all these press folks into this tiny theater, turned on the projector, and, wouldn't you know it, it ran too fast. Not enough to bother the visuals, but enough to make all the voices sound several tones higher:

Paul Burke came out like Minnie Mouse, I had a voice only dogs could hear, it was ridiculous.

And remember, it's not as if we were still at the dock or had dinghies at our disposal. They'd long since pulled up the gangplank, and we were stuck in the middle of the ocean, watching this turkey. This was truly purgatory. People laughed at all the serious parts. Jackie Susann got up at one point and left the screening: once people started laughing when the demented guy in the mental hospital scene was drooling and I was singing to him, it was enough to drive any best-selling author to her "dolls." I've read since in her husband Irving Mansfield's book that she had cancer then and was going through her own horror. At any rate, she went to her room, took a bunch of sleeping pills, and I never saw her again until it was time to get off the boat.

The rest of us, however, just got silly. We kept running around the companionways, trying to stay away from the press—we certainly didn't want to be interviewed about this—and have our own good time. Sooner or later, though, we all got trapped and had to talk, and lie, about the socially redeeming value of this movie.

Although it amazes me, there are a number of people who got something out of that picture. Whenever someone comes up to me and says, "I saw you in *Valley of the Dolls*," my instinctive reaction is to say, "I'm sorry you wasted your money." But I found I have to be really careful, because there are those who actually made a connection. There is in fact a cult following for this film. There are "*Valley of the Dolls*" parties and people dress up as Neely on Halloween. Extraordinary!

Personally, I try my damnedest never to see that movie. Almost everything I've done, even if my work could have been better, I can look at and not feel ill at ease. But there are a few things—still photos from *The Patty Duke Show*, those album covers, and *Valley of the Dolls*—that I can't to this day look at comfortably. I can't even look back and say, "Wasn't that a gawky kid?" or "Yeah, she had a silly hairstyle but she was all right." You would think after a certain amount of time you could get past the embarrassment, but it's still very hard for me. It's not a question of dealing with my history, I do that every day. It's that I feel I look silly and my work is bad. I take a great deal of pride in my work, and I can't have much about that nonsense.

TWENTY-ONE

T he summer of 1968 started on an up note. Once again, Harry and I were supposed to live together in New York. He would be hanging around with his old buddies, and he was working on a script (though it was going nowhere fast) and I was going to star in a film called *Me, Natalie*.

The project was produced and directed by Fred Coe, the *Miracle Worker* producer with the great lap, and I took it because I loved the part of Natalie. I really clicked into this lady. She's described as an ugly Jewish girl from Brooklyn, and certainly, when people looked at me, that wasn't their first thought. But her lost, waiflike quality, with an edge of humor and sarcasm, was something I could very easily relate to, as was the film's premise of recognizing the pain that's making you feel ugly when you're not. Which is probably why I was able to do the work despite the crises that developed.

Determined to find herself, Natalie moves to the Village and becomes a hippie. Then an artist moves in upstairs, this Italian god played by James Farentino, whom I knew very well and adored, and a charming love story develops, different from anything I'd ever played before. There are a lot of crises; it turns out he's married but he says he's going to get a divorce, and Natalie tries to kill herself by jumping into the

East River, but she can't even do that because it's only ankle-deep.

One of my clearest memories of the film concerns a high school dance Natalie goes to where she really looks like the dog of all time, I mean the makeup and costume people really went out of their way for this one. And this hoody-looking kid comes up and says, "Hey, wanna dance?" She looks around to make sure he's talking to her and says, "Sure, why not. I'm not doing anything else." They dance a little and he says, "So. You put out or what." And she says, "What? You put out or *what*? You mean, *at least*." And she walks away. The actor who played the kid was Al Pacino. He was doing something off-Broadway, but no one really knew who he was. Yet he had real presence, he made quite an impact with those two or three lines. I remember thinking, and saying, "Jesus Christ, this guy's good."

By the end of the picture Natalie's happy being herself, but she gives up the artist, which is something I argued vehemently against. There's no way that young woman would give up that man. Staying together may not be as noble an ending, but it's real, and I think it would have made a more successful picture. But by that time I'd lost all my credibility with the producers; my daily behavior was such that no one was interested in what I thought the ending should be.

The first snag that happened on this New York fantasy trip was that Harry didn't come east with me. He said he was staying behind to rent out our house, something he was having difficulty doing. So, very disappointed, I went to New York without him but with very specific instructions to find an apartment in the East Sixties, between Fifth and Park avenues, but preferably close to Fifth, plus a house on Fire Island. Meanwhile I was having my teeth fitted and my nose fixed and my eyebrows bleached and trying to develop a character. But I pounded the pavements with a real estate person and came up with his dream apartment on East Sixty-eighth, and I also rented Annie Bancroft's beach place on Fire Island. That made it all the more imperative to find someone for the house in Los Angeles, so I would call home every day and talk to Harry, but he still wasn't having any luck.

I was also getting very involved with Bobby Kennedy's primary campaign. Except for really unavoidable events like the Cuban missile crisis, when all the kids at school made plans to die together, politics was virgin territory to me, I had at best a smattering of awareness. I knew, for instance, who Martin Luther King was, but I had to do catchup work on exactly what King was doing in Selma, Alabama. This was also the period of my trying to make up for the college that I didn't go to, I read and studied and worked hard at increasing my knowledge. And I truly did believe that Bobby could sweep the primaries, become president, and continue maybe a slightly different Camelot.

Right before I went to New York someone involved with the campaign asked me to go up to the University of Oregon in Eugene and speak for Bobby. I think my appeal to them was as the prototypical successful young woman: "We need people in the youth market, she's good on talk shows, she'll be good at this." For my part, I was thrilled to be "stumping for a Kennedy." I mean, my father was a cab driver, so this was quite a stretch.

I went up to Eugene and I made my little pitch, all very heady and exhilarating; my voice was shaking but it was obvious that I was sincere. It was supposed to go swimmingly for the senator, and like "Patty" and "Cathy," I thought I'd be accepted everywhere, but when the open forum started, it was a disaster. I had walked into Eugene McCarthy territory, I got hit with all the charges of "Kennedy ruthlessness," and I didn't know what the hell they were talking about. I was simply not sufficiently prepared, I didn't have the facts to back me up, and I got wiped out. They hooted and booed and chanted and carried on until I was a wreck. I had been sent out to appeal to the youth element and I'd really fixed that for him, hadn't I? I was just heartbroken. Obviously at this point I had single-handedly cost Bobby the election.

Until the New York apartment was ready, I was living very well, thank you, in the Sherry Netherland Hotel. On the night of the California primary, June 5, I was having dinner with one of my agents and some friends. There was a lot of stimulating political talk and speculation, but we were all eager to get back to our respective televisions and watch what had been predicted as a Kennedy victory.

I hadn't been in my hotel room for fifteen minutes before Bobby was declared the winner, and I called Harry. No answer. I was kind of disappointed that I couldn't share this with him and wondered where he was. Then the candidate started speaking, and it was thrilling, and I was dialing again and I still didn't get Harry. Then they followed Bobby through the kitchen and he was shot and I lost it. I thought I had hallucinated what I saw. I called Harry and there was still no answer. I got the operator and begged her to stay on the phone with me, I became truly hysterical. I kept saying, "They did it! They killed him, they killed him, they killed him, they killed him!" The operator didn't know what I was talking about, I couldn't get the name out, and then her switchboard went crazy and she had to leave me.

Even once I got some semblance of control, I wouldn't turn off the television. Wallowing in it was important to me, especially because the Rosses, without offering any reason, hadn't let me watch any of the J.F.K. coverage, not even the funeral. The entire world had a communal catharsis, and I didn't get to participate. So part of my mania about Bobby was a determination that not one more thing was going to happen without my paying attention.

Besides watching the coverage, I was obsessed with finding Harry. I kept dialing him at home, then I called everyplace I knew of that he could possibly be, and either got no answer or people saying, "No, he's not here, haven't seen him." I did that continually until nine o'clock in the morning (six A.M. California time), when he finally answered the phone.

As soon as I heard Harry's voice, I got hysterical all over again. He kept saying, "Yes, yes, it's terrible," and then I remembered to ask, "And where were you when all this happened?" It never occurred to me that he was anyplace he shouldn't have been, but when he told me he'd been at a party at the Playboy Mansion it sounded terrible to a wife who was three thousand miles away. I've been there since and I know that not very much really goes on, but at the time it was enough to send me into absolute fits. At the goddamn Playboy Mansion? Partying? No, he told me, he was out so late because he was watching the coverage. And I bought it. I certainly didn't want to even think he was screwing around.

Once I calmed down, I called a woman named Sandy Smith. We'd met quite recently but we became close friends very fast—we were like Munchkins together. I arranged to go out to see her at her house on Fire Island for the weekend, and once there we shared the kind of hysteria you see at Irish wakes, denial via a little too much hilarity and partying. That weekend and the one after it I also met her husband, Lucky Lewis, who was adorable and fun and seemed incredibly wealthy. Sandy didn't have to say a word and she got anything she could possibly desire; she just breathed and she got a boat, a house, round-the-clock limo service, I mean, this was Diamond Jim Brady. But, of course, I'm married to Mr. Beautiful, so it doesn't matter that we don't have any money, all's right with the world.

Lucky and I would travel back to the city together and on the second trip he said he was going to be in the city all week and if I was lonely, he'd love to take me to dinner, did I like lobster, he knew a lot of great places. The next day there were flowers waiting for me when I got home from work and a card that said, "I love getting to know you," with a scribbled signature I finally figured out to be "Lucky." I thought that was nice and then I forgot about it.

About a week later Harry, who'd managed to make a special appearance for Bobby Kennedy's funeral and then was quickly back in California again, showed up for good. He loved the apartment, which was done in a very stark but elegant way, and after he'd been there awhile he noticed the card from the florist. The flowers were long dead and thrown away but the card was in full view on the dining room table.

"What's this?" he said, and held up the card.

"Oh, it came with some flowers."

"Who were they from?" with that edge in his voice.

"I think they're from Sandy's husband, but I'm not sure."

"Oh?"

"Yeah, I met him at their beach house, he's a really nice guy."

I went on chattering and he was just staring at me. Finally I stopped and he said, "Why did he send you flowers? What did you do for him?"

"What do you mean? I didn't do anything for him. Are you accusing me of having an affair with Lucky Lewis?"

"I'm not accusing you of anything. I just have a right to know who sent you flowers and why."

He kept digging and digging until finally he had me saying something like "Go to hell" and then denying over and over again that I'd done anything wrong. It was a very tense evening, with a lot of ugly energy underneath. The next morning, which was the start of the July Fourth weekend, Harry picked up the card again and said, "You can tell me. What's this all about?" I kept repeating that there was nothing to talk about and he kept insisting that there was.

We were out all day on this little scooter I'd learned to ride for the movie, but in the evening, sitting around the apartment, having wine and making plans for the Fourth, he started in again.

"Look, you really can tell me."

"I'm telling you, nothing happened."

"Maybe it isn't Lucky. Who is it?"

"It's no one! I've been working! I put a funny nose and funny teeth on! I've been finding houses and apartments and going to the supermarket! I didn't *do* anything!"

And then he said, "But you'd like to, wouldn't you?"

At that point we got into almost an encounter session, a deep, seemingly loving conversation in which Harry asked for my trust in him and admitted that during his first marriage he had screwed around a lot. He said that while he'd acted on his wishes, some people just think about it, and there's no crime in thinking about it.

"Have you ever thought about it, Pat?"

"No, I don't think so—maybe."

And that was it. All of a sudden the tone changed.

"*Oh.* So you *do* think about it."

"Well, no. You asked me, and it's possible that I've thought about it. I was just trying to be honest."

Then it deteriorated into, "That's it, it's all over," and he left, saying he couldn't talk to me anymore, he needed to cool off. Whether he was really convinced that I'd had an affair, or just wanted me to think that he was convinced, I'll never know.

What I did eventually discover was the reason he took so long to get to New York: he had a lady in Los Angeles. When I did go back to California after Me, Natalie ended and went to the house to pick up some things, the pool man asked me if that blond-haired woman who'd been staying at the house while I was gone was my sister. "Oh, her," I said casually. "No, no, she's not my sister." I had no idea who she was, but I soon found out. I think that what all those accusations were about was that Harry was looking for a way out. The best defense, they say, is a good offense, and it was much easier to have me be the bad guy than him.

There were some phone conversations after he left, I begged and I pleaded, and Harry came back. He said he realized he was wrong, and we had a great day just riding around the city. But something had happened on both sides, something important had been lost for me as well. My heart was broken. I thought I was madly in love with him, and I guess, considering what I knew of love at the time, I was. But you can't play that kind of cat-and-mouse game and catch the mouse and have the mouse trust you anymore.

The result was that I started wondering, asking myself questions. If this is over, what the hell am I going to do? Jeez, could I sleep with someone else? And then I began to play the game with him. When he started again, my answer, instead of being, "No, I didn't," was "What if I did?" We baited each other until there was just a huge explosion of screaming and yelling and throwing things— we practically destroyed the elegant Fifth Avenue apartment— ending with his screaming, "Go fuck yourself," and my coming back with "I'll learn." When I fight with a spouse, there is a deadly turn of phrase that comes to me, and I won't edit anything. He left, and that was it. I never lived in that great house in L.A. again. That was the end.

We did have a couple of brief return bouts. One weekend he came out to Fire Island, we made love, and fought, and made love, and fought. Or I'd get him to come over to the apartment for an evening, to try to talk rationally, and a fight would erupt. I'd threaten to take sleeping pills (I'd concocted some cock-and-bull story and gotten someone on the set to give me some) and there would be huge fights over that. "You're manipulating me," he'd say. "You're toying with me, you're not going to do this. Stop calling me, call a psychiatrist." One time I actually attempted to take pills in front of him. Not enough to kill, only enough to aggravate. But he never knew how many there were and I certainly wasn't going to tell him the truth.

One night after work I was in especially bad shape emotionally, but I told everyone that I was fine and that Harry was going to come over and get me. I was alone in this empty studio, the same one, incidentally, where I'd done *The Patty Duke Show.* All the furniture had been removed from the set, but it didn't matter. I was drinking wine and talking on the phone with Harry and getting nowhere with my manipulation. So I took a full bottle of sleeping pills, about thirty Seconals, and I did not tell him. And I stayed at the studio until they started to take effect.

I lost some consciousness after a while, but I called Harry back, and I guess it was obvious from my speech that I was not acting, not kidding, but had indeed done it this time. He kept asking me where I was, and I wouldn't say. I know this from his telling me the story later on; I don't remember much of it myself. I finally relented, and after ruling out an ambulance because that would cause too much publicity, a car was sent for me. I was taken to the nearest hospital and I guess my stomach was pumped, but by then I wasn't there, I was totally out.

Somehow Fred Coe convinced the hospital not to admit me. I was turned over to him and went to live in his apartment. I felt terribly guilty having done something like that to Fred and the other people on *Me, Natalie.* The sense of responsibility hit so strongly that I got myself up and went to work the next morning. And as much as Fred would have liked to throttle me, I know he respected the fact that I made it through a full day and did good work besides. Because, while my mental state was deteriorating by the minute, a bunch of people were still trying to make a movie.

Unfortunately for them, this was only the beginning of my troubles. I made the rest of the picture extremely difficult for everyone involved. For several days in a row I'd be absolutely fine, then there would be another suicide threat or angry outburst on the set. And there were many, many times when the contemplation of suicide was absolutely serious but not broadcast. They must have felt they were living with a time bomb.

I had a big fight with Fred over my coming back to his apartment at four A.M. when my call was for five-thirty, and after that I left and went back to my apartment. My behavior was probably very similar to a cocaine user's, but there were no drugs involved at all (except, of course, for the overdose tools I managed to get). Somewhere along the line I'd apparently kicked into a serious manic episode, because I was insomniac, I didn't eat, my mind was racing, my body was racing, my mouth was racing, I was just running, running, running all the time.

Harry soon returned to Los Angeles. I really wasn't much of a lure to keep him in Manhattan, and that's putting it mildly. I became absolutely obsessed that I must have him back. I didn't know why, it didn't even matter anymore. And then I did have some affairs, I slept with a couple of guys. I don't remember where or how, and I'd probably have to be hypnotized to come up with their names, if I even knew them in the first place. It was that kind of hysteria— "What's the ugliest, most vicious thing I can do?"

Shooting on Me, Natalie lasted six weeks, and right near the end I had a big fight on the set with Fred Coe. It's the scene where Natalie attempts suicide by jumping into the river because the guy she's in love with is married. We were on a pier in Brooklyn, facing the New York skyline, and because it's a deep river and I'm not a great swimmer and was wearing a dress and high heels, a lot of preparation was involved.

I'd already jumped into the river a couple of times, so I was filthy, and that and the delays put me in not the best of moods. Plus it was getting to be noontime and I was hungry.

I saw some people eating hero sandwiches and I asked if they'd run and get me one, and a beer. The food finally arrived, I sat down to eat when from the other end of the pier I heard someone yelling, "*You take that beer outta your mouth!*"

At first I couldn't make out who it was, but then he came right up to where I was sitting. It was Fred Coe, and he screamed at me in front of everyone, "What do you think you're doing? Nobody drinks beer on my set." At which point I screamed back, "What do you think—you're my father?"

And Fred went into a tirade, perfectly understandable to me now, about the time and the grief I had cost him. "We're coming to the end of this goddamn movie and there will be no beer-drinking on my set!" I stood up, threw the bottle into the river, and told him in front of everyone to take his movie and shove it up his ass, I quit.

I got in my car and the Teamster driver, who'd been told not to take me anywhere, refused to move. So I grabbed my jeans and a top, hailed a cab, told the driver to take me to the William Morris Agency in Manhattan, and changed my clothes in the cab going over the bridge. I stormed in there as if I owned the place, really inexcusably arrogant, and demanded to see whoever it was who was king at the moment. When they said he wasn't there, I demanded to see the next one down, and the next one, and finally someone realized that I was making a huge scene in the reception area and they'd better get some agent to see me.

Once I got in an office, pacing up and down with steam coming out of my ears, I realized I could see the Brooklyn location from there. So as soon as whoever was selected to deal with me walked in, I just pointed out the window and began screaming, "Do you see that bunch of assholes over there?" I don't even know what I said after that, I just ranted and raved while the poor man tried to figure out what the hell was going on.

Finally, after I stopped insisting that I was going to take a beer anytime I goddamn well pleased and that I wasn't going to jump into that goddamn river anymore, phone calls were made and a truce was arranged between me and Fred.

We agreed to finish the film, just to get it over with, and Fred and I would do our best to stay out of each other's way. It was a hell of a way to act in and direct a movie, but that's what it had come to.

There was obviously a great deal of pain on my side and on Fred's, especially when you consider that our relationship dated back to The Miracle Worker days, but by the time we finished the movie I think there was a larger understanding, on his part especially, that as bad as my behavior was, it wasn't malicious. This wasn't a person out to be a bitch, this was a person in trouble.

I went back to Los Angeles when we wrapped and discovered that as far as Harry was concerned, the marriage was over. I begged a lot, but it didn't do any good. We went to a lawyer and divvied up the house and the furniture and all that stuff. I kept thinking if I didn't take anything, he would see how much I loved him and he'd take me back. We all know how well that worked out. So I took nothing and moved into an apartment in the Sierra Towers.

TWENTY-TWO

The torch I carried for Harry Falk took a long time dying. Nothing, not even moving into my own apartment in late 1968 and going through the motions of marital settlement agreements, could convince me to give up the ghost. It was impossible to believe that this was happening.

I retaliated by becoming Moby Wife. I tortured the man with phone calls, and I did truly infantile things, real high school antics like sending him pizzas he hadn't ordered. I became more and more manic, even showing up where I knew he'd be, looking my best and trying to behave in a nonchalant manner. The man would be shooting pool at The Factory or some other private club and all of a sudden, there I'd be.

I got by during the days. I'd either spend hours and hours in bed, hung over and calling for takeout food, or else I was able to pull it together enough so that no one noticed what shape I was in, or so I thought. Acquaintances who were concerned about me would try to fix me up with dates or at least invite me to dinner parties. Sometimes I'd go, sometimes I'd say yes and then cancel and stay in bed. I spent a lot of time in bed.

I was hung over most of the day because I drank most of

the night. I'd go to various haunts until I met up with some group that I knew, and eventually, sooner or later, some guy would join us and both of us would be drunk enough to go back to my apartment. I went home with a lot of men, not on a nightly basis but compared to my life-style before and after, it was a lot. Part of it was simply escape—"somebody anesthetize me"—part of it my fury at Harry's false accusation: "Okay, you think I screw around? I'll show you screwing around." They were cold acts, full of self-destruction. You don't go to bed with someone you don't know because you like him. It was anger, pure and simple, anger at myself, at men in general, and at Harry in particular. He was all I thought about.

For a while I dated a young man named Gene Kirkwood. He was a young, good-looking guy, a great dancer with a lot of energy, who really wasn't interested in me at first. We started seeing each other for lunch and developed a nice friendship and rapport.

Gene and I would drive for miles and miles and he'd tell me his dreams. He wanted to be a movie producer but his family was in the fish business; they used to keep telling him, "Come home and sell fish! Stop this craziness!" We'd go up to Mulholland Drive and he'd say, "This is where I'm going to have my house, and it's going to be on this many acres, and it's going to have this and that and the other thing." You could knock him down, you could take his money, you could do anything to him, he was undaunted. He never doubted that his ship would come in.

I became more and more smitten with Gene and eventually we did go to bed together and became sort of a couple. I even cosigned a car lease for him for a Firebird. Eventually we broke up, and he ended up being one of the producers of the *Rocky* films. And he forgot all about that car lease. I saw him on television once, going to the Academy Awards, and I said to John Astin, "That's him! That's the guy with the Firebird!"

One night at the Sierra Towers I wasn't feeling very well and I thought some soup might do me good. So I dressed in my black pants and my black turtleneck and went across the street to an Italian restaurant called Stefanino's looking very wan and pale, like something out of an Ingmar Bergman movie. Nicky Blair, who ran the place, came over to chat, but I didn't feel like it, I just wanted to have some soup.

The door opened and in came Frank Sinatra with a group of about sixteen people. They sat down at a long table that'd been specially set up, and when Sinatra, whose date was a tall, statuesque blonde, sat down at the head he ended up looking directly at me. I was eating my soup and smoking my cigarettes and trying not to feel awkward because I'd noticed that he kept looking at me. There's something about those eyes, I don't know what the hell it is, but they are riveting. I thought to myself, "The next time he looks at me, I'm going to look at him." He did, I did, we both smiled because it seemed so silly, and then we went through the whole thing all over again.

The next thing I knew he called Nicky Blair over. Nicky nodded, came over to me, and said, "Mr. Sinatra would like you to join his table."

"Oh, no, Nicky. I just came from across the street to have some soup. But thank him very much, that's very thoughtful of him."

"I think you better join their table."

"No, I really can't. Just tell him how grateful I am for the invitation."

Nicky went away, talked to Sinatra, nodded, came back, and said, "He's not taking no for an answer." I laughed and called to Sinatra, "That's really nice of you, but I'm not dressed and I'm nursing a cold." And he said, "I insist," stood up, and began to walk over. Now I was really getting nervous. I stood up, met him halfway, and I said, "This is very sweet of you." And a place was made for me toward the far end of the table.

After about half an hour, during which he kept really staring at me, Frank got up to go to the men's room. As he passed my end of the table he leaned over and, without breaking his stride, said, "You *are* going home with me, aren't you?" and I said, "Yes." It happened just that fast. I thought, "I should be wondering what the hell I'm doing, but I'll worry about it tomorrow."

He came back and declared that the party was moving

to his place, except, he whispered to one of his people, the blonde who was his date. And that was it, the blonde was out and I was in. He and I drove alone in a white station wagon to his house in Beverly Hills, with everyone else following.

There was a general sort of party hubbub at his place and then, all of a sudden, as if somebody had pushed a button, people disappeared. Nobody said, "Get out of here," it was just shazam and they were gone. And there I was, saying to myself, this is insane, what am I going to tell Frank, Jr.? And he said, "Would you like to hear a new record I just made?" What am I going to say, "No, Mr. Sinatra, I really wouldn't." So he put it on and for the first time I heard "My Way." Can you imagine? We were sitting next to each other on the couch, drinking the best champagne, and he said, "Come on, let's go to bed."

I suppose I could have said no, but it seemed to me I'd stayed so long there was no turning back, and I gave it not another thought. He had two bathrooms off his bedroom. He showed me one of them, handed me a robe, opened a drawer, and said, "There's a toothbrush in there if you want it." And indeed I had my choice of brand new toothbrushes in that drawer.

I took a shower, drank a lot more while I was in there, and as soon as I got back to the bedroom the phone rang. And Frank got very involved in a very serious conversation about his father, who was quite ill at the time. When he hung up he told me about the surgery his father was going to have, we talked for about two more hours until it was close to dawn, and then we went to sleep. Nothing happened.

When I woke up the next morning, I found my period had started during the night. I was mortified, I wasn't as accepting of life and the human condition as I am now, but he couldn't have cared less; he was much too sophisticated to worry about stuff like that. Also, he was very concerned about his father and soon back on the phone again. I went to the kitchen and Frank's buddy Jilly Rizzo was there. He offered me aspirin and Coca-Cola for my hangover, which I badly needed.

When Frank came out he drove me home and said he'd

like to see me again. And sure enough the next day the phone rang and a voice said, "This is Francis Albert. Do you want to go to Palm Springs?" And I spent a few weeks with him off and on down there, we slept in the same bed, but never was there any sex. Anyone who was around in my life during those few weeks is convinced that I had an affair with Sinatra, and I did, of sorts. Considering my friendship with Frank, Jr., however, I was relieved at how things worked out, and I suspect that when it came right down to it, he couldn't do that to his son. Also, he was still troubled about his father, and, in fact, that's how it ended. There was an emergency call, he left with the jet to pick up his dad, and I never heard from him again. Maybe he didn't want to get involved with someone who was trying to kill herself, especially since she was trying to kill herself over somebody else.

When Sandy Smith returned to Los Angeles, we reestablished our relationship. I'd gotten into the pattern of spending all day in bed and carousing all night and Sandy tried to extricate me from that. I couldn't bear to be alone, so we'd run around all day doing silly stuff, getting our hair done and our nails and fooling around in Beverly Hills. She'd drop me off at the Sierra Towers and an hour later I'd call and say, "Come get me. I can't stay here." Finally she said, "Look, Lucky's never in town, you can come and stay with me." And I did. I was "the lady who came to dinner"—I showed up one day and stayed for weeks.

Sandy and I were like a mini-sorority. We had Ovaltine with marshmallows every night, we'd sit around and philosophize until it was time to go to bed. But once she went to sleep I'd disappear. I was set up on a rollaway in front of Sandy's fireplace but I had insomnia. Some nights I'd wake her, some nights I'd be too embarrassed. I'd just go out and wend my way back around five or six in the morning.

One night, after Sandy had gone to bed, I decided I had to drive over and see Harry's new house. I knew it was off Laurel Canyon but I hadn't been there. It was pouring rain, a very dark night, all very dramatic. I went down a lot of steps, his dog, Finn, was barking his head off, and I pounded and pounded on the door. Harry finally opened it; he was naked but pulling on a robe. He was startled to see me and he started to close the door, but I stuck my foot in the opening.

"Go away," he said.

"Please let me come in. It's raining. Please let me come in."

"No, I can't."

"Please. Please. Just for a minute and then I promise I'll go."

"No. Go away, Pat. I'll talk to you tomorrow."

"No, I *have* to talk to you now."

All this time I'd managed to push the door open a little with my foot, enough to get a shoulder and half my body in. Harry didn't want to slam the door on me, yet he did not want me in that house. The staircase to the second floor was directly opposite the door, and while we were talking, down the stairs came Venus, with her flowing blond hair, wearing a white monogrammed bathrobe I'd given to Harry.

He turned on her viciously and said, "Get the *fuck* upstairs!" It was the same woman, though I didn't know it then, that the pool man had seen. She just stood there and looked at me. I think I said, "Oh, my God," but I'm not sure. I don't know why I was surprised, but I was. And Harry said, "Now will you go?" I don't remember if I said yes or just nodded, but obviously I was going.

I drove back to Sandy's at some insane speed in the rain, screaming, "No! No! No!" all the way—my throat hurt by the time I arrived. I went into her bathroom, and even though she'd tried to hide them, I found a full bottle of tranquilizers, there must have been about forty or fifty in there. I went in the other room and took almost all the pills. I had been careful, however, to take one out and leave it on the counter, because I figured Sandy would be nervous and really need it when she woke up and found me dead!

I don't remember anything more until I regained consciousness after having my stomach pumped, but Sandy has told me the story many times. She got up in the morning and was suspicious about the way I looked; I seemed to be in a very deep sleep. She roused me with difficulty but I insisted I hadn't done anything, I was just exhausted and needed some rest. She walked me from my cot into the bedroom and everything seemed fine.

Sandy left to talk to Joel, a hairdresser who was a mutual friend. "You've got to be kidding," he said. "It sounds like she took an overdose." Sandy said I was up and walking, but he insisted she go back and look in on me again. And, in fact, what I'd done was hide some of the pills in my bathrobe pocket, and, when I realized I wasn't dead, taken those while Sandy was gone. So by the time she got back I was absolutely out cold; she couldn't wake me at all.

In a panic Sandy called everybody she could think of, including Joel, who came over and helped try to rouse me. She tried Harry, who'd had it by this point; he said he didn't give a damn. She called my manager, who didn't want a doctor brought in because an ambulance would mean adverse publicity. Finally, knowing I'd been dating Frank Sinatra, she called and reached him immediately. "Aw, Jesus Christ," he said, and agreed to call somebody who could deal with the situation. And it was his doctor who got me quietly into Cedars, where I was on the critical list for close to a week. I do remember that doctor, a real show biz type, dressed to the teeth, with an attitude that suggested "I don't have time for this kind of nonsense from you Beverly Hills broads." It was not an approach I responded to.

According to Sandy I was literally foaming at the mouth because of all the pills I'd taken; she really thought I was going to die. And in terms of how long the pills were in my system, plus the fact that I'd changed my pattern and hadn't alerted someone first but had done it while everyone was asleep, this was the most serious of all my suicide attempts. Yet, even this time, in my own mind killing myself was never an end, it was only the means toward a goal of being oblivious to the pain I felt. I didn't want to live the way I was living, and there seemed to be no way out except to stop living, period.

Today I often think of how incredibly lucky I was. There was always, I guess, something inside of me that figured I'd be rescued, but if you play around that way long enough, you are going to have that terrible accident. I would always show remorse afterward, because that's what was expected; if you don't, they put you in the booby hatch. But inside, there was no sense of relief that I was alive. I didn't think, "Oh, thank God, I've got another chance," but rather, "Oh, shit! Now I gotta do *this* again."

There is one thing that is truly and permanently awful about ever having attempted suicide, and that has to do with the people who love you. One of the things I treasure most is their faith in me, their trust in me, but there's no way I can tell them, "I won't do that again," and be totally believed. They have to live with that fear, and I have to live with knowing that. The people you love most in the whole world—you've done something that will always cause them pain.

TWENTY-THREE

Harry didn't come to see me while I was recuperating. It was a calculated choice, and I think the right one. He knew our marriage was finished, and felt it would be misleading and unkind to do anything that would lead me to think otherwise. And after our confrontation on that rainy night, all overtures toward him stopped. There may still have been a longing, a ray of false hope, but really I knew as well as he did that it was over.

When I think back on Harry and me, certainly the lion's share of the disaster of that marriage was mine. Not that he wasn't deficient in a lot of ways, but that was always overshadowed by my illness. What he had to deal with was terrible, terrible—living with someone so troubled, perpetually in and out of crisis. I think Harry's immaturity and the fact that his head got kind of turned around when he came to Hollywood didn't help, but he's no less a good person because of that. He was just at his wit's end, worn out dealing with me.

I'd built myself the perfect storybook fantasy, and it wasn't good enough. Why wasn't it good enough? There's really no way to explain that. I didn't just have "emotional problems," there was something wrong inside, things were out of balance. I had a disease, but no one knew it.

And the fact that I was so young certainly didn't help, though my age was not so much the culprit as my lack of experience with life. It's like being in a pod: someone opens it, or in my case you force it open, and there you are, in a completely alien world. There are things expected of you, or you think there are, and you haven't a clue how to respond. You don't know the language or the manner or the behavior. I believe if I'd somehow been able, then, to be more the person I am now, I would probably still be married to the man. Or we'd be divorced for different reasons, maybe because one of us outgrew the other. But we never got that far, we never got to figure out if anybody was outgrowing anybody. I still think I have excellent taste in husbands. It's just that my timing leaves something to be desired.

For several months after I recovered from those pills, I went through a very lethargic period. I was overweight, I wasn't working—it seemed like I couldn't get a job. There was no night life to speak of, and no manic activity either. I was just sort of getting through every night and every day.

Then I got a call about My Sweet Charlie, which I'd previously missed out on because I'd been in the Westwood when the play was rehearsing for Broadway. Levinson and Link had now turned it into a TV movie and Bob Banner, the producer, wanted me for the female lead. I had to meet with Bob and Lamont Johnson, the director, at the same Stefanino's restaurant where I'd been picked up by Frank Sinatra. Though nobody said it in so many words, I think they wanted to look me over and make sure I was functional.

I was very nervous about being scrutinized that way, but I was excited when I passed the test and pleased that I was going to do a job and make some money. But there wasn't the feeling in me that exists now when I'm going to act, the anticipation of the process of creation. I was just sort of moving through time. I didn't really kick into high gear till we got to our location at Port Bolivar, Texas, just outside Galveston.

Essentially My Sweet Charlie is a two-character drama. A teenage girl, I guess she would be considered poor white trash, takes refuge in an unoccupied house after being kicked out by her father, a hard-shell Baptist, because she's pregnant. One night a black man in a three-piece suit breaks into the same house. He's an elegant individual from the North who came down to be in a peace march and, in self-defense, killed a white man. He's pretty bloodied, on the run from the police, and he needs this haven as much as she does.

So we have these two adversaries, the sophisticated black man and the bigoted white trash girl. In fact, my first line of dialogue was, "It's a nigger," which was very hard for me to say, it made me feel very self-conscious. Predictably, things develop between these two, from each not being able to stand the other to the point where, without ever touching each other, without even sitting next to each other, it's obvious that they've fallen in love. She even teaches him to talk like a "nigra" so he can pass for a local and go shopping at the store.

He finally decides he has to go back up North, and there's a very moving scene in which they say good-bye to each other. She goes into labor the morning he leaves, and he stops by the store to try to get a doctor for her. This time the locals get suspicious and the man ends up fleeing and being shot in the back. The last image you see is of the girl being helped into a police car. There's a discussion about what she's going to do with the baby, and you know she's going to keep it and call it Charlie. It was a lovely story, as much a love story as a racial statement about the times. And in some ways the real-life relationship between me and Al Freeman, Jr., who played Charlie, paralleled what was happening in the piece.

When I arrived in Port Bolivar I was not terribly attractive. I was overweight and looked, a lot of people said, very much like Janis Joplin. Also, I had a fever blister the size of New Jersey on my lip. Lamont, Al, the writers, and I went out to dinner the first night and Al, though pleasant enough, had a very arrogant kind of attitude that put us all off. We were so paranoid that he was going to think we were bigots that we overcompensated, even pandered to Al, which made him even more arrogant. Yet I felt my liberal heart was in the right place: even though there'd been some racial trouble in the area, I'd insisted that I wouldn't stay at a hotel unless he could stay at the same one if he so chose.

After dinner we adjourned to the producer's suite to do a preliminary read-through of the script. There's no way you're going to hear award-winning performances the first time around, but everyone ends up expecting them anyway. As I said, I wasn't the most appealing-looking person in the world, plus my clothes looked awful because I'd flown in them all day. And aesthetics turned out to be very important to Al; he himself was dressed to the nines and looked marvelous.

I don't think we'd gotten ten pages into the script when Al stopped and went into his "black power" rhetoric. He felt his character was too much of an Uncle Tom, a sellout to the white world. Levinson and Link were defending their script and I was trying to interject some comments, so I could be part of the club, and Al kept snapping at me—"You don't quite understand what it is I'm discussing here" or "I'm not talking to you." I was not nearly as articulate in those days as I hope I am now, and I was easily intimidated, so my first reaction was to sniffle, and the effort I made in holding back the tears was obvious.

Whenever Al raised an objection, the powers that be kept calmly saying, "We'll deal with that later." But halfway through the script a screaming fight erupted, provoked by Al, and, once again, I tried to interject my opinion. And Al turned around and told me to shut up. He said I didn't know what I was talking about and—this was the coup de grâce—why didn't I go away and grow another fever blister.

At that point I told Al, at a vocal level that could not be misunderstood, that he could go fuck himself. I threw the script across the room, swept up the ugly little dog I'd brought with me from L.A.—which Al had also insulted—and stormed out of the room. Frankly, I was justified, but it would have been nice if I could have done it in a more gracious way.

I stood waiting by the elevator, my heart pounding in my ears. I was sure the boom was going to be lowered on this bad little girl. I could hear my agent saying, "You did *what*?" Maybe it was a holdover from my years with the Rosses, but I never felt that I was going to receive support if I made trouble, even if my actions were completely justified. And yet I knew that in this case I was right. This was not part of the creative process, the man was simply a rude son of a bitch.

While my mind was racing, the elevator was taking forever. It was one of those old relics that just *eeeek* their way down. Then I heard the door from the suite open and slam back against the wall. I kept pushing the button and looking straight at the elevator door: there was no way I was going to look down the hall and see who'd come out. And before I knew it, standing beside me was Al Freeman, Jr.

"We need to talk."

"I don't want to talk to you, I don't want to talk to anybody. I'm too angry and upset."

The elevator finally arrived, I got in, and he did too. And he followed me all the way to my room, talking the whole time, apologizing, recognizing that he'd been a prick (his word) but insisting that though this thing had gotten out of hand he was sure if I was willing to work at it we could put it back together again.

By now, of course, I was in tears and felt I had nothing left to lose. So I invited him into my room and we talked for about twenty more minutes. I told him how deeply he'd hurt me, that I was not thrilled to have a fever blister myself. Then he said, "Let me just call the producers and tell them we're at least talking to each other, because they're all pissing in their pants upstairs." That made me laugh for the first time.

After he hung up, he called room service, ordered some brandy for himself and Coke for me, and proceeded to absolutely enrapture me. He talked for hours and hours and I was just agog. His manner, his eloquence, the obvious brilliance of his mind, his grasp of politics and black history, were dazzling. And he applied all that to the script, talked about how we could make it better, it didn't have to be this white-bread thing they were trying to shove down everyone's throats, we could really make a statement here.

Before Al left that room, we'd become allies. We were united for a cause and we stayed that way throughout the picture. I cleaned up my act, lost weight, and the whole experience became a very intellectual, very stimulating time. I couldn't wait to get up and go to work, to meet Al on the ferry going from Galveston to Port Bolivar and have him talk to me about what he'd seen in *The New York Times*. The crush I had on him was really more for his brain and his charm than wanting a physical thing, and gradually I realized that I'd rather have the crush than the actual love affair.

Al and I spent almost all our time together. We rarely hung around with the rest of the folks in the company, which is unlike me; I usually pal around with everybody. Because of the racial situation, being with Al was difficult in Port Bolivar, which was a depressing place anyway because of the weather. The air is so heavy there that you're wet all the time, sweaty and smelly, and your clothes are wet, too, even hanging in the closet they're wet. Al and I were flat out told we'd get in trouble at certain clubs: "You go one night, you go another, just don't go there together."

Al made a lot of trouble for Lamont Johnson, and I, of course, was now his cohort, so I was always backing him up. There were long discussions and arguments about scenes, and the poor guy was trying to direct on a television schedule. When Lamont wouldn't agree with him, Al would say, "Okay, the hell with it. If that's the way you want it, I'll do it," and then just walk through the scene. But when push came to shove, and the cameras were rolling for what was obviously going to be a valid take, he'd pull it together and give a performance and so would I. Basically, though, we were "the defiant ones" all over again.

Which was too bad because Lamont Johnson is the type of director I like to work with. He is a very urbane man, with a magnificent voice, and he knows enough not to plumb your soul with endless discussions. He gives you an idea of what he believes the scene is about, and then he has the courage to let you do what you do. I've worked with a lot of directors who don't have that much sense, who go in there and just stomp on your sensitivities. Not that I believe actors are all little rosebuds that need to be handled with velvet gloves, but just as people need a physical space around them, actors need that same kind of space emotionally. If, without my being overpowered by a director's affection, there exists a healthy respect and confidence between the two of us, so he doesn't interrupt when I'm playing a scene, he's going to get what he wants and he knows it.

The *My Sweet Charlie* shoot lasted four weeks, and one day, with only a week left, Bob Banner, the producer, came into my motor home. He'd always been very friendly to me, warm hugs and stuff like that, but this time there was something in the air. We chitchatted for a while, and then he said, "What I'm about to tell you is very confidential, but I feel you should be filled in. It's suspected that at least one person in this company is involved with drugs. We're not sure how far it's spread, but there is a great deal of concern. The police have become involved, it's a very touchy situation."

"Really?" I said. "Who?"

"Well, I'm not exactly sure."

"What kind of drugs?"

"Marijuana."

"No kidding."

Now, Bob must have been thinking, "Jesus Christ, this woman is either absolutely psychotic or the most brilliant actress I have ever met." Because what I didn't know was that prior to his coming to see me, the local police, acting on a tip, had searched my hotel room and taken a stash of grass out of my closet. The one thing I had going for me, however, was my height, or rather lack of it. The shelf was so high that even if I stood on a chair it would have been impossible for me to reach the stuff.

Bob didn't tell me any of this. I didn't learn what had happened until much, much later, so I went on asking these innocent questions and assuring him that I would put the word out that everyone should clean up his act. Because in those days drugs were not all over the place the way they are now, especially not in the South.

I don't know if I'd convinced Bob or if he just wanted to finish his picture and get out of Port Bolivar as gracefully as possible. But he called Universal, and the story is that someone there called the governor, and the governor called the local authorities and said, "Lay off that company, and lay off the girl."

I've never had any idea who planted the drugs in my room, or tried to find out why; maybe some of the townspeople thought Al and I were having an affair and felt threatened by that. Nor, once I returned home, did I make any effort to clear my name. It hadn't occurred to me that it'd been muddied, but indeed it had. People at Universal thought I was using drugs, and for years I had the reputation of being a doper.

If it hadn't been so damaging, that would have been funny, considering that the only time I'd tried marijuana, years before at a party, it had made me nauseated, and I didn't know what a bong was until my kids told me. As for cocaine, I never even saw any until a driver on a TV show offered it to me, and his ears must still be burning. If I had been doing drugs during those crazy years, that would have been easy compared to what I went through. As dreadful as any addiction is, at least you know what you're dealing with.

During the filming Al told me that his next project was directing a brief run of the LeRoi Jones play, *Dutchman*, in Cincinnati, and he asked if I wanted to costar with Cleavon Little. I was incredibly honored, even if I wasn't paid very much. Al could have asked me to stand at the top of the Empire State Building and whistle "Dixie" and I would have done it.

It was a great experience, palling around with Al and Cleavon. But Savannah, Al's wife, was cold to me, which tainted Al's attitude toward me and, of course, tainted mine toward him.

Work on the play was very difficult—it was a tough role, that of a hooker who picks up a black guy on a subway. We were not really ready on opening night, but we got through it, and when I came offstage I was exhilarated just to have accomplished that. I looked around for Al, and they told me he'd left. I thought that meant he'd gone to some restaurant where we were supposed to meet him, but no, he'd gotten on a plane with Savannah and left town. I guess he saw the first ten minutes of opening night and then took off. I could not believe my ears.

I started calling him in New York, even though I knew he couldn't have arrived yet. I did that throughout the night until I reached him. I was hurt, enraged, appalled by what I considered a severe lack of professionalism in a director. When he got on the phone I screamed something like, "What the fuck is the matter with you? How could you do this?" He didn't say much, and for whatever reason, it was clear that we could never recapture the spirit we'd shared on *My Sweet Charlie*. I was going to have to just bite the bullet and move on. I was beginning to learn to make the best of things, a lesson I would learn and forget often over the next few years.

TWENTY-FOUR

I remember how the whole thing started, with a television appearance and a phone call. It was March 1970. I'd been on *The Merv Griffin Show*, I'd lost weight, my hair was very full and very sexy, I looked quite good. A couple of days later I got a message from the switchboard at the Sierra Towers that Desi Arnaz, Jr., had called. I knew he was Lucille Ball's son, but I'd never met him, I had no idea why he'd called, so I kind of ignored it.

A few days later there was another message, this one saying that Desi wanted to talk about my doing some recording. But when I returned the call the first thing he said was "We've never met but I saw you on *The Merv Griffin Show* and what can I tell you, you looked magnificent, you're so pretty," and so on and on. After I thanked him, he asked me if I'd recorded recently and said that now that he was producing as well as working with his group, he'd love to get together and talk with me about it. We agreed to meet Friday night, and I swear that's what I thought it was about. I thought I was going to a strictly business dinner.

Friday night came and Desi showed up in his Astin-Martin, and I didn't immediately think, "Wow, what a great-looking guy." I was just waiting to talk records. I don't know why I asked him this question, but at one point I said, "How

217

old are you?" and he said, "Nineteen." We drove to another house to meet a couple of his buddies, then on to dinner at La Scala, where Desi drank and there was a little talk about records but not much. When he drove me home he asked if he could see me to my door. I asked if he wanted a drink and he said, "Well, maybe I'll have a little nightcap." We sat around for a while, just chatting, and that was the first time it hit me that I was on a date. I'm a little slow about these things sometimes.

Desi called the next day and sounded different, much more personal. We agreed to have dinner Monday and it quickly became apparent that records were the furthest thing from his mind. I had to go to New York for a couple of days and he was very distressed about that. I arrived in the city on St. Patrick's Day, and when I opened my hotel room door there were green flowers waiting for me and a note that called me his special little Irish leprechaun. I felt a little skip of the heart, and that was it. I called him immediately, and when I got back to L.A. we started going everywhere and doing everything together. It was the beginning of the romance. Though I've at times hesitated to say it, the truth is that I loved Desi Arnaz. I loved him very much.

Almost immediately, Desi and I became the media couple of the moment. Not only were we both young and attractive, but, having grown up in the public eye, we were both celebrities, lovers who needed no introduction. We hit all the right spots every evening, like a kiddie version of Elizabeth Taylor and Eddie Fisher: the fan magazines just couldn't get enough of the story.

Desi was extremely bright, a very mature, gifted kid, and there was a lot of philosophical discussion and spiritual exploration going on between us. What I loved about him most, though, was his youthfulness. Zipping around in that unbelievable sports car, going to this house on the beach and that house in the mountains, always with an accelerated, living-on-the-edge energy—his was the kind of young and carefree existence I'd never experienced.

And though Desi did his share of drinking, overall his life was very healthy, full of tennis, touch football, bicycle riding, and water-skiing. At the time I wondered how he was able to throw back so many gin and tonics and smoke so many cigarettes and still be able to get up the next morning and handle all that activity. The secret was that while I was twenty-three, Desi was only seventeen.

I didn't learn or even suspect Desi's real age for quite a while. I'd seen him served liquor in restaurants, he always acted much more mature than his age, and, don't forget, he'd straight out lied to me. People have said, "Oh, come on. He had one of the most publicized lives in Hollywood, his birth was the most famous goddamn thing that ever happened on television. You could have checked the year." Who goes around checking years? If you're in love with somebody, you believe him. I'd asked the guy how old he was, he'd told me, that was all that mattered to me.

Once I discovered how young Desi really was, I was shocked, but that was nothing compared to the reaction Lucille Ball, who was the source of that information, had when she found out we were seriously involved. I've raised kids who are now in their twenties, and if one of them had come home at age seventeen with a twenty-four-year-old divorcee and gone up to his room with her, I would have died too. So I hold no grudge against Lucy for that kind of initial reaction. I do, however, still feel bitterness for the sorrow that she caused me by steadfastly refusing to see that I had only the best intentions toward her son.

While Desi's father, Desi, Sr., was always extremely gracious, Lucy was just the opposite. She bore no resemblance to the woman we all saw on TV, and I don't just mean that she wasn't putting the bowl of spaghetti on her head. For whatever reason—the age difference, my divorce, the rumors about my drug use—Lucy felt she was in a crisis situation, and her attitude was efficient and cold, with barely a veneer of politeness. While I can certainly sympathize to an extent, when she took out after me she had the wrong villain, because I was nothing but absolutely honorable and gracious and in love, not the rapacious fiend she seemed to think I was. Lucy from time to time tried to tolerate me, at least I think she did, because I was invited over for the occasional dinner or movie, but I honestly don't believe she tried hard enough. And sometimes, in later years, I'd wonder if there weren't moments when Lucy thought back and said, "Jeez, maybe Duke wasn't so bad after all."

The romantic intensity between Desi and me was very great, but we hadn't been together for more than two or three months before it was broken up for the first time. Lucy accomplished that with a series of ultimatums. Either he stopped seeing me or he was out of the house, he was out of the will, they'd do something to me because I was screwing around with jailbait, whatever. Desi called me and said, "I can't be there, I can't get out of the house." Then he said, "We've got to cool it. Maybe she's right, maybe they're all right." He never said, "It's over," but it was apparent.

I was deeply crushed. I sort of went into hiding for a while, then I called Desi and, not surprisingly, cried a lot. He and his family were going to Hawaii and I begged to go, but he said no, I couldn't. But I followed him there on my own, which absolutely enraged Lucy. I was feeling very similar to the way I'd felt about Harry, not thinking, just obsessed. But there was also anger in me; I didn't like the way his mother was treating me, as if I were some kind of miscreant. But in my desperation to prove what a wonderful person I was, I did every wrong thing I could.

Desi called me when he got back from Hawaii, he told me he was sorry for the way things were going, that he loved me and we'd work something out. We began getting together again, though not so much in public because we didn't want his mother to get furious. But little by little he began to let her know that he was seeing me again.

The situation between Desi and me, however, never returned to the way it was before Lucy's ultimatums, and one of the reasons had nothing at all to do with either of them. During my period of hiding after that initial break I'd met and had a brief secret affair with John Astin. He was separated from his wife and children but he was still married, and when he told me he was going back to his family, I thought that was the end of it. I didn't know how much I really cared for John, and I certainly didn't know that just before we'd split up I had conceived our son Sean.

TWENTY-FIVE

I hadn't had any sort of contact with either John or Ethel Ross for almost five years. While I was at the Westwood, Harry had made a deal with them; he'd given them fifty thousand dollars cash and bought them off. It was "go away" money so that they wouldn't pursue any contractual claims on me, and it worked. But now, in the spring of 1970, I was going through a period of soul-searching and I decided to write them a letter.

The basic thrust of the note was my desire to bury the hatchet. "All that's happened is too complicated to go into," I wrote, "but I've been thinking about you both and hoping that things are going better for you. Even though we can't have the same relationship we had before, I want to reestablish contact and say that some things are clearer to me now, about where my mistakes were as well as yours."

I showed this letter to my father figure of the moment, David Licht, my manager, the man who'd been so worried about the press when I took all those pills at Sandy's house. He thought I had rocks in my head; he advised me that under no circumstances should that letter be sent. He didn't give any reasons, but since I still tended to accept authority, I listened to him. And John Ross died within two weeks, on May 1 in Palm Springs. He was the second father I didn't get to say good-bye to, and the pain of once again having to experience that lack of resolution was especially hard to bear.

The phone rang late one night and it was Joey Trent, another Ross protégé, whom I also hadn't heard from in years. The conversation was extremely brief.

"Patty? It's Joey."

"Yes, I know."

"You know what?"

"J.R. is dead."

"Can I come over?"

"Yeah."

No one had told me anything, my knowledge was intuitive. I don't even remember having the thought, I just said, "I know."

Joey came over to the apartment and told me that Ethel did not want me to call her, did not want me at the funeral, did not want any part of me anywhere. And I asked him to plead my case. I said, "If she really doesn't, I'll stay away, but I think John would have wanted me there. Maybe if you appeal to her on that basis, she'll relent." He did, and Ethel did relent. I had felt extraordinarily peaceful when I first heard about John's death, as if he were up above, taking care of me, but the strength of Ethel's anger and hatred for me was so unsettling that I went into a very insecure state that I would later learn to recognize as premanic. I wasn't able to calm down enough to eat or sleep.

Though Ethel finally allowed me to come down to Palm Springs for the funeral, the condition she set was that I couldn't be with anyone, I had to do everything by myself. We embraced when I arrived, or I should say I was the one doing the embracing, because Ethel was just rigid. Her mood was subdued and efficient as she asked everyone else to go away. "Come with me," she said. "He's in here." She opened the door of the chapel and waited there until I'd finished.

It was just a little chapel, the casket was open, and I stood there and looked at him. I was really torn up. I looked at his hands and at his rings; I remembered how proud he'd been of them. I remembered my own fear of dying, and John telling me, "We have to worry about that a lot sooner than you do." I bent over and carefully placed a tiny note in the casket. It said, "I'm sorry. I love you." I cried, but only a little, because she was there.

Afterward there was a reception at their house, to which I was not invited. I had a room at a local hotel, and Joey Trent came and visited with me there. I stayed up all night drinking coffee, talking with Joey, and trying to track down other Ross protégés by phone after he fell asleep.

Then came the funeral. I was allowed to go to the cemetery but, again, I had to be on my own. So I stayed way behind this little procession of cars. I sang "Danny Boy" to myself while I drove; that was his favorite song. I fell asleep before I got there and ran off the road; you can imagine how that woke me up. At the graveside I stayed with the crowd, all local people, not with the family. I felt very awkward. And then I left and that out-of-control treadmill inside me kicked in, I didn't have a calm moment for the next three weeks. That brought me to June 7, the night of the Emmys.

My Sweet Charlie had been nominated for eight Emmys, including one for me for best actress. Desi and I were seeing each other again, his mother was obviously not thrilled, but nobody was threatening anybody, so I was on a high. I asked him if he'd go with me to the awards and he said absolutely. Feeling very up and filled with love for the world, I wanted to do something nice for my mother, whose birthday happened to be June 7 as well. She'd never been to an awards ceremony, and even if I didn't win this time, it would be a nice party for her to go to. So I sent her a plane ticket and brought her out to L.A.

My mother came, but no matter what I did it wasn't good enough, it wasn't right. I'd take her shopping, she'd say she liked the clothes, and then after we got home she didn't like them anymore. She just sat there stone-faced, I couldn't even make her smile. And not helping my mood was the fact that even though I'd told no one, I was pretty sure I was pregnant. I assumed at first the baby was Desi's, but when I became more clear-headed and carefully counted the days, I realized the timing was off, it had to be John's. I did not tell him, though. He was married and to me that meant there was absolutely no hope of our getting together.

Came get-ready time on the evening of the Emmys and

my mother began crying and she wouldn't tell me why. I
tried to get her dressed, but each piece of clothing involved a
twenty-minute coaching job from me. When she was finally
finished, she became even more distraught. She didn't like
the dress, she didn't want to wear it, she didn't even want to
go. I was so hurt, so angry, I really felt like popping her one.

I did a lot of yelling and she did a lot of staring into
space. I did a lot of begging, and she continued to stare into
space. And then, finally, I said, "All right, goddamn it,
here. You wear my dress"—which she'd said she liked—"and
I'll wear something else." And while she was changing into
my dress, it was as if something snapped in me, all I could
hear in my head was a nonstop litany of "fuck-it fuck-it
fuck-it fuck-it fuck-it fuck-it."

I went to the closet and put together the most ridiculous-
looking combination of stuff to wear, an evening dress topped
by a crocheted long sweater and then tied around the waist
with some red yarn. It was really bizarre. People began
arriving, Desi, David Licht and his family, and though I tried
to cover it up with party-party-party excitement, it must
have been obvious that I was not behaving in a way that was
familiar to anyone. We drank a bit of champagne in the
stretch limo, but that was the only booze I had all night. I
kept looking at my mother to see if she was getting a little
excited. Maybe she was, maybe I just didn't know her well
enough to tell when she was excited.

By the time we arrived at the ceremony, I was very
wired, there was some kind of momentum growing in me. It
wasn't excitement about the awards or anything like that; I
didn't understand what it was. First Al Freeman, who'd also
been nominated, didn't win as I felt he deserved to, and that
flipped another switch inside me. And then I won.

I can't exactly describe what happened between my
sitting there, hearing my name read, and my acceptance
speech, but any sense of the reality of what goes on at those
events, of what your behavior is supposed to be like, just
went away. John's death and the whole Ross experience
came back to me, the fact that I was pregnant and unmarried
scared me, my mother had finally come to an awards ceremony where I'd won and she didn't seem to care, all these

thoughts were like a bunch of old-hag demons, pulling and tugging at me and calling my name. And I kept trying to hang on.

I've seen a tape of that acceptance speech and though I really wasn't as nuts as people later talked about, it was obvious there was something wrong with me. I tried to talk in metaphor, and that didn't work. I wanted to be gracious to the other women who'd been nominated, but it didn't come out right. I talked about enthusiasm; John Ross had taught me that the word was derived from the Greek and meant "the god within." I thought I had the ideas strung together right, but it sounded disjointed. And when I used my hands to sign a message to the deaf, the camera shot was so tight that my hands weren't visible. To people watching on TV, it looked as if I was just blankly standing there.

When I got offstage, David Licht and a publicist for the network were waiting for me, looking very nervous, and I didn't know what was the matter. Then all of a sudden I got very angry, I told someone to take the Emmy. They thought I meant them to hold it for a minute and I said, "No, no, take it back. I don't want this. It doesn't mean anything to me." Partly I was upset because Al Freeman hadn't won; I felt since the play was a two-character piece that giving an award to me and not to him was silly. Today I'd know how to make that kind of personal gesture to Al, but then, I was just this young, emotionally upset, crazy girl.

The publicist had tried to keep me from going to the press area, but the flow just pushed me there. Then I was up on a platform answering questions angrily and accusingly, telling the world I was rejecting the award. I said I was getting out of show business, I was going to be a doctor. It was as if some other creature took over inside me and was picking answers out of the air, the more outrageous the better.

Desi and I and the rest of the group went to a club called Pip's to party, but I kept switching from hyper to angry to confused, making everybody, including Desi, very uncomfortable. A lot of whispering went on, and I kept demanding to know what everyone was whispering about all the time. We went home early, my mother and I stayed alone in my apartment, but I didn't sleep. I cried a lot, but I didn't know why. They were the kind of tears that come from a very old hurt.

The next day David Licht called and said he was coming over to see me at the apartment, which was highly unusual. When he arrived he asked me to please go into the Westwood Psychiatric Hospital again. I said, "Absolutely not." I was feeling very lucid at this point, very clever, at least ten steps ahead of him. A couple of days later we had a similar encounter, and I told him I knew I needed help but I didn't think the Westwood was the answer. He continued to implore, in fact, he became so distressed that I felt sorry for him. Finally I said, "Okay, screw it, what's the difference? I'm not doing anything else this week anyhow."

We showed up at the Westwood the same day. And as soon as I got there I knew there was no way I was going to stay in that place. So when they handed me the standard forms to sign, I decided I was going to read every last word on them. And as I read, I started to cross out things like their right to give me shock treatments and intravenous chemical therapy.

Finally David Licht said, "All right, what's this game you're playing now?" I told him I'd go in if he wanted me to, but I wasn't going to allow them to do anything they pleased to me. He asked the staff person if that was okay and was told, "No, we can't accept that. If she doesn't sign the form as is, we can't admit her." Then David, this huge bear of a man, started literally begging me to sign, but I was adamant about shock and chemicals. Finally something acceptable was worked out and I was admitted, but from that very minute I started scheming how I was going to get out.

The next day I saw my old friend Grandpa again. The last time he'd seen me I was a frightened little girl who wouldn't open her mouth. Now I was this terror, screaming, "I'm not taking your goddamn drugs." You can imagine what must have been going through his mind.

I wound up being at the Westwood about three days, at the end of which I had a physical encounter with an attendant. I'm talking about fighting down halls and through doorways. I eventually managed to wiggle out of his grasp and escape. Like the time before, at Mount Sinai, the attendant was trying not to hurt me and I took every advantage of the situation. The amount of power a person has when she is so completely out of control is extraordinary. Once I got outside the building I just ran and ran and ran until I saw a cab and told the driver to take me to the Sierra Towers. I was eventually convinced to go back in, but that didn't last very long either. I was way beyond anyone's power to control, especially my own. I was as close to a severe nervous breakdown as I ever want to get, on the brink of losing my mind for real.

TWENTY-SIX

On June 24, 1970, a man I barely knew asked me to marry him. Less than five hours later we were husband and wife. The relationship lasted thirteen days. If he walked into a room today, I wouldn't recognize him. His name was Michael Tell.

It all started earlier in June with *The Paisley Convertible*, a bedroom farce I was going to do onstage in Chicago only because I needed the money. As I was leaving the Sierra Towers one morning I heard a man asking the switchboard operator if there were any apartments available to sublet. I introduced myself and the man told me his name was Michael Tell. I said I might be gone for a couple of months, and asked if he'd like to see the place. He came up, said it was fine, and I told him I'd get back in touch if the play came through.

I called him in a day or two to say I was going to Chicago, and he asked if he could come over that evening to see the place again. Like a fool, I offered him a drink, which he took. He looked at the apartment, but how long can you look at a one-bedroom apartment? He told me he was a rock promoter; I didn't even know what that meant. Could he buy me dinner? No, not really. Could he go out and get us some sandwiches? No thanks.

Next day he was back, this time with a deposit for the apartment. I was cleaning out some shelves and he noticed a Monopoly game on the floor.

"Oh, I love Monopoly," he said. "Don't you?"

"Yeah."

"Gee, we ought to get together a group and play before you go."

"Yeah, that'd be fun." Whatever.

Later that evening the phone rang and it was Mike. "I wanted to show some friends the place I'll be renting. How'd you like to play some Monopoly?" I don't know why I said yes, I just said yes. The game ended about three A.M. and he asked if I'd like to have lunch the next day. And still, no romantic thing ever clicked in my head. As I've said, it's not the first thing that occurs to me. Not that I can't be sensual or sexual when I want to be, it's just that ever since high school I've thought of myself first as the buddy, the pal.

I went to Chicago, and Mike kept calling me there; it became apparent in the phone calls that he was attracted to me. I was charming back—this was a pal—but I was always aloof. I never felt anything for him romantically, not then or later. Meanwhile I was having problems of my own. I became a complete insomniac in Chicago, and on top of that I was beginning to experience morning sickness. I was physically exhausted, just bouncing off the walls.

I think I managed a whole two days of rehearsals but I'd been sleepless for at least ten days and it was obvious that I was sick and incapable of performing. David Licht was called and though the theater people were very angry, I was excused from the play. I was so out of it, I left my Oscar, which the theater had insisted on for a lobby display, as well as two dogs I'd acquired, behind in Chicago.

David Licht tried to talk me into going into a hospital, but I refused. I just wanted to go to bed. I'd called Mike and told him that while he wouldn't have to get out of there in ten minutes, I needed the apartment back. When I arrived I asked him to call Desi and tell him I was there, and then I completely collapsed. I don't have any idea how long I slept, it could have been days.

Then Desi called. I talked to him on the phone and got

hysterical as usual. Mike was there, being very solicitous. Was I hungry? Did I want some coffee? Could he do anything for me? I sort of sat around staring for most of the day. Mike left and Desi came over and we argued about his spending more time with me, the regular stuff.

After Desi left, Mike came back and I was very upset, going on and on about being pregnant and not being married.

"You want to get married?" he asked.

"Yeah," I answered. It was *that* simple. Never did the word *love* cross either set of lips.

"You mean it?"

"Yeah."

"When?"

"Now."

"Great. We'll go up to Vegas, we'll call my parents, they'll set it up."

And within two hours we were on a plane to Las Vegas, where the ceremony took place in one of those silly chapels. His family was there—I remember being amazed how it had all been pulled together so fast. I think there was a bridal bouquet, but that's as far as my memories go. I've been told the ring was borrowed, and that I talked through the entire ceremony, and while that's entirely possible, I have no recollection of it. David Licht saw the news on TV and had a fit. He called Sandy Smith and said, "Where is she? She just married some asshole I never heard of!" Sandy said, "She didn't tell me she was doing it either," which was the truth. I hadn't told anyone, I'd just gone and done it.

What was my reasoning, if you can call it that? Maybe I wanted to be the good little Catholic girl, which meant finding a husband since I was pregnant, but I don't remember thinking that. What was in my head when I said, "Yeah," the thought I didn't say out loud, was, "I can get along with anybody. I can marry you or I can marry Joe Blow across the street or I can marry the waiter at Hamburger Hamlet. My life is worthless, it doesn't matter anyway." It was, on my part, at least, a purely self-destructive act.

As to Mike Tell's motivations, it's sheer speculation. I don't know a thing about him, not a thing. Similarly, I don't think the man could possibly have been in love with me: he didn't know me. He had these Mike Todd delusions, had me telling people we were going to build an ark in the desert as a rock promotion because it was going to rain for forty days and forty nights. Maybe he was an operator who saw an easy mark. Or maybe he was just as crazy as I was.

After we got married, the first thing I did was go around to various casinos paying off his markers. Wherever we were, Mike was always on the phone, wheeling and dealing. He never ate, the guy weighed like eleven pounds. And that was before he'd go into the steam room and "shvitz." Really, he made Gandhi look fat. Though what was visible between us on the surface was a forced, hysterical kind of gaiety, in fact our whole time together was a most unpleasant experience. I remember not excitement, not happiness, but utter panic. It was like being pinned to the side of a centrifuge, unable to escape.

At one point Mike decided he wanted to see his relatives in New Jersey, and, not wanting to deprive my new husband of anything—this new husband in a marriage which incidentally was never consummated—I figured, what the hell. He thought it would be fun to rent a Learjet. And while we were at it, we'd pick up my dogs in Chicago. It was on the way, wasn't it? The total bill, I've been told, came to fourteen thousand dollars.

Things really fell apart in New York. I did a *Dick Cavett Show* on which I said very few things which made any sense and Cavett was ruthlessly unsympatheic; he just used it for all it was worth. John Astin, I later learned, happened to see this show and couldn't figure out what had happened. What was I doing married to this guy? I announced on the air that I was pregnant, but who was the father? John wondered. And why was I behaving so strangely?

After the show Mike and I went back to our hotel and had a huge argument. There was a table set up like a bar in the suite and I just started taking glasses off it and throwing them at the plate glass window. I'm talking about forty glasses; the window did not break but there was shattered glass everywhere. Then, panicked, I called Annie Bancroft; I hadn't seen her in a long time, but I told her I was in real trouble. And she helped me. She came to the hotel and got in touch with David Licht and arrangements were made for me to fly back to Los Angeles immediately and be hospitalized for rest.

I told Mike he had to get out of my apartment, that this marriage was insane and I was going to divorce him if I couldn't get an annulment (which I did receive about a year later). There was no conscious decision-making process going on for me here; something inside simply said, "Whatever roller coaster this is you're on, it's over. You have to stop this. Now." And I never saw or heard from Michael Tell again. Not a word.

Physically, emotionally, even financially—because David Licht had put a stop to my account—I was looking at the biggest accumulation of trouble even I'd ever seen. As far as I knew, there was absolutely no way out of this feeling of hopelessness, craziness, and loss. If I hadn't been pregnant, I would have committed suicide. Not one of those "someone will save me" attempts, but for real. And it turned out that it was being pregnant that finally provided me with the start of a way out.

TWENTY-SEVEN

From the moment my pregnancy became public knowledge, the question of who the father was was on everyone's lips. The fan magazines really had a field day with that one. I didn't have to read them to be aware of what they were saying; people didn't hesitate to let me know. And there was such a glut of stories that for a while you couldn't go into a supermarket without seeing the headlines or collages of pictures of me and Desi or me and Lucy that looked as if we might have been together although we really weren't.

I considered those stories to be sleazy, slimy, and scurrilous; I suffered a great deal from them and I still do. People who tell you that stuff doesn't affect them are either lying because it's necessary to cover their feelings, or else they've been through so much that they have become inured to it to a certain degree. Why did a woman as famous and respected as Carol Burnett sue the *National Enquirer* and go through all that trouble over a line in an article that probably was meaningless to all the rest of us? Because it wounded her deeply in an area that was important.

My crime during that time—and it was indeed a crime— was that out of fear I allowed people to assume the baby was Desi's when I knew otherwise. In fact, there were times when

I would nod in agreement or say something in such a way that, without straight-out declaring, "This is Desi's kid," I was implying as much. And I took no active part in disclaiming Desi as the father, which when you get right down to it was just as bad. One of the ways that I'm able to live with that and everything else that went on during our relationship is that Desi knew then and knows now that no matter how screwed up I was, or how thoroughly I might have been messing up his life, those were the actions of a person who really did love him but who was too sick to be fully in control of her actions.

The motive for my behavior was all kinds of terror. I was unmarried, pregnant, and I thought, "I can't tell John, John's married. I can't tell Desi, because if I tell Desi about John, he'll throw me over and then where will I be? Desi doesn't seem to mind the way things are, maybe I can just leave it alone and it'll go away." I was out of touch with reality, allowing the world to believe what it wanted to believe; like an addict, I would agree to anything if it would get me through the next hour. If you said I had three heads, I'd agree with you. If you said, "Let's get married this afternoon," I'd agree with you. If you said, "It's Desi's baby," I'd agree with you.

Although I have always been hurt by the speculations about Sean's parentage, not the least of those affected by the cloud I created has obviously been Sean himself. He's, of course, well aware of all the rumor and the scandal, although when he was little he used to get confused. He'd watch *I Love Lucy* and when Desi, Sr., came on, he'd say, half horrified, "Mom, *that* one?" or he'd get Desi confused with all those other Hollywood "juniors"; once Sean saw Sammy Davis, Jr. on some show and said, "Now, that's the guy everyone thinks is my father, right?" Other people also get mixed up; they lose track of time and ask my younger son, Mack, "Isn't Lucille Ball your grandmother?"

Once John and I got together we started talking to Sean about all this when he was quite young; we wanted to safeguard him against some kid bringing it up in a playground, the way children repeat things they hear. We knew we couldn't stop people from speculating till the cows come home, but we wanted him to hear the truth. So he knows about my confusion at the time, about my certainty that John is his father because of the timing of conception, and as far as he's concerned, John Astin is his father, period. He can be very sweet about it also. He said to me recently, "Dad's my father because he's been my father, because he changed my diapers and taught me Little League. I believe that his sperm made me, too, but even if I didn't, that doesn't change the fact that he's my dad."

Still, we're all aware that the more popular Sean gets, and the more interviews he has, the greater the possibility that he'll be asked the sixty-four-dollar question with greater frequency. But he's a remarkable kid, and he's got his own way of not so much putting on blinders as separating the wheat from the chaff. He considers what kind of a person it is who'd be asking a question like that, and doesn't allow himself to be hurt by someone who shouldn't be in a position to hurt him. His attitude is, "I've got other things to do, I can't be bothered with this stuff."

Even so, I myself haven't quite stopped worrying that this issue of his parentage may come up again for Sean in a crisis, the way it sometimes does for children who are adopted. And in truth, John had to adopt him, because there was only one name—mine—on his birth certificate. Sean has talked to me about that too. "Isn't it silly that my own father had to adopt me!" As I said, he's a remarkable kid.

Just because I'd managed to extricate myself from Michael Tell didn't mean that I'd succeeded in calming myself down. I'd still do things like rent a plane to take me from Las Vegas to Palm Springs when there was no urgency about the trip whatsoever. That was purely manic behavior—spending money for things you don't need, having no idea why you're spending it, just feeling compelled to buy, to do, to go. On one particular trip there was a stewardess who went by the name of Bobbie Jo. She was a tough, nasty cookie, with platinum hair with black roots, and eyebrows that were all tweezed out and then penciled in. She claimed to be the daughter of a famous gangster, and she certainly looked the part.

Bobbie Jo, however, told me a very sad story about the trouble she was having supporting herself and her baby. Now, I didn't know this woman from a hole in the wall, and the flight from Vegas to Palm Springs is not very long, but before we landed I'd invited her to live with me. I told her we'd take the plane back to Vegas, pick up her child, and then find a house in the desert where we could raise our babies together.

And that's exactly what I did, except that in the next two weeks we made friends with yet another stray woman and invited her to stay with us too. Not to mention the four dogs we had somehow accumulated. Then the other woman left and I had to go back to L.A. to be near my obstetrician, so Bobbie Jo was left in charge. Right before Sean was born I got a message through my agent that there had been a problem with the house and all the dogs were in the veterinarian's kennel in Palm Desert.

I spoke to someone at the kennel and was told that the dogs had been left alone, unfed and locked in the house for more than a week. The neighbors had complained, the police had broken in practically with gas masks, and found a disaster. The dogs were so hungry, they'd eaten the walls; they'd chewed on the plaster to get filled up. Since there was no way out for them, they'd relieved themselves everywhere and spread the excrement all over the house. It was an utter nightmare—as if some ritualistic weirdness had taken place there. It cost me an absolute fortune to pay for the repairs to that house. And all my furniture was gone, not to mention Bobbie Jo. I was never able to track her down again.

When I'd moved back to L.A. I'd gone first to a bungalow at the Beverly Hills Hotel, and then, presumably right before the law came to take me out, I rented an ugly furnished apartment on Doheny Drive. That's when the manic phase ended, the depression started, and I crashed. For the last month and a half before Sean was delivered, I stayed in bed twenty-four hours a day. I barely ate, slept sometimes, but mostly I watched television around the clock. I saw no one and did nothing. I'd go for my doctor's appointments, that was it, and even that felt like a real chore. The only excitement I experienced was when a sizable earthquake hit.

I'd never been in one before and I kept screaming at God, "You son of a bitch! You couldn't let me have this baby! You couldn't just let me see what it looks like!" I thought it was the end of the world.

When I went into the hospital to deliver, Lucie Arnaz came and sat with me. We had been friendly off and on, and I think she felt there should be someone with me and she seemed the logical choice, given that my mother was in New York. It was very sweet of her, especially because the tiny little room they put me in barely had space for the bed and a chair. I was in there for a day and a half, which seemed like an eternity, and then the doctor came in and announced they were going to do a cesarean. I didn't question why, but I heard from a nurse later that the doctors couldn't hear the baby's heartbeat. The reason was, the baby wasn't even in the birth canal yet. That's how I wound up having a cesarean—they listened to his ass instead of to his heart.

I was incredibly happy with Sean (Gaelic for John, like my father and Sean's) even though he was so tiny he had to be put into an incubator, and it was terribly frustrating not to be able to hold him until the third day. I was in ecstasy over my son, but there was a kind of melancholy that went along with it because I was alone. Without grandparents oohing and aahing and especially with no husband, I felt the picture wasn't exactly the way it was supposed to be. In fact, I felt like a scarlet woman. I'd like to be able to say I was more sophisticated than that, and had a truer grasp of what was important, but I didn't. I felt outcast and unclean, as if I really didn't fit anywhere. These folks didn't want me. Those folks didn't want me. My mother wasn't there. My sister wasn't there. My brother wasn't there. And there I was, like Blanche in A Streetcar Named Desire, dependent "on the kindness of strangers." It had been a pattern in my life, so part of me was accustomed to things being that way, but how the baby would fit into this pattern presented a new wrinkle.

I must say, though, that Desi, Sr., came to see the baby along with his wife, as did Lucie Arnaz with her husband, all behaving as if he were part of their family. And I thought, considering the ugliness of the circumstances that had been created by the movie magazines, and the fact that there were reporters literally camped out in the stairwells of the hospital, that was a very brave and gracious thing to do. And I don't know that I've ever really told them that until now.

Lucille Ball, however, did not come to the hospital, which, considering the media circus, was probably wise. There were so many photographers around that Sean's name couldn't be used on his little bassinet or on the bracelet they put on his wrist. Lucy had tried very hard to be kind when I was pregnant since everyone thought Desi was the father, but in the end she was not going to sacrifice her son by giving her official sanction to the relationship. I was not her idea of how Desi was going to spend his life.

In truth I had thought about marrying Desi, as a way out if nothing else, but he'd told me specifically that he wasn't interested, that he never wanted to get married to anyone. I'm sure there were times when he thought the baby was his, as well as times he was convinced it wasn't, but either way he definitely didn't want any part of that whole scene. It had been a great game for a while, but it was getting too real, is probably how he felt. He didn't want to play anymore.

I think I'd always known somewhere in the back of my head that having a child and being responsible for a child would cause me to behave in a more responsible way, and that's exactly what happened. Once Sean was born, all those vague words became a reality, something I could touch. There was no more running, running, running. I bought a small house and spent a lot of time alone with the baby. Within a couple of weeks I became almost a recluse. Having a child may have been only a Band-Aid on the disease I had, but it was one of the bigger, cleaner, stronger Band-Aids, something I was able to count on until the real thing came along.

TWENTY-EIGHT

Although I barely remember it,
I first met John Astin at an ABC affiliates convention when
I was only seventeen. He liked to claim that he was attracted
to me even then, and while that may be true, he told those
stories only to confuse people so they wouldn't find out that
we'd conceived Sean while he was still married to someone
else. In fact, we found each other very early in May of 1970,
and what brought us together was a mutual obsession with
death. That's how we met, over a conversation about the
fear of death.

It was at a wrap party for a mutual friend's film, both of
us had had quite a lot to drink, and we found ourselves part
of a bunch of people sitting around a table having a conversation about whether President Kennedy would have remained a hero had he lived. I'd noticed John earlier, because
he's an extremely handsome man (he'd starred as Gomez in
TV's *The Addams Family*), tall and slender with a great voice
and eyes that can look like a Frenchman's bedroom eyes or
those of a basset hound. And when he gets involved in a
conversation, the scope of things he considers is extraordinary and usually unique, so he seemed quite fascinating to
me.

When the conversation turned to J.F.K., I happened to

be turned in John's direction and I noticed a look on his face that had nothing to do with Kennedy at all. I immediately recognized the terror in his eyes, the panic about death that I, of course, shared and that's so enormous, the word *fear* doesn't begin to do it justice. It was as if my own adrenaline had started to really pump. John had apparently noticed a similar look on my face, and we just kept staring at each other.

Finally, I got so agitated I couldn't stand it anymore, I wanted to scream, "Am I seeing what I think I'm seeing?" I began climbing over the people sitting between us, saying, "Excuse me, excuse me, excuse me," and when I finally got next to him I just said, "You're probably going to think I'm very weird, but do you have an obsessive fear of death?" And he smiled that charming, wonderful smile of his and said, "Why, yes." And I said, "Me too!"

Then I started jabbering, jabbering, jabbering. I found myself desperate to commune with this kindred spirit, which is not a phrase I use lightly. I truly believe souls were meant to spend time together, and that John and I are two such souls.

At any rate, we went home and spent the night together. A few days later John went down to San Diego to do a movie and I visited him there a couple of times. He was wonderful to be with, brilliant and older, sixteen years older than my twenty-three, in fact, and a magnificent lover. It was very passionate, very loving, and, or so I thought, very temporary. He told me he was separated from his wife, Suzanne, that the marriage had not been good for many, many years, and, of course, I felt sorry for the poor, misunderstood husband. At that point in my life I was pretty confused about whom I loved and even what love was, but still I felt I really did love this man. I wished and fantasized that this could be a real relationship that could work out, but I sensed that he was so concerned about his wife and their three sons that the odds were he was going back there. So I tried not to get too attached.

Once the momentum of my manic episode got rolling, with John Ross's death, the Emmys, and Michael Tell to cope with, it was as if the whole thing with John had never happened. Then he called me after *The Dick Cavett Show*, and I admitted I was pregnant but even though I was sure by then the child was his, I told him I didn't know who the father was. Everything was denial, denial, denial.

That's the way things stayed. No one knew about us at all, until Sean was about eight months old. At that point, both John and I were cast in a Link and Levinson TV movie called *Two on a Bench*, a fairly silly love story between a hippie and a right wing guy, very different from *My Sweet Charlie*. We reestablished our sexual relationship and one day John told me that he had been doing some "calculating" —that's how he talks, other people might say "I was thinking about it and I figured out," but not him—and according to when Sean was born and the last time I'd been with Desi, the child was not Desi's but his. I admitted he was right but said I had figured I shouldn't go around telling that to people since he was married and had three children.

John and his wife had separated again before the movie started, and he finally went to Suzanne and said he was going to move the rest of his things out. He didn't tell his wife he was going to live with me, and as he was walking out the door, she said to him quite sardonically, "The real tragedy is you'll probably go out with some big-titted Hollywood starlet. Why don't you find yourself somebody nice, like Patty Duke." It was totally out of nowhere, and it's the first thing John told me when he came to the house: "You're not going to believe what she said."

So John and I began our life with each other, in late 1971, still undercover. For several months we went literally nowhere together, the idea being there'd been enough nonsense in the magazines, we weren't going to give them anything more to play with. It was perfect for me, idyllic. I was romantically in love with this man, he symbolized security, it was as if all those puzzle pieces that had been broken and mutilated were now being properly put back together.

We went back east at Christmas and told John's parents that we planned to get married. Being introduced as the intended mate always made me nervous—there seemed perpetually to be some dark cloud hanging over me—but his folks were wonderful. I felt instantly welcomed with unrestrained love and have evermore. It was the first parental relationship I had experienced in which I could do absolutely no wrong, and I cherish it to this day.

It was kind of a nirvana, those early times with John. He truly seemed to love unconditionally, and I obviously had long been in need of that kind of safety in love. We were literally bankrupt, even though we didn't file, and there were slings and arrows thrown from outside, but we were in a home filled with love. We didn't have much else in it, but it was a home. And we were a pair of hippie types, willing to live on bread and roses, and that felt awfully good.

John and I always wanted to get married, right from the beginning, but we had to wait until his divorce was final. It's not that I don't think commitment can exist without a ceremony, I just believe in the institution. I'm a person who puts a great deal of stock in symbols, and this is a very special one, which we as a society have passed along from generation to generation as a meaningful expression of love and bonding.

The wedding took place on August 5, 1972, in the rose garden of John's folks' house in Bethesda, Maryland. The heat and humidity at that time of year were not to be believed, the steam was practically coming up from the grass, but the whole event was just lovely. Everyone was there, including my mother and a lot of my relatives. I wore an off-white lace dress with flowers in my hair, and eighteen-month-old Sean, his little Shirley Temple curls bouncing, wore a dark blue suit with short pants. I tried to get him a three-piece suit, even though he was barely walking, but they didn't have one small enough.

The wildest dresser of all, however, was the man who married us, William Wendt, kind of a renegade Episcopal minister. He had on an orange robe appliquéd with giant butterflies of a reddish color. A musician friend of John's named Willie Ruff went out behind the trees and played a love theme on the French horn, and that soulful, other-worldly sound coming out of nowhere really flipped the emotional switch for everyone.

John and I both shed tears and promised each other things like "forever." Since he got to speak first, he stole something I wanted to do, which was to sign "I love you," so

I ended up laughing through my tears. Then Father Wendt asked if anyone had something they'd like to say, and relatives and friends from both sides chimed in with their approval and good wishes. Then he asked, "Is there anyone else?" and that's when Sean said, "Da-daa, Da-daa!" and everyone roared. Father Wendt said, "Well, I guess that about says it all. I now pronounce you man and wife." And we partied on the lawn until four o'clock in the morning, then went on to a tiny old hotel in Annapolis, where we stayed up until ten, laughing and opening our presents. It was wonderful.

Our second son, Mackenzie, was born on May 12, 1973, and I was thrilled. This time we'd done it exactly the way you're supposed to: we'd gotten married first and *then* we'd had the baby! And I loved being pregnant; perfect strangers are nice to you. We didn't have a name for our son, though, until he'd been delivered. I kept saying, "This one's going to be a girl" just to keep everybody interested. I knew it wasn't so: all John can make is boys. Still, we couldn't come up with anything until right after he was born. I asked the anesthesiologist if he could ask John, who was standing by the door, what he thought of the name Mackenzie, which moved John greatly because that was his mother's maiden name. It hadn't hit me until I saw the baby that Mackenzie was a great name. Mack. Quarter-pounder. Absolutely.

After we were married, as a sign of love and commitment I added Astin to my professional name. It was something I knew John would like and I liked it too. It brought a certain maturity to the name I wanted to establish. And though I've been accused of using it because it starts with A and would help me for billing purposes (I swear, I've actually heard that!), the simple truth is I was proud to have chosen to be married to him, and proud of his choosing me, and I wanted to show it.

John had another impact on my name, and my identity, that was much more long-lasting and profound. It began in the earliest days of our relationship, when we were still undercover—and under the covers. We used code names in leaving messages for each other; his was Jack Allen, and mine was "Sally, Mr. Riviera's secretary," which John commemorated by getting me about a dozen miniature "Sally" license plates from all over the country.

"You're not a 'Sally,' " John said to me casually one day when this had been going on for a while. "And you're not a 'Patty' either. What are you?"

"No," I said, smiling. "I'm an 'Anna.' My name's Anna."

"Well," he said. "Why don't we call you Anna? That's your name."

My initial reaction to that was one of sheer delight mixed with nervousness. I felt I was ready to be Anna, to reclaim myself, but as much as I loved the idea, I was afraid to get too attached to the name, afraid it would last a bit, as it had with Harry, but never stick. At first I felt ludicrous introducing myself as Anna, but John was so dedicated to it, he didn't merely philosophize or talk about what ought to be, he acted. In situations in which the two of us were working together, which happened frequently, he never called me anything but Anna, and that helped people get used to it. It was much tougher when I worked without him; then I got called every name under the sun, because no one could quite remember what they were supposed to call me, but even there Anna won out.

Because of what I'd been through with the Rosses, being Anna again was much more than a superficial change, it symbolized what felt like the rebirth of the core of my soul. Working from the outside in, my new/old name became a powerful emotional tool. It wasn't just that I stood taller around the house because I no longer had a babyish name; I could feel, almost day by day, the sensation of this person who was myself coming back to life after all those years. John was responsible for giving me the freedom not only to use the name Anna but to *be* Anna as well, which was truly a lifelong gift.

For a while, during the transition period, John would revert to my old name when he was angry and wanted to hurt me. Then it was, "Okay, Patty Duke, if that's what you think," which was like waving a red flag in front of a bull. I'm not so sensitive about Patty anymore, however. My names are part of me and I them; all of them are okay now. Patty may not be my favorite, it doesn't feel like me anymore, but because it symbolizes a large part of my life that I'm no longer trying to reject, I don't shudder anymore when a stranger calls me Patty in a shopping mall. I turn around comfortably and say hello. That's my name for that minute, and I'm at ease with that because I know it's only for that minute; I'm able now to be myself whenever and wherever I need to.

TWENTY-NINE

After Mackie was born, John's three sons, twelve-year-old David, eleven-year-old Alan, and eight-year-old Tom came to live with us, and my honeymoon with John came to an abrupt end. It had always been rough when the kids stayed over on weekends, and I was simply not equipped for their presence full-time. I remember very few major arguments with John until they came, and then we argued all the time about how to raise them. People have babies and they learn about children as they go. You don't, when you're twenty-four, take on a kid who's twelve. Especially when you've had the retarded development that I had, and when the twelve-year-old is seriously rebellious and acting out all over the place.

The problems with David had started even before Mackie was born. He was an unhappy kid and Suzanne was having a bad time with him; like me, she was a very volatile person with limited patience. Even before John and I were married she told him that she couldn't deal with David, that we had to take him. So we did, and the good part of me wanted to help this kid, to be the Great All-American Heroine. The competitive part wanted to be a better mother than Suzie. But David and I did not get along; we never managed to get on the same wavelength. For a while one of us would be kind and the other would be difficult, and then we'd switch roles. John and I kept David for six months, and then he decided he wanted to go back and live with his mother, which was devastating to me.

Then, after Mackie was born, came the real crisis. There are many versions of the story, and for all I know the kids may well have provoked her, but the upshot was that one day Suzanne told them to go live with their father. They called, and we ran to get them; we hardly had a choice. There was great excitement about whether she would show up at our house and create a scene, but, in fact, with very few exceptions, she had no contact with the kids until quite recently. Suzanne must have been in terrible pain, and though I don't approve of her actions, I understand now, as I didn't then, the kind of spiritual and emotional fatigue and depression that leads to such behavior.

The major contact we had with Suzanne was in 1974, when it was determined that I would adopt the boys and she decided she wanted to fight it. The kids brought up the idea before I did. They had all kinds of quirky little emotional reasons like wanting to write *mother* instead of *stepmother* on forms at school. I thought it would make them feel more secure, and both John and I wanted it because in the event something happened to him, at that time I had no legal standing in regard to these three children—I would've been unable to retain custody. But I had no desire to alienate the kids further from their mother, so it was made very clear to the boys what this was all about, that it had to be their choice, and no one would be pressuring them to do anything.

Adoption day was very difficult for everyone, initially because it was the first time the three boys had seen their mother in a long time. Suzie, who's a very attractive woman, looked strained, even distraught. First the boys went in individually to the judge's chambers, and then Suzie and I were called in while everyone else waited outside. And she proceeded to be the worst witness she could possibly have been for herself; I hated to see this poor woman in that kind of misery. I was so broken up that my lawyer, Mitchell Dawson, who treats me like an equal, not like a daughter, told me if I didn't pull myself together, I was going to have to leave the courtroom.

It was a few months before we heard that my petition to adopt had been approved. It was great to get the news. It felt like a milestone, a chance for a new beginning. I hoped maybe all the screaming and ranting and raving that had gone on between the kids and their mother wouldn't be repeated with me, but it pains me to confess I was unable to handle the situation. The frustration level was so great, I would scream my brains out at them. I would try to whack David, but he was too fast for me. It was everything I swore my life would never be if I had children. My God, the years of misery that went on in that house while publicly we were a perfect couple with an adorable family!

For one thing, I hated our house. It's very pretty now, but then it looked like Tobacco Road or a movie set that had been aged to resemble a deteriorating building. We lived in a pigsty, the accumulated mess of dogs and cats and birds and rats in cages, not to mention five kids. My reaction followed cycles, and at certain points I'd try to be very detached and say, "Okay, fine, the hell with it. I don't have to clean it up, I don't have to yell about it." Everyone thought that was wonderful, of course, but then I'd explode again, I'd scream, "Who can *live* in this mess?"

If I'd thought about my position as a stepparent more realistically, it might have made things a whole lot easier. From the moment the kids arrived, I assumed I was going to feel exactly the same about them as I did about Sean and Mack. I thought it was a crime if I didn't. John's attitude was, "Isn't it wonderful that she loves them all the same? They're all brothers, they're all sons," but it simply wasn't true and trying to make believe it was true was an enormous burden on me and eventually on everyone. If I'd treated them as I felt toward them, which is what all the experts now tell you to do, it would have been so much more honest, and a lot of the games that developed between us never would have gotten started.

A crucial element in all this was that because I loved John and he loved me I wanted to do everything I could to please him, I wanted to be the good little wife. Taking the children in was what he wanted, so I wanted it too. As for adopting them, how could that be anything but pleasing to a man who says, "The most important thing is that if I die, you will raise them."

So I'd try and do things his way. Oh, how I tried to be reasonable and understanding and gentle and kind and rational—for the first fifty-six times I'd ask them to do something. Then, at the fifty-seventh time, I'd scream my bloody lungs out. And that's when John would walk in the door and say, "Now, Anna, you're supposed to be the adult here. There's nothing wrong with the children; it's you." And then, of course, the heat would be off the kids because John and I would get into an argument that would last till morning.

What you have to understand is that John had the capacity to tune things out to such a degree that it became a family joke. You could talk to him for ten minutes and then come back an hour later and say, "What do you think about what I asked you?" and he'd have no recollection that you had even been in the room. He did that with the children too. Of course he was patient with the kids. He didn't hear them!

When David and Alan made and set off genuine Molotov cocktails in the backyard, for instance, the extent of John's reaction was: "Boys, I don't think that's something you should be doing." I could see their eyes go blank, the way one actor sees another actor's go blank when he doesn't know the next line. They knew if they sat there long enough, John would get finished umming and aahing and pausing and rationalizing and they'd be set free. Which is exactly what always happened.

Those kids never knew the meaning of limits, and it hurt them. When they started using marijuana, I said, "They're doing drugs," and John would answer, "No, they're not. I asked them and they told me they weren't." I would persist, but he would flat out refuse to believe me over the boys. He would say, "Why don't you like David?" He forgot I was closer to their age than I was to his, and even though I had had a very different childhood, I could see exactly what they were doing.

David left the house when he was eighteen. It was one of the worst times I've ever been involved in, but I felt his leaving was the best thing. I knew staying wasn't doing him any good. He'd come in at two in the morning with six or eight of his friends, waking up the little ones, maybe taking a dozen steaks out of the freezer and cooking dinner in the middle of the night. But more than any specific incidents, it was the way David manipulated John and me into hassles that I couldn't bear anymore. John begged me not to do to David what his other mother already had, and the realization that I was doing that broke my heart, but finally I said, "Yes, I am. Because now I know how she feels."

Al, the next oldest, left without being asked; he didn't want to be obligated to us and chose to live on his own. He's a follower of Swami Muktananda, bright and sunny and happy as a clam. I have great admiration for Al; he's fully self-supporting, he owes nothing to anyone. In fact, my relationship with all three of the boys, David and Tom as well as Al, has evolved so that it is now the best it's ever been. We're in touch often, and all the feelings between us are richer and more accepting. They're either working or in school, they have ambition and initiative and goodness, and they're doing fine. I just wish I could have made the road easier for them. I did not.

THIRTY

I was getting into my car outside a restaurant called The Bistro in Beverly Hills one afternoon near the end of 1970 when a man came up and started to talk to me. He said his name was Joe Stich, and I guessed he wanted a date, but somehow we started talking business talk and he gave me his card. And when I had a breakup with my manager, David Licht, I gave him a call. He and a guy named Bob Irwin (which turned out to be an alias) came to see me and convinced me they should be my business managers.

What I knew about business could fit on the head of a pin, and in those days I wasn't thinking clearly enough to realize that an attempted pickup in a restaurant parking lot is not the best recommendation for someone who is going to be given carte blanche to handle your money. I would sign anything these guys put in front of me. I just didn't want to be bothered by what I felt were unimportant details.

In early 1972, when John and I were together but unmarried, I was on location in Duluth shooting a scary film called *You'll Like My Mother* about a young pregnant girl who was in all kinds of jeopardy. I got sick with what turned out to be a kidney infection, but the production company thought I was malingering so they called Irwin, my business manager, who told them—and me—that in his opinion, John was the real problem, that he was jealous of the working relationship I had with Irwin and was causing me unnecessary grief. "It's all his fault, look what he's doing to you," Irwin said. "If you weren't taking care of John's kid David as well as Sean, you wouldn't be exhausted all the time." I happened to be going through a period of doubt about my relationship with John, and here was an ally saying, "See? See? Poor thing, look what he's doing to you." The reason Irwin attacked John so roundly, I later found out, was that John had become suspicious of how he and Stich were handling, or mishandling, my finances and had started to snoop around. Irwin retaliated by trying to poison my mind against John. Unfortunately, I bought it, hook, line, and sinker.

So when John came to Duluth to see me, I wasn't able to just calmly talk this out with him. A major scene developed, with some of it, unfortunately, taking place at the hotel, where other people could hear. The upshot was that the company told John that he had to get out of town because he was upsetting me, that I wasn't working up to my capacity. None of this was true, but the scene between John and me was not something you'd want others to witness, and John got a bad reputation for disrupting a production.

I was able to confront these men only months later after I was brought into an office in a Sears store in Los Angeles where I was trying to buy paint. The Sears people took my card away, said, "Come with us," and informed me how long it had been since Sears had seen any of my money. That was the day John finally decided he had to tell me what he'd known for a long time but had hesitated to bring up. He'd been afraid that I wouldn't believe him and that that whole Duluth chasm would open up all over again.

The embezzlement scheme used against me was complex enough that it took the district attorney's office two years to prepare the indictment. Over the three years those guys had been my business managers, I'd accumulated six hundred thousand dollars worth of bills, hadn't paid my taxes for three years, and was in danger of having my house foreclosed on. Once the grand jury acted against Irwin and Stich, they immediately brought a countersuit against me for two million dollars for slander. The reason they sued was to be able to take my deposition, during the course of which questions were asked which were designed to spook me.

"Isn't it true that you slept with Mr. Stich?"

"No."

"Isn't it true that you were hospitalized for alcoholism?"

"No."

"Isn't it true that you were hospitalized for drug addiction?"

"No! You can get the records."

"We're not interested in records. We just want to know what you have to say."

The plan was obviously to get me so upset I'd drop the case rather than have to go through questioning like that in open court. And I did freak out, I went home on the Friday afternoon before the trial and didn't get up until Monday morning except to beg John to find some way out so I wouldn't have to do this. There was much hysteria that weekend. Monday came and the attorneys didn't want me down at the courthouse until it was close to my time to testify, so I waited at home, a nervous wreck, with John. Even though I felt, "If I did it with a porcupine, what does that have to do with the fact that these people stole my money," I sort of accepted the fact that I was going to be humiliated in court.

Then the phone rang—the sound almost sent me through the roof—and John answered it and said, "Oh, I see. Uh-huh. Okay, okay. Well, you fill me in later." It turned out my former managers had pleaded nolo contendere at the last minute. It was the only piece of justice I ever got. As for getting my money back, I received three checks through the Department of Correction. One was for fifty dollars, one for seventy-five and one for twenty-five. That was it.

The money crunch, already hideous because of the embezzlement, got worse in 1973 when a Writers Guild strike in Hollywood made it impossible for us to work because we weren't going to cross any picket lines. So John started asking agents about theatrical work, and that's how our five years as touring actors, a regular Lunt and Fontanne, began. The official story was that we loved the theater so much we couldn't resist dragging the whole platoon on the road, but the fact of the matter was, we started because we were flat broke.

So when Mackie was two weeks old we hit the road with *A Shot in the Dark*. Our first stop was one of the oldest summer stock theaters in the country, Elitch's Gardens in Denver, which had a wonderful history but happened to be located in an amusement park, where a roller coaster inevitably drowned out our best lines. The play was a piece of utter fluff but it was surprisingly difficult to do, like keeping up an old, cold soufflé. And the real problem was, because of my experience in *Miracle Worker*–type dramas, audiences thought they were coming to see the more serious *Wait Until Dark*. So it took a good twenty minutes to get people off the dime and realize that this was only a silly airhead comedy. Until then, there was dead silence out there. It felt like playing to a backdrop.

The burden of keeping the play alive fell largely to John. Both in that play and the others we did, I was a very good straight man, and most of the time I was comfortable with that. There were occasional skirmishes, however. I'd come offstage and shriek at him for killing my one and only laugh, and if he could manage a word in edgewise, he'd point out to me that in fact I'd stepped on my own laugh, which would really annoy me.

Most of the time, though, I thought he was an exceptional performer and I stood in awe of his gift. He taught me an awful lot about timing in those kinds of plays, about having the courage to wait, take a line, get the laugh, and then get off. All in all, we worked very well together and while we were performing we almost always had fun. If nothing else, being onstage was one of the few times during the day when we could talk to each other without being interrupted, even if the dialogue wasn't our own. Nobody said, "Mom! Dad!" There may have been a whole audience of people out there, but we were alone.

We got through the first season making, I think, ten thousand dollars a week plus a piece of the house, and that was all John needed to know. This was going to be our new way of life. Next came *The Marriage Gambol*, which we did for two seasons until I really got bored with it. The last place we played it was Seattle, and not only was that the one time we were not a hit, we were a big, bad bomb. I wasn't used to that, I was very spoiled, and I couldn't handle the failure. Within the space of hours I'd switch from deep depression and lethargy to crying and running around the house, threatening to kill myself, to finally taking the car and driving off in the ever-present rain. And then I said I wasn't going to do the show. "I don't have to do the show. There's nobody to see the show. They hate me. I'm not doing it." I was really in a bad way.

As a sign of rebellion, I decided to get my ears pierced. John didn't want me to. We had an argument in the tea shop next door to the place I was going to get it done, and finally we accosted some old lady who was sitting there, minding her own business, having tea and crumpets. I said, "Excuse me. Could we ask you your opinion? This is my husband. I want to get my ears pierced, and he really has severe reservations about it. What do you think?" Now, mind you, I'd checked her ears out before I asked and they were indeed pierced. But she said sweetly to me, "I think you should do as your husband says." It was the first time I had the urge to punch an old lady!

Instead, I turned to John, who was sitting there smiling, and said, "The hell with you, I'm getting my ears pierced." The process really hurt, and wouldn't you know it, I got a dreadful infection and had lobes the size of grapefruit. But John never said a reproachful word, just, "Poor thing. Did you use your alcohol? Aw, poor thing." And I thought, "Oooh, I'm gonna kill him."

While all this was going on, John and I got sent the script for *My Fat Friend*, which Lynn Redgrave had done on Broadway and which was currently the hot play on the circuit. I read it and I hated it, I thought it was the most vicious, ugliest play I'd ever read in my life. But since we were in this for the money and everyone was saying we'd be fools not to do it, I figured, what the hell. And it was not until John and I started playing the piece that I recognized that this was a much more profound play than I had ever realized, that what I'd thought of as viciousness had its roots in genuine understanding.

Although there are other characters, the heart of *My Fat Friend* is the relationship between (what else but) a fat woman who runs a bookstore and her neighbor, a gay man who's in the closet during the day but a flaming queen at night. A gorgeous young man comes into the bookstore and he and the fat lady fall madly in love. He goes off for a while and the gay man puts her on a regimen so that she loses a lot of weight and becomes a very attractive woman. But when the young man comes back, it turns out he didn't love her: what he'd loved was her fat. And that's when you realize that what you've been watching is a beautiful love story between the woman and the gay guy. Without actually saying the words, they tell each other about that love, but with the realization that the relationship can never go any further.

As Henry, the gay man, John was magnificent. He felt an obligation to the gay community not to do a heterosexual's version of a gay guy. He wanted the dignity of the man, and the dignity of his sexual preference, to be organic. He was a smash, but no one knew that in rehearsals, because in the theater John is very slow in developing a character. He really wrestles with it, and carries the book for a long time, making everyone else extremely nervous.

I'd first experienced this in *A Shot in the Dark*. With that play John was so slow, I thought, "My God, we're going to have a major disaster. He's going to get out there and just stare at me." I began suggesting, "We'll write things down. You carry papers anyway in the scene, you can just look at them," but John kept insisting he'd be fine. Opening night came and as I waited offstage he sounded so letter-perfect, I thought he'd taken the book out there with him and cleverly hidden it behind the potted palms.

Our first scene together started out fine, but then came that great, dreaded pause. It was in a situation where I couldn't help him out by paraphrasing his line, so we just stared at each other. I looked at the two other guys in the scene, I looked back at John, and thought, "Poor son of a bitch. Oh, he must be dying." And then it hit me—the next line was mine. And not only did John paraphrase my line, and his, and get us back on track, but he looked at me so caringly that I thought, "That bastard. Never again will I worry. He can carry the goddamn book until they pull up the curtain on opening night and I'm not going to worry about *him*."

With *My Fat Friend,* John was truly working at a snail's pace. I don't think he knew word one for about six days. It was making the director very anxious, so I told him the story about *A Shot in the Dark,* but I don't think I accomplished anything except scaring the man about my abilities. And John was brilliant on opening night, and not just because it's astounding to witness this man who didn't know his ass from page eight two days before suddenly not only saying the whole play, but performing it. And he kept improving during the run; there was one time when he was so convincing in a scene that even I wondered, "Where is he getting this from?" I was so busy admiring him, I lost my concentration in the scene. This was not the man I knew. This was the guy from the play. That performance revealed a whole new horizon for John's skills and gift.

The last thing John and I toured with together was *Rattle of a Simple Man.* I had a lot of trouble with it. The play, about a country bumpkin who goes to see a hooker and falls in love, was dated by the time we did it, and I never felt really comfortable in the role, partially because I had to take my clothes off down to a bra and little bikini panties.

We were doing fine, however, until we opened in Chicago and I got creamed by a critic, which sent me into another tailspin. It wasn't a review of my performance, it was a negative review of my life and an attack on the respectability I was working so hard to develop and maintain. The piece ridiculed the concept of John and me as a couple, the idea that I was pretending to be a great married lady of the theater when everyone knew what I'd really been up to for the past few years.

That article had a very intense negative effect on me that lasted for months. Months. I thought, "Jeez, I've been so good and it doesn't mean anything. They still write that crap about me. Okay, now let me be bad." That idea came more in feelings than clearly defined thoughts, but the upshot was that I became more and more obstreperous. There were no pills available in Chicago, so I didn't try that. But there were screaming, raging, one-sided fights I picked with John.

The result was that I flatly refused to do any more of this kind of nonstop touring. John tried to talk me into continuing. He kept saying what great fun we'd always had, how it was the best time ever. John truly did love touring. Sometimes all of us flew from playhouse to playhouse, and sometimes we drove with the whole family, including my mother and a housekeeper, and John really got into the whole Dad's-behind-the-wheel-and-we're-off-to-sights-unseen mystique.

But because touring was a whole lot of work and I was tired, I hated it. We rented people's houses and I didn't want the kids to break things or mess anything up, so there was constant tension about situations that John was totally unconcerned with. For him, overshadowing everything was the fact that we were in "the theater," while for me it was always summer stock. I wasn't in the theater, I was in the laundromat. And I was in the bowels of hell emotionally. I even had my analytic sessions long distance over the telephone.

Generally we would play eight performances and travel on Sunday. If we were smart, we'd pack Friday night, but we weren't always smart. And packing was an enormous chore. The amount of luggage was unreal, because kids come with a lot of garbage and show folks come with a lot of garbage too. I certainly wasn't going anyplace without my coffeepot and my curlers and my this and my that. We even schlepped our own costumes—it really was born-in-a-trunk time.

Each kid had his own footlocker in which he was allowed to put anything from games to stereos. If it fit, fine, if it didn't fit, it didn't go. It was a nice theory but it worked only on paper because it didn't take into account the inevitable shopping bags. My mother had gone through her entire life having a love affair with shopping bags, so we had lots of them. Invariably the kids would put their wet bathing suits into the paper shopping bags that tore rather than the plastic ones that didn't. And always when we left someplace, something was left behind.

I especially hated Sunday mornings. I was tired, I didn't

want to fly, I didn't want to pack another frigging Pamper, I didn't care if the kids went stark naked. John was very good about the daily life chores like doing the laundry, which was fortunate because I really didn't even attempt to be more generous of spirit. The boys learned almost immediately the best thing to do was just get out of my way. "Just don't have anything to do with her, try not even to look at her." It was chaos, pure chaos.

And when we bought a van and drove instead of flying, it was only marginally better. This wasn't a motor home, this wasn't a bus done up for a rock star, this was a van, with an ice chest and baloney sandwiches and the kids having to pee in paper cups because John tried hard not to make bathroom stops. For a while we couldn't get them to pee in the cups, and then they didn't want to pee in anything but the cups. We'd get to the house and they'd demand their McDonald's cup to pee into.

Some experiences were worse than others, some were better. We did six weeks of *The Marriage Gambol* in Milwaukee in the middle of winter. It was cold, it was snowy, it was rainy, it was five California kids who were used to going out anytime they pleased cooped up in a hotel. Can you imagine five male Eloises? They were into throwing things like chairs and lamps at each other and through windows and John kept saying, "We're having the best time, aren't we?" I'm surprised we didn't all turn on him like rabid dogs and kill him, a family of Cujos eating the father.

The best time for me was always Cape Cod. Something about the artsy atmosphere there really appealed to me. The boys loved it too. They had their mini Cape Cod affairs, it was very romantic for them. They had to put up with the horrible noises I make in the night, but everybody survived. Even if I don't, I think they will always look back on that period as a terrific time in their lives.

THIRTY-ONE

In 1977 I did a film with Daisy Gerber, a friend of John's who was studying at the American Film Institute. Daisy was very involved in psychic phenomena and the film was taken from *The Fifty-Minute Hour*, a landmark book on psychiatry. It was about a woman who had an extraordinary eating disorder. She didn't just binge on pizzas and chocolate, she ate the boxes they came in, she even tried to eat the cans. It was quite intense.

Daisy and I ended up, as you often do on films like that, working eighteen and twenty hours a day. I went into one of my periods of insomnia and stopped eating. I lost ten pounds in a week, I was wired from here to the moon, which was probably at full tilt as well. Because we worked nights at what was then the AFI campus at Greystone, an old mansion in Beverly Hills which has a lot of strange tales attached to it, and because of Daisy's psychic tendencies, everyone was into an otherworldly mode. At the wrap party we all sat around till past midnight telling ghost stories and talking about spirits and other scary stuff.

John and I got home very late; I was still quite keyed up, but we went to bed. The radio was on, and I began singing along with a song I knew. Then another song came on that I didn't know, and I started singing along with that one too.

That quite amazed me, and I said to John, "Look what I'm doing! Look what I'm doing!"

"What? Same stuff you've been doing for years."

"No, listen, listen. I'm singing these words and I don't know the song." And though John has always claimed I was a millisecond behind, it seemed to me I was right there with it.

Suddenly I said, "Oh, my God. Oh, my God, John. There is life after death." It wasn't a sound I heard, it wasn't anything visual, it was like a revelation. I saw a nothingness, but not a terrible nothingness. And I felt the most euphoric sensation I've ever felt.

"I *will* see you again," I said. "We'll be together again." I was deliriously happy. I felt lighter and lighter and lighter—not light-headed, just lighter. "Oh, my God, John. You have to see this."

And he said "Anna" in such a way that it frightened me; there was fear in his voice and it frightened me. The more unearthly I felt, the more earthly he sounded to me. Then I started talking very fast, saying "Oh-my-God, oh-my-God, oh-my-God, I'm dying."

"No, you're not. Stop this."

"Call me back. I'm going. I'm going. Call me back."

And he did, he started calling "Anna," first in a normal tone and finally literally screaming. Still, I kept saying, "You're getting fainter. I can't hear you. Call me back. I'm going. Call me back. Call me back." It really seemed as if I were going someplace. Aside from the anxiety produced by the fear in his voice, it felt great. It wasn't the kind of out-of-body experience I've read about—I wasn't floating above myself, watching myself. I just felt ethereal.

All of a sudden I said to John, "Hit me on the back, hit me on the back!" and he began alternately calling my name and whacking me. I guess he was taking some pretty good shots, but I kept saying, "Harder! Hit me harder!" Then, suddenly, there was a sensation of no longer being light but grounded. It felt like a thud, and then I completely relaxed, except, of course, for my brain and my mouth. I said over and over, "Did you see that? Can you believe what just went on?"

John was hugging and rocking me and he said I had to eat something. I told him I couldn't eat, I couldn't swallow, but he said he'd get me some bread and milk. Then, just as with the song on the radio, I started saying everything John was saying at the same time as he said it. He claims I was slightly behind, but no matter; it was an extremely freaky experience for him and he decided to call my psychiatrist. He turned out to be on vacation, and a second one we called suggested I be hospitalized, which John was against, so finally we settled on going to Dr. Harold Arlen, who was John's therapist at the time and was to become a major positive force in my life.

John told Arlen that I hadn't slept and I hadn't eaten and I was hallucinating. I was still talking simultaneously with him, and I kept saying, "It's not a hallucination, it's real." Arlen said he wanted to see me at his house, and, not totally trusting this, I reverted to my New York roots and said, "I'm taking my brother," who happened to be staying with us.

As I was getting dressed, I began saying to myself, "Don't try to make everybody believe this. Go along with whatever they say." I knew that since we were going to a psychiatrist, rehospitalization was a real threat. I'd better calm down or I could wind up in the slammer again. Arlen was in his bathrobe when we got there, making me a milk shake, and he gave me a Compazine. We sat and talked and every once in a while I would get waves of that sensation all over again, and then I'd start to tremble in fear of being dubbed crazy instead of having had a spiritual experience. I tried to be careful in talking about both what I experienced and what I thought it meant. We must have sat there for two hours, and then the medication took effect and I did indeed gear down. They never convinced me that what I know happened didn't happen, but they did impress on me that if I had a brain left in my head, I'd agree with them that it was an abnormal experience.

What I went through that night had a number of reper-cussions for my life. For one thing, as long as I didn't attempt to deny the spirituality of the experience, my terrors and my screaming fits about death simply stopped cold. For another, it was the impetus for a temporary return to Catholicism, because that was a safe and socially acceptable place to explore the spiritual feelings and ideas I had. And it did create a schism with John that was the beginning of the end of our marriage, because not only would he not accept what had happened, he condemned it. I was upset that I was going to be hampered in finding out more about this new world because my husband thought I was totally crazy. In some areas of my life, I *am* totally crazy, but this is not one of them.

I was especially flabbergasted because we'd met over our mutual obsession with that very question of death. I felt as if I had this wonderful thing to teach and he didn't want to learn. To be rejected and scorned in that way didn't make me stop loving him, it just made me not want to be with him anymore. I felt betrayed. I couldn't bear to deny the answer that I'd begged for all my life. Whether anyone else believed it or not, it was mine.

Now, my comfort with these ideas is such that I'm not compelled to force others to believe or explore as I do. I am now extremely cautious about where I have these kinds of conversations. They scare people. For many years I myself would hear people talk about things like reincarnation and out-of-body experiences and it just wasn't for me, it didn't click. I believe that on that night, because I had fasted and not slept, because I'd been working closely with people who believed in psychic phenomena, I was in such a meditative, receptive state that the energy that allows you to know these things came through. I believe that each of us has a time to receive this message about life after life and that was mine. I also believe we all come here with it and we lose it as we go. We forget. Looking at infants has always fascinated me because I think, "Look at that baby. What does it know that I don't?" There's something in those eyes that shows an understanding of eternity that we've forgotten.

About a year later, in mid-1978, I had to deal with death in a different form when I found out that Ethel Ross had died. Initially, after John's death in 1970, I tried to stay in touch with her. It was important for me to maintain contact with Ethel; after the abrupt loss of my father and John Ross, I didn't want her to die before we were able to make peace with each other.

After Sean was born, I made the trip to Mecca to show her the baby, and there were phone calls after that. Ethel came to visit a few times after John and I moved into our house, and once she happened to say something derogatory about my mother. And John, very graciously but very strongly, admonished her and said there would be no more of that; in our house my mother was to be respected. Subsequently, my mother decided to move out to Los Angeles, and I told Ethel that she was still more than welcome to visit, and that as long as basic ground rules of decency could be observed, it would be great to continue the relationship. And I never heard from her again.

When my brother moved out to California as well, he wanted to find Ethel for the same reason I did, to resolve old hostilities as much as possible. We tried to locate her, but I probably wasn't as diligent about it as I could have been. Then one time John and I were driving around Palm Springs and I started talking about J.R. and Ethel, as I always do when I'm in that neck of the woods. We happened to pass by the contemporary furniture store they'd bought when they moved to the desert and I pointed it out to John, who said, "Maybe she's in there."

"No, no, she's been gone for a long time."

"She could still be around."

"No, no."

"Well, do you want to go in and look?"

"No, no, no, it's too late."

Within two weeks we read in the trade papers that Ethel Ross had died. So close and yet so far. Part of me was deeply, deeply shaken that she was gone. The idea that she didn't exist anymore was very frightening to me, and the idea that she might exist somewhere else was even more frightening. Occasionally while I'm reminiscing about the Rosses I still say to myself, "Boy, I'm really going to get whacked for this one."

But in another sense I felt no remorse at Ethel's death, no "I'm worthless, I should kill myself, I'll never be forgiven now" kind of thing. A memorial service was arranged at Ethel's home and my brother, his wife, Lucille, and I drove there together. We laughed all the way down, I mean *all* the way, reminiscing and telling Bambi-the-dog stories until my sister-in-law screamed that she was going to wet her pants. For all of the turmoil that everybody had endured, I thought having the kids come back laughing turned out to be a nice way to honor Ethel Ross.

When I look back on the Rosses, what I recognize now is that one couldn't have accomplished anything without the other. John had the brains, the show biz cunning and savvy, but Ethel was the engine, the motivating force. It was all theory until she forced him to put it into action. And she was a remarkable force, literally indomitable. Ethel had a kind of power over people that was almost unfair: a mere look of disapproval got right to your core and wiped you out, and the slightest nod of approval, which was all the kudos one ever got from her, could spur you on for days. I'm still not sure where this strength came from, but to everyone involved with her, Ethel's opinion was paramount.

One of the most lasting positive legacies I have from my time with the Rosses, aside from the great gift of acting, is an obsession with the truth. Because so much of my early life was filled with lies, clever distortions, and half-truths twisted to fit other people's self-serving needs, I've sworn, "God-damn you, now I will tell the truth." I can take anything that anyone says to me, I may be hurt or ticked off, but I don't completely reject the person. Unless they lie to me and I catch them. That's absolutely intolerable.

Both John and Ethel Ross have been dead for some time now, and it's been more than two decades since they've had control over my life and career, yet I'm still not sure I can consider them with any kind of objectivity. A difficult fact that I've finally accepted is that there will never be a true resolution of my feelings, I'll never finish with them till I'm dead. To me, there are people, and then there are the Rosses.

Yet my feelings have become manageable and giving them their due, not compromising their integrity, is very important to me. I feel terribly responsible to people who are dead. Try as I might to be fair, I'm afraid they're going to turn out to be the villains of this piece, and I wish that weren't so. It's obvious to me that had they not crossed my path, the likelihood of my becoming an actress was slim, and the joy of that far outweighs any of the pain. I know they started out with the best intentions toward me, but fame and success distorted their perspective.

More than that, there is a goodness about them that they left behind in me, that they would have left behind in no one else. They made me into a real believer. I believe in hope, I believe you can change things. I saw what they did to me in a positive way and what they tried to do in a very negative one. Out of the agony that living with them became, a strength developed. I know that change can happen, and that you *can* recover.

An example of that is my relationship with my mother. I'd made many overtures to her off and on during the years after I'd broken free of the Rosses, but either they were inept or she wasn't ready or maybe she was afraid.

About seven years ago I woke up one morning feeling very restless and needing to talk to my mother, who was living with my sister, Carol, in upstate New York at the time. I called and asked Carol, "What's the matter with Momma? Something's bothering me." It turned out that my mother had become so severely depressed she had to be hospitalized at a psychiatric facility. I told Carol, "It's my turn now. I'll take over."

I called Dr. Arlen and told him what was happening. Then I called my mother, and her voice sounded so weak, it was as if she were willing herself to die. I really thought we were losing her this time. I kept her on the phone all day, until my sister could get over, and then I immediately flew to New York. Her room was tiny and barely lit, it looked like a funeral home. I took my mother's hand and said, "You have to come with me. You have to trust me. I can help you."

We flew back to California together, and with Dr. Arlen's help she made a complete turnaround in only four weeks. At times I lament that it took seventy years for her finally to get a lease on life, but on the other hand it's certainly better that it happened late than never. She lives in her own apartment near my house and she's a delight to have around—we laugh and have great times together. Things aren't disguised anymore. When either one of us needs something, we speak up and deal with it. What with her hearing aid, cane, bifocals, and the rest, the kids call her the bionic grandma, but she plows right on.

Having this reconciliation with my mother has been a kind of ultimate satisfaction for me. She's the last, most important parental figure in my life, and when she dies there will have been a resolution that I was never able to achieve with any of the others. Our relationship has become almost too good to be true, and I cherish that.

THIRTY-TWO

Except for an occasional film role here and there, most of my adult career has been in television, not theatrical features, and my actor's competitiveness has made that really bothersome at times. It was mind-boggling to have a whole market shut down to me. I think the problem has been that I'm perceived as "everywoman," which is not the physical type of leading lady that's been featured in movies for the last ten or fifteen years. I'm not exotic, I'm not a willowy Meryl Streep, I've got my own kind of sex appeal, but I'm not stereotypically sexy. That's why I think if I'm ever going to be really hot in features, it's going to be in my forties. Those are the types of mature roles I would really play well.

Yet over the past several years I've stopped feeling like the bastard stepchild; I'm now comfortable being a television star. Of all the things done on TV, I get a crack at some of the best. I do some awfully good work and I've gotten eight Emmy nominations, more than any other straight dramatic actress, and it's heartening to be respected by my peers. But what really has made the difference for me is my relationship with the public. When I walk around in a shopping mall or get on an airplane, there are no great crowds of screaming teenagers (or even screaming middle-aged folks) but rather a constant flow of people who find me very easy to approach and who tell me that when they see my name on a program, they know it's something they want to watch. There is an awful lot to be said for feedback like that.

Some of my roles, for all kinds of reasons, are more memorable than others. Who will ever forget (though I'd obviously like to) a *Movie of the Week* called *Black Widow*, in which I played a spider. Actually, I played a person who was a spider, but why quibble? Every day at six A.M. I'd report to a dark, freezing sound stage and have a piece of latex in the shape of an hourglass applied to my tummy. During the shooting the makeup man would lie on the floor, blow into a tube, and make the latex pulsate. Nice, Academy Award–winning actress standing there in black bikini underwear while a guy blows into a latex hourglass. Terrific stuff. And they wanted me to have some kind of a foreign accent, but I wasn't allowed the time to develop one, so I sounded like my dog trying to do Marlene Dietrich. Oh, it was hideous, but I made some money.

More positive experiences were three performances that brought me Emmy nominations. In 1976 there was *Captains and the Kings*, in which I played a character whose personality was supposedly modeled after Rose Kennedy. I aged from about sixteen to eighty-three and just had a ball waltzing around in those period clothes and playing the great lady. I was very surprised when the Emmy nomination came, and the night of the awards show I was as nervous as I've ever been professionally. Would I be able to wipe out the memory of 1970? All five kids went, all in tuxedos, and I wanted an Emmy just for getting them dressed. When I won, I finished my speech by saying I was the most grateful to my husband and my sons for their patience with a working mother, and then I thanked John for teaching me how to love and be loved in return. I had purged the past and completed the way back, and that made the evening very important to me.

When I took the role of Martha Washington for the 1983 George Washington miniseries, I was surprised at how little had been written about her. Barry Bostwick had libraries and libraries to refer to on every detail and idiosyncrasy of George, and all I knew about Martha was that she was short and fat and had a lot of money. As far as typecasting goes, I guess they figured two out of three wasn't bad. At any rate, I conjured up Martha and said, "Look, I don't really know what to do with this. But George was younger than you, he was tall and gorgeous and did everything right, plus he was the Father of our Country, so I'm going to assume that you were just gaga over the guy and that's how I'm going to play it." I was astounded, absolutely astounded to be nominated for an Emmy, and even more astounded by Barry's not getting a nod. Out of all the hundreds of actors in that series, I was the only one singled out.

In 1979, between those two performances, came the one that was most special, and that was, once again, *The Miracle Worker.* Playing the Annie Sullivan part had always been a fantasy of mine. Even as a child playing Helen on Broadway, I'd put myself to sleep at night not by counting sheep but by going through *The Miracle Worker* dialogue, from the first word all the way through to the last. Part of my interest in the role was very simplistic: that character had dialogue and I'd get tired of having to keep my mouth shut. But more than that, I was fantasizing about being a grown-up, feeling, "Boy, when I can do that, then I'll be an adult."

Even in my adult years I'd invariably think about the play a couple of times a month, but whenever it came up in discussion the response was, "We'll never find a kid small enough to play Helen to your Annie because you're only five feet tall." I never quite bought that, and from time to time as both Sean and Mack were growing up, I would think, "Jeez, he's the right size now. We'll let his hair grow and *he* could play Helen."

Then I found out that Melissa Gilbert of *Little House on the Prairie* had gotten control of the rights and she wanted me to do it with her as a film for TV. She was fourteen years old and exactly my height, but if you closed your eyes and listened, you could almost hear her growing. The deal was struck and after much discussion of billing it was determined that I was to be billed second. And I must say, even though billing is very rarely important to me, that one hurt. This was *my* baby, *my* Helen, *my* Annie, and I thought, who is this child from nowhere? I felt very possessive about the whole thing.

Once I got to know Melissa, though, those feelings were quickly erased. She was a delightful kid who reminded me very much of myself, especially in the area of adult discipline: knowing what to say and when to say it, when to behave like a kid and when to act like an adult professional. Unfortunately, Paul Aaron, the director, with what I'm sure were good intentions, placed an arbitrary barrier between Melissa and me. His approach was, "You will not give this girl hints." Initially, that appealed to me for several reasons. I had my own big job to do, contending with people who automatically look askance at the remaking of classic films. It also relieved me of assuming the practical responsibility of the mentor role with this child. That, plus my need to be the good girl, my need not to make waves, allowed me to agree to something I was to regret seriously later on.

As you can imagine, everything about doing that play the second time around carried a terrific emotional charge for me, and that included sitting around a plain table at a rehearsal hall and going through the initial reading, something that is usually not much of an experience. Because I knew all the lines by heart, I had to pretend to read the script, and occasionally I got caught; someone would notice that I was on the wrong page yet had all the dialogue. I was petrified and thrilled at the same time.

The most important thing to me in playing Annie Sullivan was that I not do an imitation of Anne Bancroft, so much so that even when it came to something I would have done quite naturally and organically, if it sounded the slightest bit close to a rhythm Anne had, I would change it. Sitting there during the reading, I heard all these ghosts in my head. Annie, certainly, but also Torin Thatcher, Patricia Neal, and all the rest. I could hear them in my head just as if there were a tape recorder playing. Plus there were all these live voices which were different from those I remembered; they weren't lip-synching with the tapes in exactly the right way.

It was an extraordinary sensation to be among strangers while experiencing the realization of such a private fantasy.

At the end of the reading, I had to go into the bathroom for about forty-five minutes. I could not stop crying. It wasn't the catharsis yet, but I was getting there.

We'd rehearse the piece during the day and then I'd drive like a maniac so I could wash my hair, set it properly for the character, and perform across town in *The Goodbye People*, with Herschel Bernardi and Peter Bonerz, which was how I was spending my nights. I did that for three weeks, at the end of which I had lost twenty-three pounds and was utterly exhausted. We were four nights short of the end of the play's run when I stood up onstage in the middle of a performance and my legs just gave out. "I can't do it, guys," I said. "I just can't do it." I finished that performance, but I just couldn't go on doing both.

There were many epiphanies during that rehearsal period, but two instances especially stand out. First was putting on the underclothes prior to trying on my costume. For me, wearing a Merry Widow like the one I'd watched Annie Bancroft put on all those nights when I visited her dressing room just before the curtain, that was the passing of the mantle, and when the wardrobe woman held it out to me, I lost it.

The other moment came the first time we got to the miracle and Annie Sullivan screamed, "She knows!" The pain in my chest from this wild combination of a heavy heart and an enormous sense of release was, I thought, more than I was going to be able to bear. The years of wishing to play it, wishing to have that stature, the years of screwing up my life, and then this great gift, the pot of gold at the end of the rainbow, this moment of forgiveness for my transgressions. I thought I would die. Wherever it went from there, no matter what anyone thinks of my performance, that moment in rehearsal, that was my orgasm.

The next step after rehearsals was going to Florida, where we were going to perform the play onstage for two weeks prior to returning to L.A. for the filming. Melissa, however, was having difficulty with her role; there was almost a dullness of heart in her work. I could sense her anxiousness, and in addition I'd very quickly gotten to like her and wanted to help if I could. I was also trying to fill a giant's shoes, but she had the giant standing in front of her, staring her in the face every day. God knows what went on in her head.

I had so far kept my promise to the director, but it turned out he wasn't helping her either. I'd come home every night and say to John, "When is he going to tell her what to do?" It's all very well to want actors to find things for themselves, but this is not a treasure hunt. In my opinion there comes a moment when the search is over, and if the person hasn't found the key to the role, then you have to tell them where it is. Melissa was a very bright young lady. If you told her what to do, she would do it brilliantly and bring her own creativity to the task, but she wasn't used to plunging in on her own. One time I slipped and started talking to Melissa's mother, who would continually ask me how her daughter was faring. Finally I said, "Barbara, she needs help. She can't find it by herself." She said, "Tell her." And I said, "I can't."

Among the specific problems Melissa had was, paradoxically, that she is very graceful. Helen was not graceful, at least not in the elegant way Melissa was. Melissa had very long hair, and in those days she had a habit that many young girls have when their hair falls into their faces of swinging their head and brushing it back so the hair flies through the air. It's very romantic-looking, but it isn't Helen Keller. It should have been a very jerky move, as if she were annoyed by it, not a Farrah Fawcett fling. A more serious problem, however, was that Melissa was not getting the correct sound for that critical "wah-wah" moment.

The combination of all these factors made me feel loaded for bear when our plane took off for the trip to Florida. I sat next to Charlie Siebert, who played Captain Keller, and who has since become a valued friend, and as I was working on my third glass of wine I told him my problem, which by that time was no secret to anyone. Melissa was sitting directly in front of me, baby-sitting her little sister, and finally I turned and said, "The hell with it, Charlie. I'm gonna tell her."

I tapped Melissa on the shoulder and I said, "When you get a chance a little later, I want to talk to you about your part. I'm going to have to break a promise I made to the director, but I feel I'm more honor bound to you than I am to that." And she said, "Oh, great, thank you, thank you. I'll just give Sarah to my mother and we can talk right now."

And she turned around and over the back of the seat we began to chat. The first thing I said was, "If you touch your goddamn hair again, I'm going to break your hand!" She laughed, and I gave her some other notes, both general and specific. Most important, I gave her Arthur Penn's direction for me for the wah-wah sound. I'd never told anyone that—it was Arthur's and my secret, complicated for me by my crush on him. It was very hard for me to do, like giving her a love letter. And, of course, she was embarrassed by it just as I'd been when Arthur gave it to me. But when we began rehearsing in Florida, there were immediate results. She took those couple of little tips, put them to work for herself, and continued to improve until we opened.

Opening night for me was what opening nights are always for me, tripled. John flew out, nominally for the performance, but what he really came for was to hold my head while I barfed. I spent two or three hours that day in my dressing room bathroom, with my costume protected by a huge barber's cape. There was no threat of my forgetting lines here, they'd been engraved in my head for twenty years, but still there was real terror.

And wouldn't you know it, there was trouble even before I got onstage. During the opening scene, with baby Helen still in her crib and the doctor talking to Mrs. Keller, he accidentally knocked his bag off the table and everything the actor had insisted on putting inside, bottles and stethoscopes and little mallets fell from the second floor of the set bouncing and rolling all over the stage. So while the baby was going blind and deaf, the audience was roaring with laughter. I turned to Charlie Siebert and I said, "That's it! That's it! I'm not going out there! That's it."

When I did first walk out on that stage, I felt tiny, and my voice was shaky. I copied a few things from Annie as a tribute to her, very private and backstage, like sitting on my suitcase the way she'd sat on hers. A lot of that first performance was a blur, I was driven purely by adrenaline, but there were moments of sheer ecstasy just knowing that I was doing it. We got a standing ovation when it ended, lots of curtain calls and all that kind of fun.

One of the curious and scary things about that brief stage run was that I occasionally felt my manner with Melissa getting a little too Ethelish. One night during curtain calls, for instance, she was absentmindedly picking her nose. She realized where she was, the audience began laughing, and she sort of looked down at her finger and then took my hand. It wasn't my place to say anything, but I was livid. She was not Half-Pint on that stage, she was Melissa Gilbert playing Helen Keller, and that kind of behavior was not adorable. I felt so close to her, I wanted her to be so good and so perfect that when the curtain came down I turned and said, "If you *ever*, wherever you are in your whole life, behave that way again onstage, *I* will find you and *I* will whack you. You are never to be anything but dignified during a curtain call, and don't you ever forget it." Boy, did that make an impression. Whew. She certainly didn't fool around in curtain calls anymore; she may not even have picked her nose anywhere since.

One of the bittersweet aspects of getting involved with the remake was being reunited with Fred Coe. I had not seen him since 1968, when my behavior on the *Me, Natalie* set had not been up to the standards I would have liked, and certainly not up to his standards, so our parting had not been pleasant. It was good seeing him again under saner circumstances, but he was in very poor health, in fact he could barely walk. He was hospitalized for open heart surgery during the filming and he died on the table. His death really hit me hard. I remember going to work the next day and wailing out loud in my car. He was my last connection to the past, and I missed him so.

When I think about both film versions of *The Miracle Worker*, it's inescapable that the second wasn't as powerful as the first. Not that some things about the remake weren't improvements. The play's original ending was restored, you have the boom-boom-boom momentum of the miracle, Helen giving the keys to teacher, sitting on her lap, kissing her cheek, and teacher signing, "I love Helen forever and ever." For me, that will always be the ending. And even though I still admire the courage of not going to closeups in 1961, I think in the newer version the more personal, quieter moments were well captured because they were done in that television closeup style.

One reason we had to go to closeups in the remake, however, was that the director was unable to build emotional momentum any other way; the choreography of the production was in general lacking in intensity. And doing the picture in color bothered me. Even though *The Miracle Worker* really is a black-and-white movie, you can shoot something in muted colors and come pretty close to that feeling. But the house they used was a yellow gingerbread and it looked wrong, like something from *Oklahoma!* Everything was a little too vibrant for my taste.

As for my own performance, if people were going to dislike it on its own merits, I was prepared to live with that. My fear was that instead, people might accuse me of having done an imitation of Anne Bancroft. I hadn't watched the original for many years, but the night we wrapped I called John and said, "I'm finished and I'm coming home. I'm having a large drink and I'm going to watch *The Miracle Worker*." And I did. And a fascinating thing happened. For the first time I realized that that ghost of a voice I'd kept hearing, the one whose rhythms and patterns I was so afraid of imitating, wasn't Annie's after all. It was my own voice of all those years of reciting the play as I lay in my bed at night. There was no similarity at all between that ghost in my head and Annie Bancroft. "I'll be a son of a bitch," I said. "I fought myself."

And though I'm in general ambivalent about awards, I have to confess that the Emmy I won for *The Miracle Worker* is my favorite acting honor. My enthusiasm wasn't even dampened by not being able to accept in person; there was a Screen Actors Guild strike and I had to watch the ceremony on a snowy little TV on a cross-country train—John and I were touring again. I don't know whether it was the competition with that authority figure of my youth or wanting to be recognized for having the tenacity to hang around long enough to play the Annie Sullivan role or both, but I wanted that award and I was thrilled to have it. It was the perfect end of a perfect fantasy.

My last involvement with *The Miracle Worker*, unfortunately, was a sour one. I'd always been fascinated with the later years of Helen and Annie Sullivan, and my enthusiasm fired up Ray Katz, one of the producers of the TV version, who in turn convinced William Gibson to write a new piece called *Monday After the Miracle*. I was shown an early draft, which we all knew wasn't there yet, and I was told they'd get back to me when the kinks were worked out.

The next I heard about the project, however, was an article in *The New York Times* announcing that it was going to be done as an Actors Studio showcase directed by Arthur Penn and starring Ellen Burstyn. I was shattered. And suddenly, Ray Katz was unavailable for my phone calls or my agent's. When we finally got in touch with him, he said he had done what he could, but he could not convince Arthur Penn and William Gibson to use me. He didn't go into details about what their objection was, and he didn't apologize. I was devastated.

About ten weeks later I got an urgent call from Ray Katz saying that things had not gone well in the showcase and there was renewed interest in me. Even though I knew better, I got caught up once more in the excitement of possibly doing the show. But the same thing happened a second time: I got turned down without any reason being given. Even forgetting about our past relationship, to have a director of Arthur's stature reject me out of hand was a hurt that was insurmountable for a while.

As an actress, you can reject me for a lot of things, and though I won't like it, I'll get by. But *The Miracle Worker* is something else. It's intertwined with a very complex emotional history, and being rejected for that play touched a raw nerve ending. When people speak of my career, even those in the business, rarely do they remember that I started in live television and had played many roles before *The Miracle Worker*. I'm an actress because of Helen Keller; that role was the very foundation of the one area in my life that remained steadfast while all the rest, more often than not, went to hell in a handbasket. Being rejected for *Monday After the Miracle* was like being stripped of my epaulets. It was as if someone had said, "You're *not* Helen Keller anymore, and you're *not* Annie Sullivan either!" If I'd had more perspective at the time, more of a sense of humor, I'd have been in a lot better shape.

THIRTY-THREE

From almost the moment he began to talk, my son Sean was constantly saying, "Can I be in the movies? Can I be in the movies? Please. I can act. Please! Please! Please!" I mean the kid has been running for mayor since he was eighteen months old. John and I didn't ignore him but we really played down that acting bent. Initially, my approach was, "No kid of mine will ever do this." Given what I'd been through, it was the most honest attitude I could have.

It was John who helped me realize how unreasonable I was being, who pointed out that my situation had been unique, that the chances, thank God, of our sons having similar problems were slim to none. These kids weren't being given over to the Rosses or anyone like the Rosses, they were staying with their parents, no matter what. John also used a clever lobbying tactic. He'd say, "Hey, this is an honorable profession. What are we so ashamed about? If we were doctors, we'd want them to be doctors. If we were in the dry-cleaning business, we'd want them to take over that." All those arguments helped to allay my big fear, that it was bad enough to screw up your kids under any circumstances, but to put them into show business, with all the special risks that entails—that was a heavy-duty responsibility.

Then, in 1981, when Sean was ten years old, I was offered an *Afterschool Special* about child abuse called "Please Don't Hit Me, Mom." I wasn't particularly interested, but out of courtesy I agreed to read the script, and when I saw that there was a lovely part for a boy Sean's age, I thought, "What the hell—it would be kind of fun to do it with him." I discussed the idea with John, who hemmed and hawed as he does, and finally he said, "Okay. Take a shot at it."

I didn't feel it was terribly honorable to blackmail the production company by saying I would do the show if they'd use Sean, so I told them I would do it if they'd just audition him, no matter what the outcome. They were delirious at the chance, for the P.R. value if nothing else. And when Sean got the part, he was jumping out of his skin, he was so happy.

Sean was absolutely adorable to look at, and given the irrational behavior he'd witnessed, courtesy of me, he had no problem understanding the feelings of the kid he was playing. The only thing he had a problem with was a scene in which I had to scream at him. Screaming was something private that happened at home, you didn't do it in front of people. He was so embarrassed, he would laugh on camera, which was not exactly what the director had in mind. We were having a real problem, so at one point, just before a take, I looked at him not like the character but with a genuine mean-mother look. Sean was brilliant in the scene, but the poor kid was petrified. I instantly regretted what I'd done, and I told Sean so as soon as the scene was over. I said it was something I would not repeat—from now on he was on his own. He could stink up a scene for all I cared, I was not going to put either of us through that again.

Sean loved everything about the whole movie-making process. He loved the equipment, he loved the people, he loved the attention, he even loved the doughnuts. He just took to it like a duck to water, which frankly didn't surprise us at all. Because Sean's true gift, which becomes so apparent on a set, is that he is completely guileless. His confidence is not an ain't-I-the-cat's-pajamas kind of thing; it comes out of a wisdom, far beyond his or even my years, that this kid just has. And, of course, that makes everyone just want to hug and touch and love him, which can lead to difficulties.

The problem is not with other actors, who, in my experience, are awfully good at parenting a kid on the set. But the people who need something from the child—the director, the assistant director, the wardrobe and makeup people, the crew—will find themselves, even if they're against it in theory, pandering to that kid to get what they need out of him. That makes it very difficult for the parent to monitor and control the child. And if the kid is getting all kinds of approval for what may be aberrant behavior, it's very confusing for him as well: "Mom and Dad keep saying it's wrong, but everybody else seems to like me. Maybe Mom and Dad are wrong."

I've very often found myself, for instance, going to people on a set and saying, "Excuse me. I know you enjoy Sean (or Mack) and that you want to do something nice for him, but I'd really appreciate it if you wouldn't give him any more candy. Why don't you play a game of cards with him instead." I had a problem with one guy who was just crazy about Sean and wanted to be the bad guy with him behind Mommy's back. He was feeding him crap all day long and, because Sean is a high-energy kid anyway, if you shoot him some sugar, forget it, you're scraping him off the walls. I told Sean that if he didn't cooperate, I would go so far as to have memos typed and put up around the set. He said he'd be good, but by then he was out of control—we were finding Hershey bar wrappers and Winchell's doughnut boxes under his bed—so up went the notice. It was very humiliating for him, but once you make a threat like that, you have to follow through.

As opposed to Sean, Mackie was very shy, and at first I didn't believe he'd be able to act. I thought if you told Mack to do something he didn't want to, he would either cry or go stand in the corner until he turned blue, and he certainly would never repeat something more than once for anyone. But the competition between the two boys is intense, and once Sean was on his way, there was no holding Mack back. And he has amazed me with the way he takes direction. His instincts are great, but unlike Sean and me, who are largely instinctive, he's a very intellectual actor, terrific at sizing up a situation, figuring out how to allow the director to believe Mack's taking his direction, and then doing it the right way. Sean doesn't have the time or the patience to go through that.

Mack has been a regular on *The Facts of Life* for the past few seasons, and as pleased as I am that they want him in every episode possible because he's such a draw, I do have qualms about his being in a series. There is always the danger of bad acting habits and sitcom tricks developing; they're very easy for anyone, even an adult, to fall into. And because of the hours he has to work, not only do we have scheduling problems as a family, he's spending most of his time with adults, and that's not as balanced a situation as I'd like it to be.

On the other hand, because Sean and Mack and I have so much in common now, the conversations we have over the dinner table are stimulating and fun. I'm so proud of the work they've done, I really wish parents didn't have to hide just how proud they are in order to be socially acceptable. To go into a theater in Westwood when Sean was in *Goonies*, to sit down in a seat and look at a forty-foot screen with that kid on it—I don't know that I will ever find words to describe how that felt. It was a validation of everything I'd been through, everything that was important to me. Even though his father and I were separated by that time, we held hands in that movie and we both cried. We cried with pride, and with love.

When it comes to relating my own past to their careers, however, I find that very little applies. One of the things I've discovered in general about raising kids is that they really don't give a damn if you walked five miles to school. They want to deal with what's happening now. Sometimes my experience can be helpful. I can remember, for instance, how left out I felt when everyone else got to party after a wrap and I had to get back in the pumpkin. So I try to arrange some alternative fun instead of just saying, "Get in the car, you don't drink vodka anyway."

Because of my experience, however, I have laid down strict rules in certain areas. For instance, there is no such thing as these kids getting home from school and then being dragged to three or four auditions that afternoon. Although we're all ambitious, we're not *that* ambitious. I don't want the boys getting involved in the seamy competitiveness that takes place when you look at a kid who happens to be your size and you hate him already. And I don't want them dealing with rejection on a daily basis. I don't believe in telling people not to take that stuff personally. When I've auditioned and failed to get the part, of course I've taken it as a personal rejection, because they were rejecting me. What else could they have been rejecting—the chair I was sitting in?

The other area in which I'm a real tough cookie is money. All expenses that would normally be taken out of a kid's salary, things like clothing and professional photographs, are paid for, at my insistence, by John and me. It's probably overkill on my part, but I feel strongly about this issue because I was so used by the Rosses. Even though Sean and Mack are acting because they want to, even though they're enjoying themselves, they're also having to give up a certain amount of kid time, and I believe there's a premium on that. And I know the day will come when they're going to say, "I could have done this, I could have done that," so at the very least I want all the money they earn to be at their disposal someday.

Finally, my sons know that until they reach their majority, their parents are the ones in power. They are aware that their situation is under constant reevaluation and that one day their father or I could say, "We've been looking at this, and we really feel it's time for you to stay in high school and play with the other guys."

They know that whatever they get out of acting, and it is considerable, it's not worth the expense of their essential selves. Their parents are really taskmasters when it comes to that. If I feel they're becoming distorted emotionally or spiritually, getting an elevated opinion of themselves, I'm very tough with them, nearly cruel sometimes. I try to cut away the fat and leave them intact. I remind them that there were moments when I thought I was hot stuff, too, but now I'm scrubbing the floor. Right, wrong, or indifferent, that's who I am and they're stuck with me.

When it comes to raising Sean and Mack outside of their acting careers, I deal in more obvious limits and fewer thoughtless indulgences than I did with David and Alan and Tom. On the one hand, the lines of communication are very open—we have great laughs, they know everything there is to know about me. However, Sean and Mack don't have the same freedom to run off to the local hangouts. I have been through kids who've had substance problems, and I do not intend to go through any more. If I have any regrets about my first three sons vis-à-vis my second two, it's that I wish David and Al and Tom could have learned one tenth as much from me as I did from trying to raise them—and failing. I don't mean that they're failures, but that I didn't do it the way I would have liked. I really went to school on them, and that's been invaluable in raising Sean and Mack, and in raising *me*.

One phrase we use a lot around our house was so abused by the Rosses, I thought I would withhold it until the penalty of death was imminent, and that's "I love you." Sometimes we use it to say, "I feel vulnerable," sometimes, "Hey, I'm reassuring you," but never is it used in that completely thoughtless, transparent Hollywood way the Rosses had. I've decided that from the moment we walk out the door until we come back home our sensibilities are so assaulted by the world at large that we have to soak up (and not in a panicked way) as much love as we can get, simply to arm ourselves. It's like going to the gas station for a refill. We humans need to hear "I love you," and we need to hear it as often as we can.

THIRTY-FOUR

Working on *It Takes Two* wasn't like work at all. Never did I dream that I would fall into a situation that satisfying, and never did I dream that it could end so quickly and mysteriously. But those strong, positive feelings had a crucial side effect. During the show's run, in 1982, I had a serious manic attack, and it's only because I felt in such a positive, healthful, safe atmosphere that I didn't cover up again, but had the courage to face the consequences.

The show came together very quickly. I'd met with Paul Witt, Tony Thomas, and Susan Harris to discuss an earlier series, and we'd made a lasting good impression on each other. I had excellent relations with ABC, partially because their top programming executive, Lou Ehrlict, had a son who played baseball with my kids and John was their coach. And both Richard Crenna and I were represented by the same agency. So when the idea for a comedy about a high-powered chief of surgery married to an equally high-powered legal type came up, it took just a twenty-minute meeting before Ehrlict said to one of his henchmen, "Well, what are we all hanging around for? We're going with this, aren't we?" And that was it.

What I loved about *It Takes Two* was that not only was

there a sophistication and intelligence to the characters and the situations we dealt with, but the show also dared to be a little old-fashioned. These folks were not insulting each other all the time, their love for each other and their children was apparent. The show was able to be nice without being saccharine. Even though my part had some problems, the bottom line was I woke up every morning, remembered where I was going, and grinned.

A total of twenty-two episodes of It Takes Two were filmed, and although we weren't off the charts, our ratings were very healthy; even Cheers was invariably behind us. We were seemingly the fair-haired children of the network, and we thought we had a hit. Every once in a while we'd be lying in bed rehearsing and Crenna, whom I adored working with, and I would turn to each other and say with a giggle, "We could be doing this for ten years." I would have been very, very happy to stay there, it felt that good.

Why the show was pulled after those twenty-two shows is something I've never gotten a satisfactory explanation for. What I believe happened is that ABC, panicked and committed to too many new shows, gave Witt-Thomas-Harris an impossible choice. They could have either another season of Benson, which would give that show five years, enough for very profitable syndication, or they could have a second year of It Takes Two. Not surprisingly, we became the sacrificial lamb. That was the year I was voted a People's Choice Award as the most popular television actress for my work in It Takes Two. How do you decide not to stick with something so well liked one more time?

The manic attack I had during the series was touched off not by anything emotional but by an injection. I have suffered on and off from nodes on my vocal chords, and occasionally, when I'm smoking too much and working too hard, I will get laryngitis. We had a show that night, and I needed a quick cure. I went to a doctor who was recommended by someone at the studio, an extremely reputable man who didn't know my history. He wasn't the type who doled out cortisone left and right, but the "show must go on" stuff was being heavily laid on. I was insisting, "In two hours, I have to talk, and I have to talk well." So he gave me a shot, and I did talk well, but since cortisone and manic-depression don't go together at all, the injection instantly kicked off an episode.

Insomnia hit that night. By morning I began having severe diarrhea as well as an overwhelming feeling of nervousness and edginess. Had to go to work, couldn't get out of the bathroom. I finally pulled myself together, but I couldn't eat, I couldn't drink, and I had that old familiar feeling of my motor running but not going in any particular direction.

These symptoms continued for about a week. By then I'd lost a good deal of weight, I was completely dehydrated, and if I wasn't hallucinating, I was certainly paranoid and having extremely volatile encounters with John. Physically I was in such a weakened condition that even navigating was rough, so the show was giving me a ride to the studio. One day I was trying to read through the script but I kept rushing to the bathroom to be sick. Finally, I passed out there and was taken home. Dr. Harold Arlen, our psychiatrist, was called. He came to see me and it was agreed that if I felt well enough, I'd see him in his office the next day.

When I walked into Arlen's office, I was very shaky. He said, "Now, I don't want you to be frightened by what I'm about to say to you. I suspected this before, but because it's such a delicate thing to pinpoint, and because it's something you really don't want to be wrong about, I wanted to be as sure as I could. I think you are manic-depressive."

From that moment on, I wasn't frightened at all. It was such a relief, almost like a miracle, really, for someone to give what I'd gone through a name and a treatment, and I am ever in Dr. Arlen's debt for having the skill and insight to diagnose me. The odd thing is, when I was a kid and had those panic attacks, usually related to dying, I used to pray for a pill. I'd say to myself, "There must be a pill. There's a pill for everything. There must be a pill for this." It turns out that there was.

The best way to describe what goes on during manic episodes is to talk about the mood swings, from very high euphoria to very low depression. In the manic phase, you're wired, you're edgy, your speech pattern changes. You talk very quickly, almost as if you're on speed, and one of the reasons I was often accused of being on drugs is because the behavior is similar to drug-induced activity. And when you're in the real pit of the depression, you can look zonked out, as if you're on Quaaludes.

Insomnia is a manic trait, as is spending a lot of money. Someone entering a phase will suddenly go on a wildly irrational shopping spree, buying things they not only don't need or want but will never use. We're not talking about spending too much money at the department store; we're talking about buying five or six cars in a week or, in my case, flying all over the country in private planes to places I didn't want to be with someone I didn't want to be with. Yet even though it's the disease that's creating these situations, there's a certain amount of responsibility I still insist on taking for the way I acted in them.

The treatment for manic-depression is a carefully regulated, twice-a-day dose of a chemical already present in the body, Lithium. New tests are run periodically to make sure the level of treatment is safe, because everything from climate to stress to how you're eating can affect the dose. This is not a drug that makes you high or alters your mood; if you've got daily irritations—your children aren't listening and the dog is eating the rug—you don't take Lithium and feel better. All Lithium does is help correct an imbalance that's already present in your body's biological systems. Most people who have this condition are born with it, but it can remain dormant, in some cases forever. Different things can trigger it, and by the time I was twenty-four, I'd experienced every trauma on the list, including the separation of my parents and feeling abandoned first by my father and then by my mother.

There are, however, people who are definitely diagnosed as manic and who, for whatever reason, choose not to take their Lithium. Some people are talked out of it by nutritionists who feel there is a natural way to deal with the problem, some people get tired of the pill-taking routine, some people resist the whole notion. Eventually, however, and it could be as long as a year or so later, all of a sudden there's a manic attack or a depression, and they're right back to square one.

For myself, I would rather accept this as a condition I have, recognize the tremendous positive change in me, and say to myself, "This is it. For the rest of my life I take a pill in the morning and a pill at night." Some creative people are especially resistant to Lithium; they believe that creativity is born of nutsiness and if you're insane, you're a genius. In fact, I've found that my creativity has been enhanced by the treatment, that the comfort I now feel with myself allows me to take much bigger risks than I ever would have before. The down side of the drug is so small compared to the release of my power over myself, why mess around?

The difference Lithium has made in my life starts with the absolute basics: being able to get up in the morning and not be afraid, not having the very first thought in my head when I wake and the very last thought before I go to sleep be of death. I have a sense of self-control in every area of my life—control of eating habits, control of sleeping habits, control of money-spending—that I never experienced until after Lithium therapy began. Even basic organization, something as simple as listing ten things and doing them, used to be impossible for me because I couldn't organize my thoughts.

And while I still have a great deal of anger in me, much of it left over from what I went through with the Rosses, my ability to control my temper is light-years ahead of what it was. The only people who would probably give a bigger testimonial for Lithium than me are my kids. These are the people who witnessed and suffered the most during those times when their mother was out of control.

One night, a few months after I'd begun with Lithium, it was around midnight and I kept hearing a thumping from the wall my bedroom shares with Sean's. I opened the door and I saw a person half-in and half-out of Sean's window, and I let go with the most blood-curdling, unearthly scream I have ever produced. The person dropped to the ground and I ran to the front door and started screaming, "Call the police, call the police!" Then as the intruder fled around the corner, I recognized his shirt and realized it belonged to one of Sean's friends. Now I wanted to kill Sean because his friend had scared me to death. I started yelling, "Sean, you little shit, get up!" On my way to Sean's room I ran smack into Mackenzie, who was sobbing and howling, his whole body just racked with agony. I turned to him and said, "It's okay, it's okay, I thought it was a burglar." And he said, "A burglar? Oh, thank God! I thought you forgot to take your Lithium."

All of which emphasizes one of the key points about Lithium. It's not a panacea, it doesn't do away with life's little (and not so little) problems. When I started my Lithium therapy, it didn't mean I ended my fruitful psychiatric work with Dr. Arlen, it meant I could begin. I could face life as a garden-variety neurotic, not a green, squirrely monster. Lithium is not a cure for living. It's a tool.

THIRTY-FIVE

That man in the White House may not have noticed, but in my life 1985 was a presidential year, and not once but twice. I played America's first female president in *Hail to the Chief*, and then I became the real-life president of the Screen Actors Guild. Not bad, I couldn't help thinking, for a scrawny kid from East Thirty-first Street.

Hail to the Chief was like manna from heaven. Just when my usual money problems were peaking, boom, there's a series. Not only was it a Witt-Thomas-Harris production again, but the cast was a group of creative actors I enjoyed working with, high-powered, high-performance horses every one. I thought the pilot was the best thing I'd ever read for half-hour television. We came out of the chute very well, and then, just like *It Takes Two*, suddenly the show was off the air for no apparent reason.

Not that we didn't have our problems. For one thing, the follow-up scripts didn't have the genius of the pilot. The reason for that depends on whom you listen to, whether we made the network nervous and they clamped down or Susan Harris went off and gave most of her attention to *Golden Girls*. Whatever the cause, we wound up with a very poor bastardization of what had gone before, a show that wasn't even bizarre anymore, just silly.

The other difficulty was that even though I enjoyed the show, I did not like my part. My character became deadly dull. The woman never took a stand on anything, she never even had a position in family arguments. The writers chickened out, they were afraid to give me any kind of character quirks because I was the president. Since they didn't know what else to do with me, I became the roll-call person. If you needed to know who the characters in a scene were, just wait a second and the president will tell you. My entire part was a memory contest for what name goes with what face.

Another thing that hurt the show, something I heard constantly from folks on the street, who in general liked the absurdity of the thing, was that they were uncomfortable with my husband, the First Man, if you will, screwing around on his wife all the time. It worked in the pilot because you never saw the other woman, but once she was brought into our living rooms, it set people off. Now I was in a very awkward position, because if I said that to the writers, it would look as if I had an ego problem, that I was afraid my part wasn't big enough because the bimbo of the week was getting that airtime. And that really wasn't the case at all. My position was, if you want the American public to respect and like this woman, if you want them to buy the premise that she's the president, her husband can't be that disrespectful or none of your big jokes will work. I kept quiet, however, and I think I did myself and the show a disservice.

Despite all of this, I was shocked when the show was canceled after seven episodes. Everyone in the cast was in shock, every single one of us. I haven't a clue why we were dropped, to this day no one has even tried to explain. I never expected to see ten years out of that show as I had with *It Takes Two*, because the material was too bizarre, but I did expect a full season. Afterward I told myself, "I need to know why this happened so that it won't happen again," but really, there's no formula you can learn from. What am I going to say? That I won't work for ABC again? Who am I kidding? It's one of the three shops in town. The next person willing to pay the price gets the body. That's the reality.

•   •   •

Despite my abortive appearance for Robert Kennedy and some sporadic antiwar rallies during the Vietnam era, I really date my serious political involvement from my involvement with John. There was much political discussion in our house on a daily basis, and not just around the dinner table. The discussions that went on between John and his brother Sandy and Sandy's wife, Lena, and eventually me were truly exciting and inspirational. They made me want to go out and mix it up in the world.

John's an extremely well-educated man, a stimulated and stimulating thinker, but I'm a doer, so I stole from his thinking and went and did. I don't love danger, I don't want to commit professional suicide, but I've had to face the fact that I no longer like playing it safe either. If a situation arises in which I can be involved, and it's something that I feel is vital to me or my kids or just other people, I'll take a shot at it, even if somebody says, "Hey, you may not work on such-and-such network anymore." I really want to know that I've participated.

Something very critical to my letting go of apathy happened in 1980, during my return to Catholicism. Three celebrities, LeVar Burton, Dick Van Patten, and I were asked by Catholic Relief Services to go to Mauritania, Ethiopia, Djibouti, and Kenya to make public service announcements and help raise money to fight famine in Africa. I'd been asked to go the year before, and frankly, I just hadn't felt equipped to do it. The second time I was asked, I felt a combination of being too embarrassed to say no again and wanting to be able to deal with it. I desperately wanted to stretch and grow and find other purposes for my existence. I was looking for the larger picture, and for answers to the questions, and they were not to be found, as I used to think, in the bathroom puking up overdoses. So even though I was very fearful, I went.

Before I got to the relief camps, I tried to steel myself to imagine the worst, most horrifying thing I was going to see, so that the reality would be less of a shock. I thought the sight of all these thousands of starving people would be the first assault, or the noise they make, the wailing and agony that sounds otherworldly. But the first assault was the smell.

It wasn't the smell of excrement, it was the smell of decay, of death. The total impact of the camps was so overwhelming, so grotesque, I couldn't even begin to absorb it.

Very shortly after the visit to the first camp, in Mauritania, a headache began that stayed with me for two weeks, a headache that no amount of aspirin or anything else could get rid of. Sitting under the stars one night in Kenya, stars so close you feel you don't even have to straighten your arm to touch them, I had to face the fact that what this headache was caused by was repressed rage.

First there was my own impotence. I mean, what goddamn good was my public service announcement going to do in the face of all this, no matter how much money it raised? Then there was the anger at man's inhumanity to man, at the way none of the systems we've set up really work. I'd even confronted Father Kaiser, the Catholic priest who was with us, in the middle of a shantytown where death was happening all around. "What do you say to these people?" I demanded. "What's the answer? You're supposed to know."

But this one night under the stars in Kenya, there were a bunch of us sitting around the camp, and we began to hear really boisterous singing off in the distance. Someone got curious so we jumped into the Land-Rover and headed off. We found maybe two hundred people, members of the Kakama tribe, people whose children were dying during the day, singing and doing this ritual jumping dance with such jubilation, such joy.

We pulled up and they were thrilled to have visitors. They loved Father Kaiser because he was big and gawky and silly-looking in the hat he always wore. They wanted him to jump with them, and since the man can't walk and chew gum at the same time, his attempts had them just roaring with laughter. Then they wanted the "little mama" (guess who) to do it, and I was just bent over double, I was laughing so hard. Then I stood up, and my headache was gone.

What I realized then was that for all my bleeding-heart concern, I couldn't begin to make a difference in the lives of these people, and past doing what I could to feed them, maybe I didn't even want to. They were sick and dying and yet something inside them came alive and celebrated the stars and the moon and the fact that they can jump three feet off the ground. I'd never experienced anything like that night.

That trip to Africa lasted a little more than two weeks; my next serious political involvement took eighteen months. That's the amount of time I took off in 1981 and '82 to work for the passage of the Equal Rights Amendment. Given my chronic lack of financial stability, that was quite a decision. But I believed that if we changed the packaging and the P.R. for the movement, something the right wing is so adept at doing, and made it less threatening to the mainstream, we could turn the tide.

I said to my activist gay women friends, who were essential to carrying the movement for a long time, "I know we're Johnny-come-latelys, but just as a political maneuver, step into the background and let us more mainstream-looking folks go into the Midwest and talk about our husbands and our children. As long as the means are honorable, isn't the result all that counts?" Unfortunately, I didn't have the power and the confidence to go out and recruit more women like me, and I never got a lot of support for my position. I understand that, but given how things turned—or didn't turn—out, I think it's regrettable.

Though over the years I've gotten myself involved in so much public service work I've grown fearful of becoming "caused out," two areas still get as much attention as I can possibly muster. One is fund-raising for AIDS research and awareness; any group that comes to me about that gets my help. The other cause is nuclear disarmament, and what involved me there was a promise I made to my son Mackie.

Mackie was having something called "night terrors." He would start out of his sleep, absolutely terrified, and no amount of consoling helped. We'd just have to wait until the screaming was spent. Unlike my own early fears, he at first didn't seem to be terrorized by anything specific.

But eventually it became apparent to me from conversations while we were watching the news that Mackie was not just concerned by the potential of nuclear holocaust the way most of us are, he really was quite preoccupied with it. He's always been very articulate, but instead of talking about his fear, he'd ask a lot of questions. Did I think anyone in power was crazy enough to push the button? What if someone flipped out and did it? What if this, what if that? From my experience with the Rosses I knew telling him not to worry wasn't going to help, but I didn't know what to say. Frankly, I was just as scared as he was.

One week *Newsweek* came out with a cover story about *The Day After*, the TV movie about post-holocaust society. Mackie saw the magazine lying on the breakfast table and started asking me these questions again, until I felt, "If he asks me one more like that, I'm going to scream." And then he said, "How come you're not involved in any of the nuclear freeze groups? You do the E.R.A. and famine relief, you do this and you do that, but what good is it going to do if we all melt?"

"Mackie, please. I can't get involved in one more cause. There are people out there doing it."

"Yeah, but there aren't enough people doing it."

"Mackie, you know I have little enough time at home. Don't send me out there. I can't do this."

And he kept challenging me and challenging me. Then tears welled up in his eyes, he started to cry, and he told me how tired he was of being afraid. Finally, he just said straight out, "What are you going to do about it?"

"I don't know what to do about it," I said, "but I'll find out."

I said I couldn't promise him that there wasn't going to be a nuclear holocaust, or that we're not all going to drop dead from who knows what, but that if there was anything I could do in my limited way, I would. And I did, and Mackie has fewer night terrors now. I have nothing really to offer the nuclear freeze movement except one more voice, one more person with the ability to show up and give a speech, and Mackie's smart enough to know that. But that someone who loves him is making an effort is a consolation to him. It's that simple.

Although I've now been a Screen Actors Guild member for twenty-five years, I had absolutely nothing to do with the union until the second half of the *It Takes Two* season.

That's when one of the show's regulars, Richard MacKenzie, and a friend of his, Paul Kreppel, who years later became my campaign manager, asked me to become involved with an organization that was formed to support the merger of SAG with AFTRA, one of the two other actors' unions. That's how my appetite got whetted to understand not only the purpose of unions but also what goes on in them.

Several things attracted me to working for SAG. For one thing, although doing a series and running a family might seem like enough for anyone, it wasn't for a person with my high energy level. And after I'd gotten involved, what hooked me was a combination of enjoying the sense of personal affirmation and seeing that I had an effect. "My God," I said to myself, "I can make a difference." I began staying abreast of and taking a serious interest in union matters, and I stopped throwing away mail from SAG that didn't say "residual" on it.

I'd been seriously involved in union work for about three years when I got a call on a Saturday morning from Ed Asner, the outgoing SAG president. I could hear a hubbub in the background and Ed began, "A group of us are in a meeting here . . ." Ed and I had met several times at various functions and although he'd never said word one about me succeeding him, my intuition plus the tone of his voice and the circumstances of the call made me guess what was on his mind, so I jokingly said, "You've got the wrong number." Then he said, "I don't want to pressure you," and I said, "Oh, my God," because I realized my guess was right. I told him that I needed a couple of hours to think it over, or a hundred years.

Once I decided I would run for the office, I really wanted it. I didn't want to even think about losing. Although I was sure that some people might be voting for me because they recognized my name or admired my work or thought I was good on talk shows, I was determined to be totally prepared. I worked really hard doing my homework. I gathered boxes and files and stacks of material, and come nine o'clock every night I was in my room reading. It was exhausting, but I didn't want to be standing at a press conference taking questions and have to say, "I don't know.

Let me ask my press secretary." I have too much ego not to get completely behind anything I begin.

Aside from the things that had initially interested me in union work, I realized that part of the attraction was that it would be a great way to practice politics in a relatively safe environment. I'd had thoughts of running for public office, and this would be a way to see how I liked the political process. And what I've found since I've been elected is, quite frankly, that given how stressful and time-consuming an experience it's turned out to be, I think I've had enough. Besides, being a manic-depressive is a political liability. I know that Lithium works, but convincing voters of that is a different story. *The New Yorker* did run a charming piece comparing my career to Ronald Reagan's, and people began asking me if I'd thought about national politics. But now that I've experienced the kind of pummeling that goes with the territory, I'm not at all sure I want to be king, or even queen.

Winning the SAG election, however, felt great. It wasn't quite like getting an Oscar or an Emmy, because there was an element of worry attached to the excitement. Now I had to put my money where my mouth was. Personally, the most important thing was finally receiving indisputable proof from my peers that I was respectable, respectable enough to be the leader of the fifth largest union in the United States. That was very moving and important to me.

I can remember going in to work at SAG the morning after the election to accept the gavel from Ed Asner, driving along Sunset Boulevard and passing all the houses that had some, usually unpleasant, memory for me. This person had said I was unstable, that person had called me a dingbat, that manic episode had happened—I was ticking them off as I drove. I wish I could say that I was thinking about what a victory for liberalism the election was, or that it was great for the women's movement, but I didn't feel any of that. The sense of triumph was intensely personal.

A similar thing happened when I won the Southern California chapter of Americans for Democratic Action's first Eleanor Roosevelt Award for my political and social commitments. When a group of people dedicated to a particular ideal that matters to me, that denotes responsibility and value to society, gives me an honor like that, it affects me at the very core of who I am and who I need to be. It legitimizes my father's short life, it does the same for my mother's seemingly ignorant existence. And it also makes me recognize that I don't have the right to attempt suicide, that in whatever infinitesimal way, I'm making a difference. And that makes a difference to me.

THIRTY-SIX

John and I were great at the big issues. The spiritual connection between us was so strong it genuinely felt as if it must predate this lifetime. It was the everyday living that we couldn't handle. We never lived a day—not a day—in our relationship without real stress. Coasting was unheard-of. There was always at least one crisis going on, whether it was precipitated by me or by a kid or by our finances. Still, we shared the undying hope that the time would come when the crises would clear and we would have peace. It never did.

One of the first areas where stress became apparent is in what I now see as a search on my part for limits. Sometimes, when we were touring, I'd get really haughty with John if he was directing me and say, "I'm not doing that. I don't give a damn what you want, I'm not doing it." When you've got a stage manager and other people standing there, that's very embarrassing, almost as if I were saying, "Wanna see castration? I'll show you castration!" But John had the ability to tune out, and although my hostility would have stopped a lot sooner if he'd addressed the situation with a "Hey! That's rude, you little bitch! Quit it!" he invariably just let it all slide.

The worst example of this kind of behavior occurred in

1978, on the pilot for a series called *Rossetti & Ryan* that John was directing and I was doing a guest shot on. There was one scene for which I'd done two takes that we both knew were very good, and then he leaned over and whispered that he'd like me to do it one more time. If any other director had said that, even if it bugged me, I would have swallowed the bug and done it. But although I responded quietly, so no one could see, I turned on him with great force, saying, "How dare you ask me to do it again? You *know* it was terrific. How dare you humiliate me this way in front of other people." Of course, I did the third take and because I was so angry and upset, it was the best of the lot.

We went to see dailies the next day, and it turned out some of the better takes weren't usable because the angle of the camera wasn't what it should have been, and once again I was livid, exhibiting a "how could you do that to me" kind of ugliness that I never would have shown with another director. During the drive home I opened the car door and tried to get out while we were doing sixty-five miles per hour on the freeway.

Some of this can be chalked up to my illness; people in a manic episode tend to pick fights. But some of it was also a way of punishing John for his infuriating distance, for not noticing a host of other problems or not wanting to deal with them if he did. Even more basically, I was asking him just how far he could be pushed: How far can I go before you don't love me anymore? How many times can I shoot a clever, witty one-liner and embarrass you before you pull the plug?

And, of course, there never was a limit. As the years went on, my respect for him diminished greatly because he didn't stand up for himself. He didn't say, "Look, I'm a person too. There are days when *I'd* like to commit suicide. You gonna love *me*?" It's tragic, because I'm sure his tolerance was based on love, but that limit became more and more important to me.

In 1978 I had a hysterectomy, which was traumatic because the ability to have babies had been a fail-safe mechanism for me, a way I could be sure of feeling attached and loved. On the other hand, it was a relief to be finished with

surgeries in that department and not to have to worry about
cervical cancer or, for that matter, contraception, because I
think that in the back of my mind I was for the first time
entertaining the idea of either leaving John or not being
faithful.

It was another year before the real intention of having
an affair occurred to me, and though I went as far as arrang-
ing an assignation, I chose someone who was impotent.
Wasn't that clever of me? Who knows what makes the world
work the way it does? The idea was certainly there and I'm
responsible for that. But the fact that the act was never
completed made the guilt a thousand times less.

Still, John found out about it, and we had a marathon
confrontation session that lasted close to twenty-eight hours.
I told him I didn't feel attractive anymore in a house filled
with unkempt boys who were noisy and uncaring, that I was
tired of his analyzing my every move, I was eager for someone
who accepted me as I was. Though he was absolutely devastated, John was a mensch about it and we decided to use the
situation as a way to start all over again. We embarked on a
new approach with each other. We spent more real time
together, not just taking up the same space. And even
though it didn't last, for a while I fell in love with him all
over again.

What finally happened to our relationship was that many
of the very good things about it turned into very bad ones.
At first John's love seemed unconditional, but eventually I
found out what the conditions were. Although for years I was
very defensive when people suggested this, I came to believe
that there was indeed a strong father-daughter link between
us. The all-knowing, all-seeing, all-protective and God-like
idea I had of John, an idea that I so craved at first, eventually turned out to be abhorrent to me when I was old enough
to want to be an equal partner.

As long as I was dependent and subservient and John
was the caretaker, everything was fine. Even though he was
always as supportive as he could be, he'd become so comfortable with the father-daughter, patient-doctor, mentor-student
relationship, he couldn't let go of it. If I got too healthy or
too strong, there was no basis for the relationship anymore.

I'm a much more productive person since I'm not married to John. It's astonishing to me what I've been able to accomplish in every area of my life since the divorce. The false dependency between us was very enervating; instead of feeding, we bled each other.

John and I had a few brief separations, and during those crises and all others, my across-the-street neighbor and best friend, Mary Lou Pinckert, would simply be there. We had an "I'll just run across and see if Mary Lou is making a cheesecake" kind of back-fence closeness. She had the kind of homespun, very basic bottom-line approach to life that really was a ground to me. I would be wandering around the backyard thinking of the most inventive way to kill myself and Mary Lou would be inside the house coping. That kind of selflessness is something I'd never witnessed before.

The final conflict, the one that irrevocably broke John and me apart, came in 1984, when he joined a Buddhist group. John's father, whom he'd been extremely close to, had just died, and I came home late one night to find John sitting in the den. He told me that he'd found "the answer" and that it was Buddhism. I began to weep and it turned into one of the heaviest crying sessions I've ever had, sobbing that lasted for hours until my face was swollen and distorted. I was enormously relieved that he'd found something that was spiritually important to him, that he wasn't going to die not believing.

But within a few days I began to feel very threatened. John maintained it was because Buddhism was alien to my culture, but that wasn't the problem at all. It was a deep feeling inside of me that this espousal of Buddhism was not so much a full revelation as a thinly veiled substitute for his father, for me, for everyone, that it was an attempt to isolate himself still further from the kinds of everyday concerns he'd never wanted to deal with anyway. I see nothing wrong with chanting, it does have a very salutary effect on people, but John became so obsessed with the procedure that everything revolved around it. If you said, "I'm going to have a cup of coffee," it somehow related to one of the sutras.

Also, John determined that he wanted to proselytize and convert all of us. The great ecumenical spokesperson of this household, the parent who'd insisted our children not be forced into any religion, was now beating us all over the head with his chanting. And this was the man who'd belittled and refused to take seriously what I felt was my own spiritual revelation. I was enraged. Buddhism became the new battleground.

John was already a complete vegetarian and he now wanted the equivalent of two totally separate kitchens in the house, meaning two sets of dishes, two sets of utensils, even two refrigerators, one in which there would be no meat or meat by-products, and one for the rest of us. That was fine with me; if I'd wanted to eat cat food, I wouldn't want somebody picking on me for that. The problem I had was with John's *gohonzon*, the Buddhist shrine he wanted to put in our living room and make available to complete strangers to chant at whenever they felt like it.

"Why can't you have it in the upstairs room?"

"It has to be in a more prominent place."

"Don't you have a whole building in Santa Monica? Go play over there anytime you want."

"So you're not going to allow me to worship as I see fit in my own house?"

John felt he couldn't live with that kind of religious oppression and that I still had a lot of straightening out of my head to do. And we kind of left it at that.

John and I had endless discussions during this period, and during one of them I finally asked a very basic question: "What do you want out of life?" And he said, "I want to contemplate." And for the first time in our marriage, I recognized the age difference. It finally hit me that the man was going to be fifty-six years old. He didn't have to stay on the out-of-control treadmill; he'd earned the right to contemplate if that's what he wanted to do. What I also realized was that it's not my time to contemplate, it's my time to do. I still have to gather all those little nuts before I can sit down and look them over.

Then, in January of 1985, John went up to San Francisco to do a play. He was still a notoriously slow study, so a couple of nights before he was to open I went up there on a mission. Within forty-eight hours he had to have all those words in his head. That was my olive branch, my gift to him because I loved him.

Once I arrived, I catered to any possible need I thought John had. I drilled lines with him, I made suggestions about the play, I chanted with him, both in his apartment and at a meeting hall, I ate the kind of food he wanted to eat, and if I needed to smoke, I did it in the hall near the elevator. I even bought him a *butsudan*, a rosewood cabinet for his *gohonzon*. I was going well beyond what I considered my duties as a wife, much less an estranged wife, but I was in need too.

It was about three o'clock in the morning, we were lying in bed after having drilled some lines, and a song came on the radio. It was "I Just Called to Say I Love You" and I said to John, "Oh, just listen to these words. I want you to hear these words." And, at three o'clock in the morning he picked up the phone and called his machine in Los Angeles and listened to his messages. And then he had a difficult time understanding why I was upset at being ignored. He said he really needed to hear his messages and I replied that it was considered bad form to return people's calls at three in the morning. Push came to shove, as it usually did. He told me how selfish I was being and I told him to go to hell.

I slept on the couch that night, or tried to, and sort of patched things up the next morning. I helped him with his lines again, went to rehearsal with him, ate some vegetarian food, but when we got back to the apartment and I smoked a cigarette in the bathroom, he made a great show of coughing. I was feeling more and more uneasy, and then his mother called. He got on the phone with her, and I got angrier and angrier, thinking of all the past efforts I'd made. He came out of the bedroom and said something grand and unkind, I can't remember what it was, and I punched him in the face.

I immediately apologized and made sure there was no damage done. He cursed me and left, but he called from the theater and said, "Please don't do this to me, it's opening night." So even though I'd had every intention of leaving, I went there and ran through his lines with him one last time. I stood in the back of the theater, willing every word out of his mouth, and he did fine. I saw him back at the apartment later and told him that I was going back to Los Angeles and filing for divorce. He didn't believe me, but I did it.

With all these problems, why did we stay together for so long? Because I loved him and he loved me. It's an elusive, indescribable ingredient, love is. It doesn't come in words, I can't tell you what it is, but it's as sure as anything I can taste or smell or hear. There was a sense of security in being with him that permeated my body, my psyche, all my surroundings. I felt I could touch his steadfastness. All those things that we're supposed to have as children, I was experiencing for the first time with John. There is something to be said for being adored, and he adored me.

On the day the decree became final, I walked in the door after being in court, and John was phoning me. He still couldn't believe it. He said, "'You didn't *really* do it," and I said, "Yeah, I did." And he talked a lot about how divorce doesn't mean forever. And that was it. The kind of love we had for each other never goes away, but although the kids, especially, have a hard time understanding this, being in love or loving isn't necessarily enough. Quite simply, there was nothing more I could bring to his life, nor he to mine.

In the fall of 1985, I began work on a TV movie called *A Time to Triumph*. The SAG campaign was going on, that was certainly taking up time and energy, but I needed to work, I needed to act, and as usual I needed the money, so this was once again a godsend. *Triumph* was based on the true story of a woman who joined the army in her thirties so that she could get medical benefits for her ailing husband. That meant location work at Fort Benning in Columbus, Georgia. It felt like quite an adventure, me the pacifist playing a soldier. I didn't know the half of it.

My first day on the base I was introduced to a pair of drill sergeants whose job was to get me through different stages of basic training so I'd look as if I knew what I was doing when we did it on film. One of the sergeants did most of the talking. The other one, the quiet one, was named Michael Pearce. Married, age thirty-one, eight years younger than me, and an eleven-year army man, he'd just come out of drill sergeant's school. He'd been sent there from Airborne, a much more exciting place, and much more to his liking. Mike had never wanted to be a drill sergeant, and I find it silly even to think of him that way—screaming in people's faces is not what he does best. When he was told they needed a couple of drills to teach Patty Duke, he didn't even want to go for the interview, but they said he had to and he ended up one of the two chosen.

When shooting started, the other sergeant had to be hospitalized and couldn't be around, so Mike and I were thrown together for more time than we otherwise would have been. He was still just Mike-the-drill, but we went through a rigorous schedule together—I lost eleven pounds the first week—and when it came time to say good-bye after that part of the filming was over, the only thing he said to me was, "I'd hate to lose contact with you. Could you be my little sister?" And that, I thought, was the end.

One Sunday morning, Mike called and said that he and his two daughters, Rayleen and Charlene, were out doing errands. Could he bring them by to say hello? I said sure, and when he asked if he could bring me anything, I asked for some Fudgsicles. When they showed up, Mike told me his wife was in the car and I said of course he should bring her in too. We visited a little, but it felt very awkward and I didn't know why. After they left, I hung around my room, kind of hungry but too lazy to go out for dinner, so I settled for a Fudgsicle. I was lying in bed reading and eating, when I suddenly sat up, startled, and thought, "Holy shit. I'm in love with Mike Pearce." I told myself I was crazy, to forget about the whole thing. Then, a while later, there was a knock on the door. I went to open it and it was Mike. "I'm not going to fight fate, are you," I said. And that was it.

I've been aware from the beginning that the combination of Mike and me seems like culture shock to the nth degree, but the fact is that the passion we feel has been so strong it's had the ability to push everything else aside. We are like epoxy for each other, the attraction is that strong; it heightens all my senses, including the sixth one. And although he's turned out to be one of the more complicated people I've met, there's also a what-you-see-is-what-you-get quality, a welcome simplicity about Mike. There's such pu-

rity and goodness in him, and those qualities come out in the
letters he's written to me; they're publishable poetry. It's hard
to believe that a drill sergeant can be thought of as a gentle
soul, but he is, and that's what I fell in love with.

But while part of me needed Mike and felt this was
someone who was meant to be in my life, there was another
part that wanted to be very honorable and wasn't at all sure
about getting involved with a man who had a wife and
children and the army. How was his wife going to compete
with this kind of romantic interlude with a movie star? It
turned out that he and his wife had been estranged for quite
a while, which was the reason for the tension I'd felt that
Sunday morning. But I insisted he go back and really talk to
her, have them both realize that once our traveling circus left
town, they might be able to pretend this hadn't happened, or
at least learn something from it. I would have hated not to
see him again, but I loved him so much, I could have done
it. But things between them had gone too far, and the papers
for the divorce were signed soon after I left Georgia.

When our engagement was first announced, I'd have
conversations like this once I got back to Los Angeles:

"I understand you're engaged."

"Yes, I am."

"And what's his name?"

"Michael Pearce."

"What does he do?"

For a while I cheated and said, "He works for the
government," but then, after a long pause to set them up, I
said, "He's a drill sergeant in the army."

"He's what?" came the invariable response.

"Drill sergeant—you know, like Lou Gossett in the
movie."

"Now, let me get this straight. You're going to marry a
drill sergeant?"

"Yep." I'd find myself laughing. "The pacifist and the
drill sergeant."

Actually, it didn't matter to me what people thought as
long as it didn't hurt Mike. We talked about how that would
be inevitable sometimes, how it would probably hurt both of
us. But what I really thought was, if I can feel so good in the

company of this man, and feel so good about loving him after I thought that part of my life was over, then I pity those people who don't get it, because it's their loss. That's really how I feel.

Although it took the better part of a year until Mike was able to get out of the army and move to Los Angeles, we talked a good deal early on about his fitting in. Never was there a question about who was going to change life-styles; I could just tell Fort Benning wasn't for me. And even though I'm not the Hollywood party type, occasionally I do have to go to them, and I wanted to feel that he'd be able to survive in my world without smothering who he is. We've come to call that "crossing the Big Street," and though it hasn't been easy by any means, Mike's been able to do it, not just because he looks so good in a tuxedo but because he feels comfortable within himself. Watching him work at that, exploring who he is and what he wants, is watching true bravery.

Mike and I were married on March 15, 1986, about six months after we met. We thought about waiting, but our separation, his being in Georgia and my being in Los Angeles, had been very hard on us, so our getting married that fast was, in part, indulging our insecurities. That hardly means, however, that it was done thoughtlessly; I mean, it seemed pretty damn fast to me too. And it was important to me to consider all the ugly things that I or anyone else might come up with and be able to address them honestly. I wondered if maybe I wasn't doing this for shock value, or to get even with John. I worried about the age difference for all of the hackneyed reasons, like my not looking as good as he does for as long as he does. I worried about inflicting the same kind of Pygmalion experience I'd been through on someone else. But against this was: if it felt right to both of us, then why wait? Of all the reasons that were logical and practical, we couldn't find any that was strong enough to counteract the feeling of wanting to go ahead and be man and wife.

One thing I've never been able to do is live my life by looking down the road. Of course, it is the nature of this business not to be able to look too far into the future, and you do tend to live in the style of your profession. But I also think that, without sadness or fear, I recognize the fragility of life. When I was thirty, ten years seemed so far away, and here I was at the end of those ten years, pushing forty. What was I waiting for? What was the worst that could happen? That I would experience similar unhappiness—and cause similar pain—to what I came through with John. But if that was the worst that might happen, I didn't want to sacrifice the best that could happen right now. Because couldn't the worst happen anyway? None of this means, though, that I for one minute thought our marriage was going to be easy. It's worth whatever Mike and I have to endure for it, but it's not going to be simple.

We got married at Lake Tahoe, in the middle of a snowstorm so big it closed the airport. I got my first look at the chapel the morning of the ceremony, and it was hideously overdecorated. "Take it out, take it *all* out, everything," I screamed. "I want it to look very Presbyterian!" And by seven o'clock they were ready. I, however, was not. Having decided that I couldn't get through the day without a glass of champagne, I was just getting into the shower ten minutes after I was due at the chapel. Mike called. He thought I'd changed my mind. And when I did finally arrive, you could hear everybody laughing because the organist had lost the sheet music for "Here Comes the Bride." To top it all off, the ceremony was performed by a Reverend Love. And everybody cried.

We'd rented seven Lincolns for the wedding party, and, looking like a gangster's funeral, we went from the chapel to Caesars Palace, where we had a great party. We just hooted and hollered and jumped around and danced and laughed. And on the way out, my mother won 150 quarters in a slot machine. The next day, when it was time to head back to Los Angeles, we discovered that even the Reno Airport had been snowed in. Undaunted, we rented a Greyhound-size bus which we dubbed "Camp Run-A-Muck." The ride home took eleven hours, but the kids entertained us most of the way, singing and telling jokes and carrying on. Even though we got in at six in the morning, nobody was complaining.

•   •   •

Embarking on a fourth marriage is not exactly what you have in mind when you're sixteen and fantasizing the way you're going to live your life, and financially, I've always been in a mess and I still am. Up until very recently I've been very unsuccessful at life as we prescribe it in our society. But ever since I was eight years old, the one thing I've done that guaranteed I'd feel alive and part of a family structure was acting. It is as vital to me as having the right amount of oxygen in the air. I'm not a dancer, but *A Chorus Line* put me away, because I so identified with the life force that dancing represented to those kids. That's what acting is to me. It's what I was sent here for.

Looking back now at the ebb and flow of my life, it exhausts me in precisely the way you get tired when you hear someone else talk about a particularly daunting trip they took. Because so much of it now seems to have happened to someone else. I know that history is part and parcel of my being, but I can't feel the pain anymore, and I can remember wondering if that would ever happen.

And there's another part of me that's really tickled by the whole thing, that can say, "Yup, wasn't that funny? Wasn't that terrible? Isn't it amazing that I survived at all?" I'm still my own harshest critic and most demanding taskmaster, but I have moved into a time of being much more accepting of whoever it is I am. I have horrible times, I have great times, I have so-so times, but I wouldn't trade my life today for anyone's, not anyone's.

I've survived. I've beaten my own bad system and on some days, on most days, that feels like a miracle.

ABOUT THE CO-AUTHOR

Kenneth Turan, the film critic for *Gentleman's Quarterly*, has been a staff writer for the *Washington Post* and *TV Guide*, and film critic for National Public Radio's "All Things Considered." He is the co-author of several books.

BANTAM BOOKS
GRAND SLAM SWEEPSTAKES

Win a new Chevrolet Beretta . . .
It's easy . . . It's fun . . . Here's how to enter:

OFFICIAL ENTRY FORM

Three Bantam book titles on sale this month are hidden in this word puzzle. Identify the books by circling each of these titles in the puzzle. Titles may appear within the puzzle horizontally, vertically, or diagonally . . .

Bantam's titles for June:

FIRST BORN
_____

CALL ME ANNA
_____

SAMURAI STRATEGY
_____

In each of the books listed above there is another entry blank and puzzle . . . another chance to win!

In July, be on the lookout for these Bantam paperback books: THE UNLOVED, TILL THE REAL THING COMES ALONG, MAFIA ENFORCER. In each of them, you'll find a new puzzle, entry blank and GRAND SLAM Sweepstakes rules . . . and yet another chance to win another brand-new Chevrolet automobile!

MAIL TO: GRAND SLAM SWEEPSTAKES
                  Post Office Box 18
                  New York, New York 10046

Please Print

NAME _____

ADDRESS _____

CITY _____ STATE _____ ZIP _____

OFFICIAL RULES

NO PURCHASE NECESSARY.

To enter identify this month's Bantam Book titles by placing a circle around each word forming each title. There are three titles shown above to be found in this month's puzzle. Mail your entry to: Grand Slam Sweepstakes, P.O. Box 18, New York, N.Y. 10046

This is a monthly sweepstakes starting February 1, 1988 and ending January 31, 1989. During this sweepstakes period, one automobile winner will be selected each month from all entries that have correctly solved the puzzle. To participate in a particular month's drawing, your entry must be received by the last day of that month. The Grand Slam prize drawing will be held on February 14, 1989 from all entries received during all twelve months of the sweepstakes.

To obtain a free entry blank/puzzle/rules, send a self-addressed stamped envelope to: Winning Titles, P.O. Box 650, Sayreville, N.J. 08872. Residents of Vermont and Washington need not include return postage.

PRIZES: Each month for twelve months a Chevrolet automobile will be awarded with an approximate retail value of $12,000 each.

The Grand Slam Prize Winner will receive 2 Chevrolet automobiles plus $10,000 cash (ARV $34,000).

Winners will be selected under the supervision of Marden-Kane Inc., an independent judging organization. By entering this sweepstakes each entrant accepts and agrees to be bound by these rules and the decisions of the judges which shall be final and binding. Winners may be required to sign an affidavit of eligibility and release which must be returned within 14 days of receipt. All prizes will be awarded. No substitution or transfer of prizes permitted. Winners will be notified by mail. Odds of winning depend on the total number of eligible entries received.

Sweepstakes open to residents of the U.S. and Canada except employees of Bantam Books, its affiliates, subsidiaries, advertising agencies and Marden-Kane, Inc. Void in the Province of Quebec and wherever else prohibited or restricted by law. Not responsible for lost or misdirected mail or printing errors. Taxes and licensing fees are the sole responsibility of the winners. All cars are standard equipped. Canadian winners will be required to answer a skill testing question.

For a list of winners, send a self-addressed, stamped envelope to: Bantam Winners, P.O. Box 711, Sayreville, N.J. 08872.